BIG SAM

MY AUTOBIOGRAPHY

SAM ALLARDYCE
BIG SAM
MY AUTOBIOGRAPHY

with Shaun Custis

headline

First published in 2015
by HEADLINE PUBLISHING GROUP

1

Cataloguing in Publication Data is available from the British Library

Hardback ISBN 978 1 47223 267 0
Trade Paperback ISBN 978 1 47223 286 1
Ebook ISBN 978 1 47223 266 3

Typeset in Bliss Light by Palimpsest Book Production Limited, Falkirk, Stirlingshire

Printed and bound in the UK by Clays Ltd, St Ives plc

Headline's policy is to use papers that are natural, renewable and recyclable products and made
from wood grown in sustainable forests. The logging and manufacturing processes are expected to
conform to the environmental regulations of the country of origin.

HEADLINE PUBLISHING GROUP
An Hachette UK Company
Carmelite House
50 Victoria Embankment
London
EC4Y 0DZ

www.headline.co.uk
www.hachette.co.uk

To Lynne, Craig, Rachael, Harriet,
Sam, Keaton and Ollie

ACKNOWLEDGEMENTS

My grateful thanks to Sir Alex Ferguson for his generous foreword. To the publishers Headline for their unstinting support in putting together my autobiography. Thanks also to my lawyer Jonathan Crystal and my agent Mark Curtis for their advice. To Shaun Custis for his valued assistance in putting my thoughts on paper, to Scott Custis and Molly Baker for transcribing hours of interviews and last, but certainly not least, my wife Lynne for putting up with me for 45 years.

CONTENTS

Sam Allardyce is one of the great characters of the game, and it's with the utmost pleasure that I find myself contributing a few words to his long-anticipated autobiography.

Having spent all of my playing career as a centre-forward, I was able to sympathise with fellow Number 9s in England on the day they were due to come up against Big Sam. My God, I wonder if breakfast was in any way enjoyable. There were many centre-forwards in those days who were not exactly shrinking violets, but nonetheless contests against the Big (Man) Brute from Dudley were certainly a test of their courage.

Whatever Sam achieved as a player could not compare to his long and illustrious career as a manager. His was not an easy route to the top, but I always believed that the learning process is more worthwhile when you start from the very roots of the game, so his first spell as a player-coach at his local club West Bromwich Albion must have felt a great honour to him.

After a two-year stint in the Midlands, he then cut his teeth as manager of Limerick where he won the league. The next three appointments were challenges which only the best can endure and sometimes tolerate. Clubs like Preston, Blackpool and Notts County have that revolving door for managers that can either kill your career or make you, and those experiences without doubt equipped Sam for greater tests ahead.

It was when he joined his next club, Bolton Wanderers, that I started to take notice of Sam's achievements, particularly when I came up against his team. When you assess the relative stature of Bolton and Manchester United, we are talking David and Goliath and more than once did David embarrass us.

I remember the first trip to Bolton when they moved to their new stadium, the Reebok. I was more than intrigued by their substitutes sitting on bicycles and pedalling away while the match went on. After the game, to get to Sam's lounge you had to pass through the video analyst's room where there were a number of boffins digesting and detailing the previous 90 minutes. Yes, he was ahead of his time and through this exhaustive use of video analysis he was able not only to assess home talent but to scout players from all over Europe who were just coming to the end of their careers with their present clubs. I can think of Okocha, Hierro, Djorkaeff, and there were many more.

Taking a club like Bolton into Europe for their first and only time was one of his major accomplishments, and quite frankly they have gone downhill since Sam left.

If there was ever an unfortunate time to join a football club then Sam's brief spells at Newcastle and Blackburn were examples of bad timing and bad luck. Both clubs changed ownership and out went Sam. Ridiculous, it seems now, but that is the football industry.

His recent spell at West Ham was a fine example of astute management, gaining promotion to the Premier League with what you could only call a workmanlike team but one that had all the character of their manager. In his last season there was only one challenge, and that was to consolidate West Ham's position in the Premier League, which he succeeded in doing so well with his skilful leadership.

Sam is enjoying his rest at the moment, but football is at a loss without him. For me, there is no way he can leave this great game as it needs its characters. Thankfully, his Scottish lineage won't allow him to quit, so on that note I await his return with great anticipation.

Good luck, Sam.

INTRODUCTION
11 June 2015

What a view. The hills of Moraira here on the north-eastern tip of the Costa Blanca in Spain hold an eternal fascination for me. The sun burns down on the dusty yellow landscape stretching towards the coast. When the clouds drift over, they bring out the green in the trees, and even on the occasions lightning flashes across the mountain tops it's a spectacular sight.

The dragonfly is buzzing across the swimming pool. He arrives at 10am almost every day and was a pest at first. But the grandkids named him Hector and he's become our adopted pet. He might be a she, but I'm not sure how you tell with dragonflies. Hector didn't turn up one day last week and we were in a panic. I actually went looking for him. That's all I have to worry about these days, wondering what's happened to the dragonfly.

This is the life. We built the villa where I'm sitting as a refuge from the madness of football. It took two years but it was the best investment we ever made. The builder was a bit naughty though. He carved out a sandstone sign in the shape of a football which reads 'Big Sam's Villa' and nailed it to the wall between the first and second floor. My wife Lynne wasn't happy and is convinced it was my idea. 'Your bloody villa, is it? What about me? Have I got nothing to do with this family? Is it all you?' Lynne is threatening to get a ladder and pull the sign down – or get the builder back to carve out another one underneath which will say, 'And Lynne's too!'

A reporter wrote that we'd named the villa 'Casa St James'' claiming it was constructed with the proceeds of my pay-off after I got the sack at Newcastle. That infuriated Lynne as well. She wouldn't want any memories of our time in a place where she never settled. Lynne is my rock. She's the foundation of the Allardyce family which also comprises our two children, Craig and Rachael, and four grandchildren Harriet, Sam, Keaton and Ollie. I've spent 45 years playing, managing, and being completely absorbed in football, with so much time away from the family that if Lynne had her way I would never go back into the game again. She's felt like that for the last few years and didn't want me to go to West Ham, the club I left this summer after four years in charge.

She wants us to enjoy life, to go on more holidays, to take the cruise to Hawaii that she's always wanted and to spend more time with the grandkids. For the first time in my life, I might be starting to agree with her. Sunderland offered me their manager's job two weeks ago. I couldn't discuss it because we had the grandchildren with us and I wanted to concentrate on them. They offered to come out this week instead to talk about a deal. I'm sure the financial package would have been tempting and, having played for Sunderland and been an academy coach there, I know what the place is about even though they've since built a new stadium.

In the past, I could never have imagined turning down such a special, historic club with its huge fanbase, but now I have no hesitation in doing so. I thank them for their interest but tell them the job is not for me. I don't need the money or the hassle. If I'd taken it, I'd have been packing to fly to the North East to prepare for pre-season training. Instead we're off to Portugal for ten days, then on to Dubai and after that I will be doing some TV analysis for BeIN Sport in Doha. Maybe being in the studio will get me yearning for the smell of the dressing room again, although that isn't always the most pleasant aroma, let me tell you. On the other hand, it might confirm what I feel today, that I'm happy out of it.

Football has given me a brilliant life and I've loved every minute of it, with all its ups and downs. But even those with the sweetest tooth get to the point where they want to try something apart from chocolate cake. I've turned 60 and I'm proud of my career. I played until I was 39 and I think it's fair to say that I'm acknowledged in the game for having a good track record. I turned a small club like Bolton into a Premier League force that was feared by the biggest teams in the land. Arsene Wenger at Arsenal never stopped complaining about our tactics; he was so embarrassed when little old Bolton got the better of him.

When I left West Ham, I was the second-longest serving Premier League manager behind Wenger. Not bad for someone who was flat broke, and not knowing where I would end up. We feared we'd lose our house which had been put up as insurance against a pub business that was going under. We were seriously struggling. I reckon that gave me the extra fight to make a go of management. I literally couldn't afford to fail. Perhaps if I'd been earning the money that players do today, I wouldn't have had the same drive. Even when a BBC *Panorama* programme about transfer dealings could have broken our family, we stayed strong. I still don't know how they were able to throw the mud they did, but I was grateful for the support of many friends.

Having ridden the football rollercoaster and come to a stop, be it temporarily or permanently, I cannot remember being so at ease with life. I might not feel like this in six months' time and might get the bug again, but we'll deal with that if we have to. Of course, it depends if somebody offers me a job, what it entails and whether it's right for us. The beauty is, coming to this stage of life, I can make better choices for myself and the family. A job in MLS in the States appeals and Lynne might like that. We've always enjoyed going to the USA for our family holidays in Florida, and I played there for Tampa Bay Rowdies in the early 1980s where I couldn't get enough of the Fannies – and they loved me too! Nothing sordid you understand, that was the name of the Tampa Bay supporters. America taught me so much that stood me in good stead for my managerial career, from diets to training techniques. They were light years ahead of us, and that summer on the other side of the Atlantic was one of the most important moves of my life.

Being a national team boss intrigues me too and that could be what entices me back. I had a shot at the England job back in 2006, impressed in an interview but missed out to Steve McClaren. I should have got it and, as I'm a better manager now than I was then, I believe I should be in the running whenever it comes round again. That's not vanity or being full of my own importance. My track record entitles me to being considered. Of course, I could manage a different country altogether. We'll see what opportunities come along.

Whether West Ham said they were getting rid of me or I said I was leaving, doesn't matter. We both came to the right conclusion in the end. Four years is long enough in any management job these days. Everything moves so fast, there's no time to build a club properly. Chairmen get fed up with their managers, managers get fed up with their chairmen, the fans want someone new and it's impossible to keep all the supporters happy all of the time. Social media pummels you constantly. Even if you win three in a row, they're on you the minute you lose. Lynne never watched a single game while I was at West Ham, she didn't even watch us on TV, yet she had a morbid fascination with the fans' website 'Knees Up Mother Brown' which she consulted daily to find out what new insults were being fired in my direction. It upset her but she couldn't keep away from the screen; I don't understand why she put herself through it.

Yet I never met one West Ham fan face to face who gave me any stick – all they wanted was a selfie. They were always supportive, thanking me for what I'd done for the club. Last night, I met a season-ticket holder while we were in Moraira having dinner. He was a dyed-in-the-wool

Hammer and was all over me, insisting he was never one of those shouting abuse or willing me out of the club. Sometimes you wonder who the hell they were.

Slaven Bilic is the new man in the hot-seat and good luck to him; he'll need it. He's been told to play the 'West Ham Way' but you won't find two Hammers anywhere who agree on what that is. I once called the supporters deluded about the so-called 'West Ham Way' and I stand by that. I've talked to my predecessors Alan Curbishley, Alan Pardew and Harry Redknapp and they don't know what it is either. They got it in the neck from the crowd as much as I did, so I don't feel that any of the flak I got was a personal thing against Sam Allardyce. It was a West Ham thing.

Is the 'West Ham Way' about playing entertaining football? Is it about winning all the time? Is it about commitment? Is it all of these rolled into one? I don't know who invented the phrase, but it's a millstone round the club's neck. If I was to try and guess what it is, I'd say it's about passion and showing the crowd you care. For the most part, we fulfilled those criteria and played some quality football along the way too, while taking a team which was on its knees after relegation back up from the Championship at the first time of asking and re-establishing it in the Premier League over the next three years.

I did a bloody good job. West Ham is in its best shape for ages. I've just been reading vice-chair Karren Brady saying that Slaven's first task is to stabilise the club. Seriously? It already is stabilised, that's where I put it. Now it's about taking it on to bigger things, which is a monumental challenge with the move to the Olympic Stadium, one of the most iconic sporting arenas in Europe, coming at the start of next season. That must be a big anxiety for the owners, David Gold and David Sullivan, who need to fill a 54,000-seater ground with entertaining and successful football. The fans won't turn up if West Ham are playing fantasy football and losing 5–3 every week. They'll soon be demanding a winning team and wanting to know why they are leaking goals.

What exactly do the board and the fans think they can achieve? Champions League football? A top six finish? I doubt that will come in the near future. It will take a long time and patience is required. Unfortunately, patience and football don't sit well together. Everyone wants a quick fix, but that's unsustainable. Instant success is built on sand and ebbs away just as quickly. To be sustainable you have to grow steadily, without risking it all collapsing and sending the club into a spiral from which it might never recover.

Given the time and a certain amount of resources, I've proved I can build a successful football club anywhere. Nobody can argue with that. As a rugged centre-half, I occasionally made my mark on the game by taking out the opposing centre-forward. As I relax with a glass of wine here in Spain, I'm content that I put my mark on the game as a manager too – for all the right reasons.

1

JUMPERS FOR GOALPOSTS

The best day of my life was when I left school. Every day after that was a hundred times better than any day at school ever was.

I didn't know how life would pan out, but I couldn't spend another minute at Wren's Nest Secondary Modern in Dudley. I was no academic but there was a reason for that. I was dyslexic, although I didn't know it at the time. Nowadays I would have had lots of help, but back then you were regarded as a bit thick. If you couldn't spell, the teachers told you to practise more and gave you endless tests. However hard I tried, I couldn't put the letters in the right order. I could just about read or write the little words, but with bigger ones I was in trouble. Once I got beyond 'the cat sat on the mat' I was stuck. I was good at covering up, I just copied what my less-challenged mates were doing. I could remember the word and how it looked, but if I had to spell it without it there in front of me, I was beaten. My work was all misspellings with bright red rings across the page, even if the content wasn't too bad.

When I became a footballer and travelled on the team bus and we had quizzes where you had to read questions out, my response was always, 'I'm not doing that stupid stuff, leave me out of it.' I couldn't do crosswords either. As there were no video games or films to watch back then, it was a pretty lonely journey. Nobody ever discovered the real reason for me not taking part though. When I did the theory work for my UEFA coaching badges, I had to ring Lynne each night to ask her how to spell everything.

I've gradually learned to cope but it hasn't been easy and I'm an interminably slow reader. No matter how hard I try, I will never get the difference between *know* and *now*. They have totally different meanings but I cannot tell you which is which. Texting was a nightmare until auto-correct was invented, and the spellcheck on the computer is a godsend. But reading and writing are still not easy, which is why I needed help putting together this book. It wasn't until my thirties that Lynne read an article about dyslexia and it all fell into place. You cannot imagine the relief at finding out my problem had a name. I've always found it funny though that dyslexia is one of the hardest words to spell of all. It's not easy for us dyslexics.

I became a patron of the Dyslexia Association and linked up with Johnny Ball who took a keen interest in the subject. Johnny was a famous figure on children's TV in the 1970s and '80s and a clever mathematician who is probably best known today as the father of DJ and presenter Zoe Ball. We worked together to promote the fact there was help out there for those in my situation. I'm fortunate that I didn't need to be reading or writing all day, but I don't understand how there are so many dyslexic actors. How on earth do they remember their scripts?

The upside is that a lack of ability in one area heightens the senses in another, and I'm an exceptionally good listener. I can retain information instantly. So much of our learning is by listening and visuals on our iPhones or computers that I find myself becoming more educated than when I was a kid. When I was playing I could remember everyone's positions at set-pieces because I only had to hear it once and it stayed with me. Nobody else could do it, and that might be one of the reasons I was captain at lots of different clubs. So many dyslexics I know are successful in what they do, so I can only assume it makes you extra determined to succeed.

Given my handicap, it will come as no surprise that I didn't pass a single exam. Not that I took any. There was no point. My dad, Bob, couldn't hide his disappointment. He was a clever man who came from Scotland where the education set-up was considered so much better. He wasn't impressed with the English system and what it had, or rather hadn't, done for me. I wasn't stupid though. I was in the B-stream, which was the second class of four and, if the teacher was good, I was good. I could do maths, technical drawing, art and pottery. I was quite interested in history too. But the thing that made school bearable was PE, thanks to a brilliant teacher. He didn't only do it within the timetable but in extra-curricular hours.

He gave every kid a chance but wouldn't accept any messing or trying to duck out. If you didn't have your kit he would find some, and if it didn't fit properly then tough. There were no excuses for not taking part. Kids nowadays give it a miss and get away with it, and we wonder why they aren't fit.

We don't pay enough attention to giving time to physical education like we do to the academic side. Consequently, we don't develop the top sportsmen and women that we should, including in football where participation is dropping at an alarming rate. For a while, there was a dedicated push by the government to support elite athletes to make sure they didn't fail in the 2012 Olympics. That's all gone now. Without physical education, you put your life at risk. Parents have been brainwashed and are obsessed with their kids being academics which is not as important as living your life as long as you can. We need a proper physical education curriculum back in schools, because I wouldn't have made it as a footballer in the education system today.

I represented my school at football, basketball, athletics, swimming and gymnastics. Basketball helped develop my spring which benefited me when it came to heading the ball and it gave me tactical awareness. You had to think on your feet, when to dribble, when to pass, when to shoot, how to protect your zone with the five men you had, or when to mark man to man.

I was a triple-jumper, strong over 220 yards, and could throw the javelin and spin the discus. I used to swim a lot, the incentive being that if you completed your 16 lengths badge, which was the quarter-mile, you got free tickets to the baths in the summer. If you did 32 lengths you got even more tickets, so we spent plenty of time there. The pool had a springboard and a high board. The first couple of times I did the high board, I almost knocked myself out. If you don't go in right it's dangerous, and they probably don't even let kids do it now for health and safety reasons. But diving was another valuable skill. I can still do a nice pike off a springboard. I was on the table tennis table at the youth club for hours and I tried boxing too but got punched in the kisser and thought, 'I'm not having that.' Gymnastics was more me. I could vault a pommel horse and do back and forward-flips on the trampoline where I learnt to keep my feet level with my shoulders and bring them back together on descending. Then I got shown how to flip over the pommel horse using a trampette which combined the two.

● ● ●

Sport was my thing from the day I was born at 1 Ash Green, on Old Park Farm in Dudley, which was a neat and tidy council estate where the houses were built in a semi-circle with grass in the middle. It was perfect for the kids and big enough for our regular 14-a-side football matches. We were typical children of the time, playing until it got dark and some-times beyond under the street lamps. We'd have challenge matches against Beech Green and Oak Green and played home and away because they had pitches just like ours. When there weren't enough kids for a game we'd practise crossing and finishing, and we really did use jumpers for goalposts. As a Wolves fan, I was Derek Dougan when I was shooting and Ernie Hunt or Dave Wagstaffe if I was crossing. One day, when I was about ten, Dad asks, 'Do you want to go to Molineux?' You bet I did. It was a magical place, and I made up my mind there and then I had to be a footballer. Dad was a sergeant with Dudley police and could always get tickets for the games. Wolves were on the slide, having been one of the top teams in the 1950s, but they could still pack in a big crowd. I didn't go too often though, because I was playing for either the school, the youth club or the town team, so I didn't have the time to play and watch.

I'm not sure how the family ended up in Dudley, because Mum is Scottish too, and I never asked my parents, but I assume it was because of Dad's job. He was a tough disciplinarian. When he wasn't dishing out a bit of corporal punishment he was working shifts before going out drinking. He was a founder member of Parkes Hall Social Club, which he built with his mates on a piece of land near our house, and though it began as a wooden shack it grew into a concert room and lounge bar with a football pitch behind it, all done with the profits they made. It's still there today. Dad was a proud committee member; it was his escape from work and the family. Most men were the same: working hard, going to the club, sinking seven or eight pints, falling into bed then going off to work again.

My mum, Mary, looked after the family and worked part-time making golf bags. We weren't well off but we weren't skint either and never went without. She was a good cook and smelt everything to check it was okay to eat. There were no sell-by dates then and we only had a pantry because we couldn't afford a fridge – they were for posh people. Mum wouldn't hear of using a tea bag. 'Tea tastes funny out of those,' she would say. She had to use a tea strainer, it was the only way. We didn't have central heating, although strangely we did have two toilets, which was quite a luxury, one upstairs and one down, and we had a black-and-white TV. There were three children: my sister, also called Mary, was 15 years my senior, and my brother Robert five years older. I was a mistake, apparently, after Mum had a rare night out with Dad! We didn't see a lot of Mary, as she joined the army when I was four and then got married, but being the youngest, I was a mummy's boy, there's no doubt about that. She was always telling the others, 'Leave our Sam alone, stop picking on him.'

Mary was occasionally left in charge when she came back from the army, and Robert and I drove her mad by fighting. It was a typical bust-up between young boisterous lads. Mary would try to drag us apart but we carried on scrambling, and then she'd give up and go to bed. Mum would come home and ask what was going on and I'd be there with my shirt in tatters, pleading with her not to tell Dad. Even when I was the innocent party, I still got walloped for fighting. We didn't have a car but Dad would hire one for the holidays. We once went to Aberlour in north-east Scotland where he was born. It's on the whisky trail and it felt like a week to get there, one of those 'Are we there yet?' trips, while Mum and Dad argued about the right route to take. Whenever we were in the car, if Mum said turn left when we should have turned right, there was hell on. The most exciting holidays were to my aunt's in Scarborough or to Blackpool. But, even on the way, Dad couldn't resist a drink. Mum and us kids had sandwiches in the car while he went into the pub for a couple of pints.

I went to Sycamore Green Primary School, which was only two greens away from our house so it was a short walk, and I had to go on my own to Sunday School with a threepenny bit for the collection. I don't know why I had to go because Dad was an atheist. I'm still not sure whether I'm religious or not. I'm not entirely convinced by it, but I'm not against it either, and as I got married in church and go to funerals, I suppose I must be hedging my bets. I played football for the school team in the last two years I was there and we won the cup but obviously I didn't pass my 11-plus to get into grammar school so I moved on to Wren's Nest Secondary Modern, so called because it was set in a conservation area. Underground was the Severn Sisters Cavern which was dug to mine minerals, and at the bottom was a canal. It was all fenced off with a sign saying 'Do Not Enter' so naturally we did. Our Robert protected me from the bullies, but by year two I was bigger and tougher so could look after myself. I got the cane a few times and learned that the trick was to pull your hand downwards at the last minute to stop it hurting. If you didn't get it right, it stung like hell. You don't get discipline like that any more which is not a good thing. I didn't like being punished but it taught me to respect my elders, which is something lacking in a lot of teenagers today. I once came home with a letter from school for being naughty and Mum and Dad had to go in and see the teacher. I can't remember what I did, but I'll tell you what, I made sure I was never naughty again once Dad got hold of me. He had to be seen to be administering discipline to his own kids because he was the number one bobby on the estate who everybody came to with their problems. He would go round and sort it out, even if he was off-duty.

Mum wasn't scared of Dad but I'm sure she got fed up with him taking her for granted. She got her money off him every week to look after us, and he kept the rest for his fags and his booze. She always made sure his meal was on the table when he came home, and on a Sunday when he'd been to the pub he'd go straight to bed when he got back. When he got up, Mum warmed his meal up for him. When I look back, it was an empty relationship but I doubt there was ever a question of them splitting up. It wasn't the done thing. We never sat round together as a family. Dad would be in his own little world reading the paper and wasn't interested in what we'd done that day. He never watched us play sports and poor Mum was always too busy.

If Dad had bothered to get out of the armchair, he would have noticed me playing a year above my age group because I was so well developed and catching the eye of George Pearson, a top bloke who managed the Dudley and Brierley Hill town team. He recommended me for the county and I got England Schoolboy trials, although I didn't make the team. I never represented my country at any level, which is why I was so excited to be interviewed for the England manager's job in my later career. You should never give up hope and I still haven't.

I was always a centre-half and a dirty bastard at that. I was playing semi-professional with Robert for Dudley Town at the age of 14. This was the school of hard-knocks and the instructions to me were simple – kick their striker: 'Let him know you're there, son.' Ideally you wanted to take ball and man and it didn't matter in which order, and refs were a lot more lenient then. You had to break someone's leg to get booked, and kill them to get sent off. I don't know how but I didn't have one serious injury in all my playing days. You would have thought with me kicking lumps out of opponents they'd do the same to me, but somehow I survived.

You grow up quickly playing semi-pro when you're a young teenager, and it was important to my development. It wouldn't happen now, because if you're good enough to play semi-pro at 14 you're snapped up by a club academy and forced to play against kids of your own age. The teacher wasn't happy about me doing it though. I scored a bullet header from a corner in a West Midlands League game and there was a write-up in the local paper which attracted his attention so I was banned from playing. 'Carry on doing that and you'll be finished before you've started,' he said. 'They'll cripple you.' He was right but I was fuming. Dudley paid me ten shillings a game and I was only getting two and six pocket money.

George Pearson tried his best to get clubs interested in me. I trained with West Brom and Wolves, and had trials at Villa, but nothing came of them. I was also promised a trial at Tottenham but they didn't follow it up. Mum was saying, 'Never mind, you stick to it, just enjoy it when you leave school, and play semi-pro.' But I wasn't giving up. One night I turned out for Staffordshire against Cheshire at Stockport County and knew I'd had a good game by keeping quiet Neil Whatmore, who was a young star at Bolton and would become a team-mate of mine for many years. The teachers warned us not to give our names and addresses out to any scouts if they approached us because they were supposed to go through the school, but I was getting desperate. A Bolton scout called Frank Pickford, who was probably there primarily to check on Watty's progress, said he was interested in me and asked for my phone number, which was a bit of a problem as we didn't have a phone. So he took my name and address and wrote saying someone would be down to see Mum and Dad the following week. I do wonder what would have happened if I hadn't played in that game. Was it a *Sliding Doors* moment? Maybe there would have been another match where I was discovered, but maybe not.

Dad decreed that Bolton's visit warranted opening the best room in the house. We lived in a three-bed end-of-terrace, but the best room wasn't used because there was never an occasion grand enough. It had the smart table and dining chairs and a fire, but we had to live in a small lounge with kitchen and a boiler and a little table which we sat round while watching the telly. When the chief scout arrived, he was shown in while Mum got the bone china out for tea. He wasted no time getting straight to the point.

'We'd like to offer young Sam a three-year apprenticeship, but he needs to come up next weekend for a trial first just to make sure. It should be straightforward and afterwards he'll meet the manager and sign up. Then he'll start next season and we'll put him in digs with a landlady.'

Dad said to me, 'Is that what you want then?' Of course it was, it was my dream. So Dad and I travelled up to Burnden Park on the train to meet the manager, the great Nat Lofthouse, nicknamed the Lion of Vienna for his bravery in scoring a goal for England in Austria. Nat scored 30 goals in 33 games for England and was a Bolton legend who later became club president. The manager did everything and meeting a wet-behind-the-ears urchin from the Midlands was all part of the job. I also met George Taylor, the youth-team coach who became one of the biggest influences on my career.

They handed Dad £150 in expenses but he complained they'd given him too much. 'Don't worry about it, Bob,' George replied, but Dad was adamant. 'No, no, no. It's only cost me twenty quid, I only want what I'm owed.' So he handed back £130, much to their surprise. It was admirable on Dad's part, I guess, but he could have given it to Mum who was always scratching to make ends meet. Dad watched my trial game, which was a rarity, over at Bolton's Bromwich Street training pitch. The rain pelted down and I had a shocker, full of the jitters because I was playing with lads I didn't know. There was me with a broad Dudley accent surrounded by people wondering where on earth I'd come from. I was totally self-conscious and thought I'd blown it. 'You'll be alright, son,' said Dad, which by his standards was quite a morale booster. But he already knew. 'They've said they're going to give it to you.' Everything got signed, so they couldn't have taken much notice of my performance in the trial. I was on my way to becoming a professional footballer. I was to start on 8 July, but it was only March. I told the school careers officer I was leaving to be a footballer and he laughed in that 'I know better' sort of way. 'You're neglecting your education, Allardyce. How do you think you're going to make it in the world?' I didn't know for sure, but I was ready to take my chances. Goodbye school and good riddance. Hello the good life.

2

EDUCATING SAM

Not many professional footballers came from Dudley but one of the most famous of them all was Duncan Edwards. He was a Busby Babe who died following the 1958 Munich air disaster at the age of 21. By general consent, Edwards was a genius of a left-half who could play midfield, up front or at the back and already had 18 caps for England by the time he lost his life. United were returning from a European Cup tie in Belgrade when they stopped off in Munich for refuelling. The plane crashed on take-off, killing seven of the team, while Edwards died in hospital a fortnight later. There is a tombstone memorial to him in Dudley cemetery and a statue was later erected in the town centre, unveiled by his mother and Sir Bobby Charlton, another United and England great who was on that fateful flight.

Everyone in Dudley was proud of Duncan Edwards. I had no pretensions about being able to fill those formidable boots, but there was a certain amount of pressure because of his memory. Mention you were from Dudley and the first person who came to mind was Duncan and you could see people looking at you thinking, 'You'll never be as good as him.' The only other player I knew of from Dudley was Roger Minton, a full-back at West Brom. He was a couple of years younger than our Robert and had twin brothers, Neil and Steven, who got complimentary tickets for the Hawthorns and would take me with them if I had a spare after-noon.

My three best pals Brian Milner, Tony Edwards, and Steven Hartleberry were made up for me that by joining Bolton I could become another footballer to grace the Dudley hall of fame. As kids we'd played together, doing knock-a-door-run, tig and British Bulldog, and went scrumping, shinning up trees and filling our jumpers and pants with as many apples as we could. I'd get stomach-ache from eating so many as we went along. We did strawberry and blackberry picking too, and I was sick from eating way too many of them as well. You had to get a stone of blackberries in a box to get paid. No matter how hard I tried, the maximum I could manage in a day was three boxes, and the farmer would give you a telling off if you left the ones higher up the branches which were more difficult to pick. 'Why've you left these ones here on this bloody tree?' I can hear him now.

Blackberry picking wouldn't pay enough in the four months I had to fill before starting at Bolton. This was 1969 and I hadn't signed some mega-money Premier League contract. Bolton were only going to pay me £4 a week and there was no signing-on fee. So I got work on a production line that built record decks, and it made me realise even more how much I had to make it as a footballer. I was responsible for checking for faults on the decks, throwing away the piece that didn't work and putting the good parts back in the trays for the girls who were making them further up the line. If the ladies got past their targets at the end of the day, there was an almighty cheer because they got a bonus. I didn't qualify but still had to work flat out to help them get the extra money, which struck me as rather unfair.

It was boring, incredibly boring. You'd get on the factory coach in the morning for an 8 o'clock start. At half past ten there was 15 minutes for a tea break, a 45-minute lunch break and at 3 o'clock you got another 15-minute tea break until you were finished at 4 o'clock. Then it was back on the coach and home. I did other jobs in the summer too for the first few years I was at Bolton, like cutting grass in the park. I was never shy of hard graft and always keen to make some extra money.

Finally, the day arrived to start at Bolton and this time it was Mum who came with me on the train to see where I was staying. She didn't like the digs and got upset, although I think it was more that she didn't want me to leave home at all as I was only 15. Dad, as you might expect, was more matter-of-fact about it all.

'You've made your own bed, off you go, it's up to you now, son. Here's a fiver, put that in the bank, that'll help ya. It's a chance you've wanted, don't bloody spoil it, just bloody get on with it.'

The landlady was an old retired woman who lived on her own on Settle Street in Great Lever, and I had my own little bedroom in a two-up two-down terrace which the club paid for on top of my wages and some expenses for the bus.

I met up with the lads who were to become good friends, like goal-keeper Barry Siddall and centre-half Paul Jones, Joe Walsh, John McGill, Peter Reid and Willy Graham. We were all under the guidance of the man in charge of the youths, George Taylor, who was one of the first tracksuit coaches. Most coaches wore a jacket and tie and stood there with a whistle directing operations but not George, he was much more involved.

Football was only part of our duties. We had loads of jobs to do outside of training, including looking after four members of the senior team whose kit you had to sort out. First came an inauguration in front of them all, which meant doing a turn while they decided whether you'd done well enough to be spared a punishment. 'Sing us a song then, Sam!' they said. I wasn't really up for that, so I tried a few jokes. Nobody laughed, not even a smile. 'When are you going to start the jokes, Sam?' they shouted before drowning me in buckets of cold water and blackening my bollocks with boot polish. It took ages to scrape it off and it didn't half hurt. Nowadays, if the police heard about that, they'd have six squad cars round to the training complex which would be sealed off and the protagonists charged with sexual abuse. I imagine it would make big headlines in the papers too, but back then it was considered run-of-the-mill banter and you had to take it or there was worse around the corner.

The players' jockey pants, socks and shirts only got washed twice a week and the sweat tops just once a week. We put them in the drying room after every training session and they absolutely stank, but we'd get hammered if we gave the players smelly gear. We also had to clean and mop the dressing rooms, scrub the boots and flatten the two training pitches using heavy hand-rollers.

Every Monday morning we swept the Burnden Park terraces, which wasn't so bad seeing as you might find a few bob lying around from spectators who dropped change out of their pockets. Bolton were getting 15-20,000 crowds even in the Second Division, where they were the season I joined, so there was plenty of scope for discovering loose change. The railway embankment end was infamous for a tragedy in the FA Cup quarter-final against Stoke City in 1946 when 80,000 people crammed into Burnden and the banking collapsed causing 33 deaths. The game was stopped but re-started with bodies still laid out by the touchline. It's a disaster which still haunts the town 70 years on, even though the club has long since relocated to the Reebok Stadium. There is a plaque on the old site, which is now an Asda supermarket, commemorating the dead.

At the end of the season, we painted the dressing rooms and slapped more paint on each other than we did on the walls. Then we prepared the pitches so they could be seeded by hand by the groundsman.

Those menial tasks were part of a young pro's education which we all accepted, but they don't do it today because of objections from the Professional Footballers' Association, which was extremely short-sighted of them. The PFA argued it was slave labour, but it taught kids discipline and made them appreciate it more when they became fully-fledged pros rather than getting it all the moment they signed.

On top of the jobs there was the little matter of training to be done. The sessions were brutal and there was no mercy, no easing you in. We ran for miles up to Lever Park and back, round the outside of the ground, and up and down the terrace steps. We weren't allowed any water either, as apparently that was bad for you. If you had too much breakfast you threw up, then George would say, 'Carry on.' Once we'd done our jobs and training, which in the afternoon did actually include some football, we were on the brink of collapse and I frequently fell straight into bed afterwards, my legs as stiff as oak trees. Somehow I found the energy to do it all over again the next day. Players don't train anything like that now. Physios get concerned about fatigue which makes you more susceptible to injury. The theory in those days was that by flogging you into the ground you learned to cope with fatigue, and when it came to playing you would be going strong at the end while the other lot wilted. Whether it was the right idea or not, we were certainly fit.

George had a big wooden board with a goal marked on it and we had to run up and shoot, get the ball back, then shoot again, alternating left foot, right foot, left, right, over and over. My left foot was hopeless, I was totally right-footed. That eventually changed thanks to George's drill, although team-mates reckoned it made me equally crap with both feet. I spent hours practising headers and clearing balls out of the penalty area. You were taught to be in the correct position, getting the right body-shape and dealing with different trajectories. I was taught to use the pace of the ball to clear my lines and realised that a clean side-foot often achieved greater distance than slashing at it. We worked on attack against defence, and getting tight on your man, but George would mix it up with a ball over your head for someone running in behind to score easily. You needed your wits about you.

● ● ●

English football has never come up with a better system for developing players through the ranks than the one we had in the 1970s. It was so simple. We started in the B-team, progressed to the A-team, then the reserves and finally the first team. The B-team was for Under-18s while the A-team onwards was open age. Every team played on a Saturday and all four line-ups went up on the noticeboard on a Friday afternoon. If the seniors were away they'd go off by coach, while the reserves stayed behind to play at Burnden at 2 o'clock on a Saturday afternoon. Reserve games used to pull in thousands of fans and were very competitive fixtures. The rest of the week was devoted to coaching, unless there was a cup replay or a rescheduled game because of a postponement. So there were five days available for practice, with Sunday a day off. Today, you get two days a week for coaching if you're lucky, because players are either recuperating from a game the previous day or preparing to travel to the next one. Youngsters can be travelling with the reserves, doing a couple of days' training, then maybe joining in for a kickabout with the first team on a Friday. They might also travel with the first-team squad as a non-playing sub, or worse still be sitting in the stands. There is no proper development route; it's all over the place.

I went straight into the B-team at 15 but suffered an unexpected affliction – homesickness. I wasn't just a bit homesick, I was in a terrible state and couldn't function. In short, I wanted my mum. It started after I returned to Dudley for a long weekend and I didn't want to go back. Predictably, my old man was saying, 'What's up with ya? Get your arse back up there.' It wasn't so easy. I was missing my mates, football on the green, and most importantly Mum's quality cooking and getting the washing done. The old lady where I was living shrunk all my clothes and couldn't cook. The stuff she served up was inedible. I was meeting up with Joe and John, who lived round the corner, and eating fish and chips. I explained this to Dad but there was no compassion, he sent me back. One day I'd had enough, so I packed my bag and took the bus to Williams & Glyn's bank to draw out some money for the journey home for good. But it was a Bank Holiday and it was shut; there was no cashpoint. I was pig sick. I told Mum how fed up I was, and was on the brink of tears.

But then came the defining moment of my life when I met Lynne, who was to become my wife, during one of our regular nights as young drinkers of shilling-a-pint pale ale at the Cromwellian Club in Bolton. The Cromwellian was the sort of place where fights broke out once everyone had too much to drink – and a thoroughly good time was had by all! Lynne was standing in a corner with her mates, pretty and petite with long dark hair, and was a right catch. I told her I made record decks for a living, which wasn't a total lie as it was what I'd been doing after leaving school, and that I played football on Saturdays. I didn't want to come over all big-time when I'd done nothing in the game. We started going out but I thought I had competition for Lynne's affections from a lad called Anthony Knowles who went on to become a famous snooker player and shortened his first name to Tony. We got into a routine where the three of us walked back to Lynne's house and I was sure he fancied her, but she says he was just a friend. When Lynne found out I was a footballer after I scored a goal for the youth team and my picture appeared in the paper, she finished with me at the bus stop, saying she didn't go out with liars. But she changed her mind after some pleading on my part and my homesickness was cured. She got to like the perks of my job, such as the players' pass which got us into the Odeon picture house in Bolton for free.

On Mum's pleading, Bolton moved me to new digs owned by a couple called Anna and Arthur who lived right by Bromwich Street. I got my washing done, was spoiled rotten by them and everything fell into place. I became pally with Lynne's sister Maureen's husband, Paul, and was always round at Lynne's to the extent that when Anne and Arthur needed my room for a friend, Lynne's mum and dad, Vera and Ted, invited me to move into their house. My room was one side and Lynne's the other, with her mum and dad's in the middle – with floorboards on the landing that creaked so there was no funny business! Lynne's schoolmate, Janet, was going out with Barry Siddall and drove a Morris 1000, so the four of us would go over to Blackpool and places further afield, which was great and a change from getting the bus. Lynne passed her driving test which gave us more freedom, and finally I passed too and bought my first car, which was a 1500cc Ford Cortina. It had blue and white fins at the back and was my pride and joy. I'd wax and polish it every Sunday.

* * *

On the field, we Under-18s were very successful, winning the Lancashire Youth Cup and getting to the quarter-finals of the FA Youth Cup before being beaten at home by Arsenal in front of a 15,000 crowd. I went from the B-team into the A-team pretty quickly, playing semi-pro reserve sides like Runcorn and South Liverpool. We were kicked and battered, learning the hard way among fully grown men. Not that I was a short-arse. They were turbulent times for the club as a whole though. Nat Lofthouse was sacked, Jimmy McIlroy took over but didn't last long, followed by Jimmy Meadows, and Lofthouse again. Bolton lost 2–0 to Fourth Division York City in the third round of the FA Cup and were relegated after finishing rock bottom of the old Second Division in 1971.

Relegation proved to be good news for the youngsters. There was a mass clear-out, which meant we were closer to our big chance. Paul Jones, Don McAllister and Siddall were forcing their way into the first-team reckoning, while Whatmore was making a name for himself too. I was playing for the reserves against Manchester United, Liverpool and Aston Villa in the Central League, which was often of a higher standard than the Third Division. But I'd be lying if I said I didn't have doubts about whether I would make it. When I trained with the first team it was an eye-opener, and Paul Jones was clearly better than me. I'd easily been the best player at school and one of the first names on the team-sheet for the town and the county, but this was the real deal. Joe Walsh, Willy Graham and John McGill all got released, which was a shock and made me fearful for my own future. Joe had so much skill, with a wand of a left foot, and could have given the Brazilians a run for their money. He could keep the ball up from the training pitch all the way back to Burnden even when we tried to put him off by shoving him.

But while my mates were let go, I was called in on my 17th birthday and given a pro contract rather than having to wait until I was 18. I got a £125 signing-on fee and wages of £14 a week which, in real terms, was not much more than I was already earning because my digs' money and expenses stopped and I was no longer the club's responsibility. Who cared? I was a proper professional footballer.

After another year with the reserves, the new manager Jimmy Armfield told me to prepare for my debut in a night match at York City. It was 5 March 1973, I was 18 years old, and this was the moment I'd been waiting for. I couldn't sleep the night before but felt okay when I boarded the bus, and after we stopped the other side of Leeds for our traditional pre-match meal of steak and toast, the boss pulled me aside for a quiet word.

'Don't eat too much and get your mind on the game, son,' he said. 'It's going to be a big night for you, but I'm sure you're up to it.'

I was going to the lads, 'I'm playing, I'm playing!' and got a 'Well done, son!' from Roy Greaves, a Bolton lad through and through, someone I looked up to as a model pro and who never stopped practising. He was two-footed, could head it, tackle, and score. He loved Bolton and spent all his career there, even turning down a big move to Liverpool. To think I was going to play in the same team as Roy. He went on to become one of my best friends.

When we got to Bootham Crescent, I eagerly started getting changed, preparing to put on the famous white shirt. In came Jimmy to read out the team: 'Siddall . . . Jones . . . McAllister . . .' There was one glaring omission – Allardyce! The lads looked at me like I was an idiot. There was a barrage of, 'I thought you said you were fucking playing' and 'Fucking hell, he's not even picked you.' There was no sympathy, they crucified me. I wanted the ground to swallow me up, I was absolutely devastated, especially as there was no word of explanation. When Armfield later took over as manager at Leeds, their captain Billy Bremner came out with the immortal line, 'The manager's indecision is final.' I knew exactly how he felt. What had I done wrong? I can't remember the rest of the night and I just sat sulking on the bus on the way back. Jimmy called me in to see him a couple of days later and was sat behind his desk puffing on his pipe. 'I know I said you were playing son, but when I saw the condition of the pitch I didn't think it would suit you.' I felt like saying, 'It was grass with two goals on it and some white lines just like everywhere else, boss.' But what could I do? He was the manager and I was just an 18-year-old, desperate for my chance. Having an argument wasn't going to do me any favours, especially as Armfield took us up into the Second Division as champions. The following season I eventually made my debut on 6 November 1973 in a 2–1 home defeat against Millwall in the third round of the League Cup. My league debut followed on 17 November, which was a 3–1 home defeat by Notts County, so it wasn't the best of starts and I only got a handful of games during the campaign.

We had a strong bunch of characters. Siddall was a mouthy so-and-so who delighted in abusing the directors on the team coach, but what a goalie he was. It was rare for a keeper to be a regular in his teens, but Barry justified his place. He was sold on by Ian Greaves, the manager who replaced Armfield. Ian knew he was good but couldn't stand him. He threw Baz's boots at him shouting, 'Fuck off to Sunderland and don't come back!' Greaves came to the club as assistant manager, having been sacked by Huddersfield. He had a sound knowledge of the game, was more experienced than Jimmy and was the perfect choice when Armfield went off to Leeds in October 1974 to replace Brian Clough who only lasted 44 days at Elland Road.

My career was at a crossroads when Greaves took over. I'd played a few times for Jimmy but not nearly as much as I wanted to, with McAllister and Jones established as the centre-half pairing. I'd told Armfield that if he didn't think I was going to make it there, he should let me know so I could find another club. I said the same to Greaves who told me to bide my time. Then a bid came in for McAllister from Tottenham, and he was gone for a reported £80,000 which was massive money for a centre-half. Rumour had it that Spurs really wanted Jonesy but he was such a lazy bastard they'd probably have got fed up with him. As it happened, Don enjoyed a fantastic career at White Hart Lane.

So Greavsie called me in and said, 'Look, you've been mithering me for weeks and weeks. Well, now we're safe, Don's gone and we've got ten games left. You are going to play in all ten, unless you are shit. If you are not shit you're staying, and if you are shit then you're going, so it's up to you. Now fuck off.'

THE BIONIC MAN 3

My career was on the line, it was make or break and I couldn't mess it up. Thankfully I came through the Greaves test, won the club's young player of the year award and I was on my way. Meanwhile, Jimmy Armfield was doing alright for himself too, taking Leeds to the European Cup final although they lost 2–0 to Bayern Munich. I'd established a partnership with Jonesy and we had a team to challenge for promotion, with Peter Reid in midfield, the former Liverpool and England winger Peter Thompson, and Tony Dunne, who won the 1968 European Cup with Manchester United, at left-back.

Dunne had been at Old Trafford for more than a decade and when he joined us he couldn't adapt to dropping down to our level. I kept looking across at him thinking, 'What the hell is Tony Dunne doing in Bolton's reserves playing with me?' But once he got used to his new life, we played in the first team together and it was reassuring to know Dunny was there on my left to bail me out. What a defender he was. He had the offside trap down to a tee and just stepped up when I did, relying on his years of experience.

Bolton fans called me Super Sam Bionic Man after fictional astronaut Steve Austin, TV's *Six Million Dollar Man*, who was rebuilt with all the latest technology after an accident. I suppose I got the nickname because I went crunching into tackles and still got up, while the other bloke was laid out flat. Greavsie wanted me to intimidate centre-forwards and give them a good kicking. 'Get through the back of them, sort them out,' he would say. He liked me to go in hard and promised if I ever burst the ball in a tackle he would give me £50. I tried and I tried but never managed it.

You could always get away with a first foul and maybe the second, whereas you would be sent off today. In the early days of Armfield the mantra was 'last one to the halfway line's a sissy' as the ball was launched forward, but Greavsie preferred us to drop off and to play the ball out from the back. Not me though, I had to give it to someone who could play! Greavsie wanted me to do the things I could do, not the things he felt I couldn't.

Greavsie didn't want his keeper just humping the ball down the middle, he wanted him to roll it out to the defence so we could have a more measured build-up. So, one afternoon at Bristol Rovers the ball came out from Baz to Dunny then across to Jonesy then up to Reidy and on to Whatty and back to Reidy who passed to John Ritson. When Baz got the ball again, I called for it but he rolled it to Ritty who gave it to Reidy who picked out our captain Roy Greaves who knocked it back to Jonesy.

This must have gone on for 15 minutes and I hadn't had a kick.

'What the fuck's going on?' I screamed at Roy. 'We've got 11 players here, you can pass to me too.'

Roy replied, 'The gaffer's told us to miss you out of it today or we'll get fined.'

'Fuck off,' I said, 'Why would he do that?'

'Because he says you're useless with your feet,' he shouted back.

Then he ran off. I was absolutely fuming but, as usual, I got no sympathy, the lads were pissing themselves. You could understand a bit of a joke like that in training, but this was while we were playing the game.

I went for the boss at half-time. 'Did you tell them not to give me the ball?'

'I never said that,' Greavsie protested.

'Well, he says you did,' I raged, prodding my finger in Roy's direction.

'Don't worry about it, you're just a big ugly centre-half anyway.'

I knew he had put them up to it. If he thought I wasn't as good on the ball as the rest of them, I was going to show him. Midway through the second half, I got it on the halfway line and pinged a 40-yard diagonal ball over their defence, we crossed it back in and scored. I turned towards the bench to Greavsie thinking, 'Is he looking at me? Is he fucking looking at me? Look at me, I told you I could play, so make sure I get it next time.' He never looked at me.

The youth coach George Taylor spent hours working on my strengths rather than my weaknesses. He thought I was the best at sensing danger, that the awareness came easily to me and I was a great header of a ball and strong in the tackle, but he did tell me I was slow on my feet, which motivated me to improve that area. To be fair, the best thing Greavsie ever taught me was to give myself an extra five yards. By dropping off, I was less anxious and better able to read the game. But I was a better player than I was given credit for, and that team was one that was all about pure football. I wouldn't have survived in it if I couldn't play a bit.

The lads knew I was a worrier and played on it. I've always been an insomniac and could never settle the night before a match, turning it over and over in my mind and going through all the scenarios. I worried about what my opponent might do and what the manager might do if I cocked up. I had this irrational fear of making a mistake and letting the team down. Defenders are natural sceptics because a bad error often results in a goal for the opposition, whereas I don't think forwards are bothered in the same way about missing chances because they are much more instinctive. I would get stomach cramps, then I'd get the runs and my armpits would sweat profusely. Yet once the whistle went I was fine, which was the same when I became a manager.

As you may have gathered, we were a piss-taking bunch at Bolton and if you couldn't handle the banter you were dead. Greavsie was not averse to joining in now and again either. You got tested every day, with the others prodding at you, looking for the weak spot. If you couldn't take it, it just got worse. If I snapped it would be, 'Look at him, big ugly bastard, he can't take it . . . he wants his mum.' They'd probably call it bullying now, but it was part of the process of making you into a player. At every club there are the smart lads, the daft ones and the streetwise, which makes for a good mix in the dressing room. There were a few scuffles, especially if there was a bad tackle in training, but nothing that got out of control. I wasn't a fighter, I was more one for the verbals, and being a big lad no-one fancied fighting me anyway.

There was always a bottle of whisky around too. It went in the skip for matches and we all had a shot before running out for the game. It warmed you up nicely and gave you a little glow. If there was any left, Greavsie put it in his tea. I once picked his cuppa up at half-time by mistake and spat it out all over the floor. It was full of whisky.

When new signings arrived they understood you had to be part of the squad, no matter where you'd come from or how big a player you were. If we went out, everyone had to come out. If we were doing a fancy-dress night out, like at the Christmas party, everyone wore an outfit, be it a horse, a cow, one of the Flower Pot Men, whatever. It was one of life's challenges, going to the gents and doing what comes naturally dressed as a bumble bee.

● ● ●

The 1975–76 season featured an epic three games against Newcastle in the fifth round of the FA Cup. There were 46,000 at Burnden Park to see us draw 3–3 against the First Division side, with their centre-forward Malcolm Macdonald scoring twice, one of which was a blinding volley from outside the box. We drew the replay 0–0 after extra-time in front of 52,000 at St James' Park and then got absolutely smashed on champagne at the team hotel to celebrate taking it to a third game. There were no penalty shoot-outs then, so another replay was scheduled, this time on neutral turf at Leeds United's Elland Road. We played our full part again but eventually went down 2–1. If that was a disappointment, it was nothing compared to the crushing feeling at the end of the season when we missed out on promotion by one point despite winning three of our last four.

Another ex-Manchester United man, Scottish winger Willie Morgan, signed in the summer and gave us a new outlet. This time we had a great run in the League Cup before going out 2–1 on aggregate to Everton in the semi-finals. It was a sickener but, once more, not half as bad as the end of the season when we missed out on promotion by one point again. This time we were beaten by eventual champions Wolves in our penultimate game and could only manage a draw in our final match at Bristol Rovers. Our failings were becoming horribly repetitive. Whenever people talks about cups affecting league form, I look back to those days and wonder what might have been but for our cup runs. It cost the players financially too. The promotion bonus was about £3,000, and bearing in mind my house only cost £7,000, that money would have doubled my season's wages. I was only on £60 a week.

We seemed jinxed in our promotion bid, but was there more to it than that? Because we played it out from the back all the time, when the pressure was on we got nervous and we gave the ball away in bad areas. So as the 1977–78 season went on, the gaffer got us playing it forward quicker, working off the front men and in the channels, and squeezing up on opponents in their own half. Greaves had also been shopping again and found the missing piece in the jigsaw to help us over the line and into Division One at the third time of asking. His name was Frank Worthington, a magician with a football who had the magic touch with the ladies too. Morgan thought he was the playboy at Bolton, but he was a schoolkid in short trousers compared to Frank.

Worthy was a real character, an Elvis Presley fan with his great long sideburns who always had a Swedish blonde on his arm, sometimes two! He was a sensation at Leicester but fell out with them, and Bolton came to his rescue. He walked the walk and talked the talk but wasn't considered 'establishment' and only won eight England caps which was criminal for a man of his ability. Frank used to joke, 'For some players their second touch is a sliding tackle,' and 'Other players control it further than I kick it.' I never asked if that one was directed at me. It was better I didn't know.

Greavsie called him the working man's George Best but everything about him was class. He could infuriate the life out of the manager in training though, and Greaves admitted in the book *The Mavericks* that he couldn't tame Frank.

'We'd be stood there, looking at each other, eye to eye,' he said. 'He was talking to me and his eyes never left mine, but he must have flicked the ball up 47 times. He caught it behind him on his neck, let it roll down, hoofed it over his back and caught it on his foot, something I could never do if I played forever. I thought, "How do you give him a telling-off when he's doing that?"'

Greaves had managed Frank at Huddersfield and said when he signed him, 'I don't know why I've done this.' He told us we'd have to control him because he couldn't. But they loved each other really and Greavsie knew he was buying a game-changer. Worthy produced the goods with the winner at Blackburn with a stunning left-foot strike from a Roy

Greaves pass which sealed our promotion in the second-last game of the season. It was extra special doing it in front of a full house at Ewood Park against our rivals. I was crying at the end, and we went off to the Playmate Club in Bolton to celebrate with me wearing my suit to get in, then putting my kit on over the top of it. I'm not sure why, I just did. We sobered up enough to get a draw at home to Fulham and lifted the Second Division trophy in front of our own fans, followed by an open-top bus trip and reception at the Town Hall. Three years of hurt were over and I still cherish that medal, a little square golden plaque which is in my study at home.

Bolton were back in the top flight after 14 years in the wilderness, and I finally pocketed that £3,000 promotion bonus which meant we could buy the detached house up the road. I also got a new contract. But playing in the First Division wasn't easy. The quality, the touch, the strength and the pace of players was on another level, which made it difficult for defenders like me. Centre-forwards like Cyrille Regis at West Brom and Frank Stapleton at Arsenal had unbelievable movement. Players were tougher too, Joe Jordan being the prime example of the ultimate hard man. I had to learn fast.

The first challenge was to stay in the team, and then to make sure we didn't go straight back down. It was important to consolidate, which we did, including doing the double over Manchester United. But any veteran Bolton fan will tell you that the truly memorable moment from that season was provided by Frank Worthington. He scored the greatest goal I ever saw in a match where I was playing, and I remember the date distinctly because it was the day my daughter Rachael was born at two minutes past mid-day on 21 April 1979. I popped in to see her and still made it in time for kick-off.

We actually lost 3–2 at home to Ipswich with Alan Brazil, who became talkSPORT's *Breakfast Show* host but was a little thinner and quicker back then, scoring twice. I netted as well with a header from Worthy's corner but nobody remembers that. This was all about Frank. Worthy was facing away from goal, going nowhere, when he nodded the ball down, juggled it up and down twice, then flicked it over his head and two defenders before turning round and volleying into the bottom corner. My description doesn't do it justice. The goal was so good it was in the opening sequence to ITV's *The Big Match* for years and can still be found on the internet. I never tire of watching it.

Years later, when doing the after-dinner circuit, Worthy would recount how, having lifted the ball over the Ipswich defence and scored, he went up to their centre-half Terry Butcher and said, 'Terry, you'd have got a better view of that goal if you'd been sat over there in the stands watching it.'

The England manager, Ron Greenwood, was in the crowd to witness Worthy's brilliance, but it didn't make a blind bit of difference. Frank was never picked for his country again despite being top-scorer in the league with 24 for a team that finished 17th out of 22. There were players who won 50 England caps who couldn't tie Worthy's bootlaces.

England has a sorry history of marginalising flair players. It's been going on for decades. Alan Hudson, Rodney Marsh, Worthy, Stan Bowles, Matt Le Tissier, to name a few – not one of them made it to double figures in England appearances. That's a scandal. We've always preferred the work ethic over the skill. Bill Shankly was going to break the British transfer record to sign Frank for Liverpool in the early 1970s and pair him with Kevin Keegan, but apparently it fell through because of a high blood pressure reading during his medical.

I couldn't compete with Worthy for headlines but I did make the front page of the *Bolton Evening News* once, as well as local ITV's *Granada Reports*, when I spent five hours in a police cell on suspicion of theft. Imagine the fun the lads in the dressing room had with that one. It was purely innocent but what a nightmare. I was about to wash the car and realised I needed special adaptors for the hose pipe, so I popped down to B&Q. To get technical, I required male and female adaptors to put on the end of the tap to work with the spray gun and screwed them together in the shop to check they fitted. My fatal mistake was not pulling them apart again, meaning I only got charged for one adaptor. A female security guard was watching and as soon as I was out of the door she took me aside and accused me of stealing. It was an honest mistake and I offered to pay the 69p for the adaptor straightaway. This jobsworth wasn't having any of it though, telling me the company policy was to prosecute shoplifters like me.

I thought she was joking but she called the police. I was hauled off to the local nick still thinking it would all get cleared up and they would understand we were hardly dealing with the Great Train Robbery here. But once inside I was formally arrested, had to take my belt off and shoelaces out and got photographed for a mugshot before being thrown into a cell. My CID mates from our local pub thought it was a joke when they saw me in there. After my solicitor turned up, I had to write a statement explaining my side of the story before I was allowed out. They wouldn't let the case drop, it went on for months with me being labelled a thief, until my solicitor got a call to say I wouldn't be taken to court. There was no apology, nothing. We were just invited to submit a claim for costs. My innocence made two paragraphs inside the paper, which was a stark contrast to the original front page. So I did an interview telling the fans how stressful the case had been for me and my family.

● ● ●

Other family matters were more positive. Lynne and I were engaged at 18, and married at St Maxentius' Church on 1 June 1974 when I was 19. There didn't seem any point waiting and I liked the idea of stability in my life. I had wanted to get married sooner and asked Lynne about six months after we started going out. But she came back with news from home and said, 'My mum says if you really love me, you'll wait.' So I did, until Vera gave us the thumbs up. I was a picture on the big day in 27-inch flares and a great big knotted tie with wide lapels and platform shoes which made me about 6ft 8in. Lynne, on the other hand, looked beautiful, although she wouldn't give me my ring until after the ceremony as she was so nervous and thought she'd drop it. Lynne's dad was battling cancer, but we were happy he was able to walk her down the aisle and we had a fantastic day.

We had our son Craig a year later, on 9 June 1975, which made me grow up quick, especially as Lynne's dad had died three days before Christmas. His death broke her heart and mine too. Ted was a scouser who loved his football, enjoyed talking to me about the game and would also come and watch me play on his days off from the two jobs he had as a printer and a railwayman. Rachael arrived four years after Craig and they were a boisterous pair, but Lynne's mum, who had moved in to live with us and help out, could calm them down in an instant. Most young married men would run a mile from the mother-in-law, but I didn't. Vera was a godsend and I think it helped her to be involved having just lost her husband. Once she moved in she never left and was with us until the day she died at the age of 89, just before I became manager of West Ham. I didn't resent her for a minute; she was a diamond. I was much more of a hands-on dad than my own father, but I suppose that was a sign of the changing times. Dad was more a reflection of the way society was in his day, where caring for the children and helping them through their tender years was women's work.

Back on the pitch, our bad run towards the end of the season, in which we failed to win any of our last eight, was a sign of things to come. We had lost our coach George Mulhall, who left to become manager of Bradford City, which was a massive blow. He was a passionate football man who played outside-left for Sunderland for years and would challenge us every day. George and Ian were the perfect double-act, feeding off each other. Mulhall's replacement, Stan Anderson, didn't work. Roy Greaves went in to see the boss about Anderson and told him he'd dropped a clanger. Greavsie threw him out, calling him 'a fucking arsehole' and adding that just because he was captain he had no right to question the manager's judgement.

Although we beat Southampton in August 1979, we didn't win another league game until a victory over Forest the following March, by which time the gaffer had been sacked and Anderson put in charge. It was a sad end to Greavsie's time at Bolton. He was a major influence on my career and someone I continued to turn to when I became a manager. He was very hands-on and was not just in charge of the on-field stuff but transfers and contracts too. You could walk into Greavsie's office looking for a rise and he'd just say, 'You're not that good, son.' There were stories of players going in to see him and coming out with less than they were on the season before. He was a hard man to bargain with.

Once, when I was dropped, I stormed into his office to find him rocking back on his chair with his feet up on the desk, towel round his neck after a shower, and cigarette in hand as usual.

'Why have you left me out?' I demanded.

'Can't see you now, I'm too busy, come back on Monday,' he replied.

'Well, you don't look very busy to me,' I said, which was like a red rag to a bull.

'I said I'm too busy, now PISS OFF.'

I reminded him of the story a few years on and he told me the reason he did it was that by Monday a player couldn't possibly be as angry about being dropped as he was when he found out on a Friday. If the team won, he had no argument, and if it lost, he would be happy the manager had cocked up and knew he had a better chance of playing the next week. It was a special little nugget of advice from a manager with experience.

It was obvious we were going down. Stan was struggling and just walked around chatting while we played five-a-side. It didn't help that our training ground had been sold off and we were practising in the middle of a dog track full of turds. We finished rock bottom of the First Division, ten points adrift of safety and got exactly what we deserved. Stan claimed he'd only taken over because Greavsie asked him to and that he wouldn't be staying, but astonishingly the board gave him the job full-time. I couldn't wait to get out; there was no way I was hanging around with Stan in charge. The feeling was mutual. Stan couldn't abide me either.

The very idea of leaving Bolton was seismic. I'd been there ten years. It was where I'd turned from boy into man and had my family, but it was time to spread my wings. I wanted more money too. I was on £70 a week and every time a new signing turned up at Bolton he was given twice as much as me. At Forest, when our bus pulled up, the man I was due to be marking, Trevor Francis, drove into the car park in a spanking new Jaguar XJS V12. Yes, he was the first million pound footballer, and I was humble Sam Allardyce playing for bottom of the table Bolton, but I was driving a Marina 1800 and it struck me that the gap between me and Trevor was far too big. My career wasn't going to last forever, I wanted a bigger piece of the pie and I wanted to play at the highest level I could. Bolton wasn't the place for me any more.

The best way to let clubs know you wanted a move was to develop a relationship with the national newspaper journalists in the North who could put a story in the paper to help you. I found out from them that the season before, Arsenal and Tottenham had made enquiries about my availability but that the club hid it from me. There was also the time West Brom boss Ron Atkinson was talking to Greavsie after a game when

Lynne and I walked past and Ron asked out loud, 'How much for Sam?' Ian turned to Lynne and said, 'How much is Sam worth then?' And she replied 'Millions!' Ron told Greavsie that if we were playing games, he wouldn't bother asking again. Lynne wonders if she ruined my chances of a move to Manchester United because Ron took over at Old Trafford a year later. I like to tell her she did!

FROM THE DORCHESTER
TO THE DEN

4

'If Ian Greaves thinks you're good enough that will do for me, so let's get this deal done. What do you want?' Norwich City manager John Bond had a reputation for being forthright and didn't disappoint.

There had been plenty of interest in me when news of my wanting to leave Bolton came out, which was a boost to the ego, but I had to sort out my own transfer because in those days agents didn't bother with the likes of me. So I consulted Alan Gowling, the rep at Bolton for the PFA, who would help with advice. Norwich, mid-table in the First Division, came in with a £150,000 bid, so I drove over to East Anglia to meet John Bond. He offered £150 a week and a £10,000 signing-on fee, with a promise that if I did well he'd take me onto Manchester City, where he expected to be offered the job when Malcolm Allison was sacked. 'Can't put anything in writing though, you understand, but I give you my word.' He was right about City; he took over four months later.

Derby wanted me but had just been relegated with Bolton. Colin Addison made a great pitch and offered to beat anything Norwich had put on the table. Stupidly, I told him exactly what the Norwich deal was rather than adding a bit on, and he gave me an extra £30 a week on top. The PFA suggested I add in some extras, so I also asked for the cost of removals and a car. I dare say I could have tried for a boat and a plane as well because Addison was very keen. We verbally agreed a three-year contract and I asked for the night to think it over.

Addison rang that evening wanting an answer. I said it looked like a 'yes' but I would have to tell Bondy first. I was concerned that if Bond went to City and didn't take me, I would be left high and dry at Norwich. Addison was fine with that and said he looked forward to me joining. Next morning at 8am, the phone went again and it was Ken Knighton, manager of Sunderland who had been promoted back to the First Division. He vowed to beat anything Derby were offering and I wasn't going to look a gift-horse in the mouth. I asked Gowling what the position was with me having agreed to go to Derby. Alan's response was that if I hadn't signed a contract, the ball was still in my court. 'You've got to do the best for yourself, Sam.'

I told Addison of Sunderland's interest and how I owed it to my family to see what Knighton had to say but that I hadn't ruled Derby out. 'Fuck off,' he said. 'You're going there, I know it.' The Sunderland contract was £300 a week, and £20,000 for signing on. It was more than four times the amount I was on at Bolton, and they were in a higher division. Baz Siddall was playing for them by now and he said Knighton was alright and I should move. But the money was so good that even if Baz had told me Knighton was a complete imbecile, I'd still have signed.

Typically, as soon as I got there, Baz had too much to say for himself again and lost his place to Chris Turner. Sunderland had talented players in Gary Rowell, Kevin Arnott, Shaun Elliott and little Stan Cummins, along with defender Steve Whitworth. It was a big club and I had fond memories of having scored my best ever goal against them five years earlier, a towering header from the penalty spot into the top corner. The TV commentator Gerald Sinstadt exclaimed, 'What a goal that was, what a goal!' A fair summary, I thought.

I was made captain and after we beat Everton 3–1 in our first home game, I drove back home to Bolton. That journey became the bane of my life and it quickly wore me down. In the winter it was horrendous and, frankly, dangerous. Even though we had a new place lined up in Chester-le-Street in Durham, we couldn't sell our house, with interest rates going through the roof and very few people buying. I was in a hotel in Washington, travelling back after every game, home or away, before driving back to Sunderland on a Sunday night or sometimes very early Monday morning with Craig screaming, 'Don't go, Daddy!' Knighton knew it was getting to me and sympathised to the point where he tried to get a bridging loan organised for me by the club. The chairman Tom Cowie wasn't interested, not helped by the fact he was involved in a ruck with Knighton. The boss had gone public about having to pay out of his own pocket for the team to stay overnight in a hotel before a Christmas home game because Cowie wouldn't stump up. I went to see Cowie myself and explained it was the first time I'd moved since I was 15 and, as he'd invested a substantial sum in me, it made sense to try and help move my family up to the area. The situation was affecting my game, made worse by the fact I was captain.

Cowie ran a car sales business and said, 'It doesn't affect my reps when they travel all over the country and don't see their families.' My argument that they didn't have to be in peak shape to play top-level football cut no ice. I was wasting my time and suggested he get rid of me as soon as possible. 'That's up to the manager, not me,' said Cowie. 'I'm not helping you.' So I asked Ken to transfer-list me, because if he didn't my form was bound to decline in the circumstances and he'd end up just not picking me. True enough, as results dipped, I got left out. One Monday as I arrived at Roker Park, I saw the directors sat upstairs in the lounge and knew what that meant: Ken was out along with his assistant, Frank Clark. It was rumoured Frank was asked to take the job, but he walked through loyalty to Ken. I was to become good friends with Frank in later years when he became an executive at the League Managers' Association and I was on the committee.

Mick Docherty, son of the legendary Tommy, was promoted to caretaker manager from reserve-team coach, having not long finished as a Sunderland player. We lost at West Brom and at home to Brighton but, incredibly, won at Liverpool on the last day of the season thanks to a goal from Cummins. Ten thousand Sunderland fans at Anfield were ecstatic. I came on as sub, but I was grateful for the extra bonus the chairman gave us for staying up – a week's wages of £300.

Docherty didn't get the job, and when new boss Alan Durban arrived in the summer of 1981 he asked me to stay but I told him my situation and begged to go. I'd got out of the hotel and been lodging with our striker, John Hawley, in a nice bungalow in Cleadon, but it was hardly an ideal arrangement and I was drinking too much because I was bored with nothing to do in the evenings. Durbs didn't pick me and it was obvious he had to sell me. George Mulhall had taken over at Bolton and wanted me, but I would have had to take a massive pay cut. I may have been miserable at Sunderland, but the money eased the pain. Then Millwall, who were in the Third Division, came in for me. Initially, I laughed it off. It was a two-division drop and travelling there from home was going to be even worse. But they matched my Sunderland wages with £30,000 for signing on and a £10,000 loyalty bonus payable at the end of the contract. I still wasn't taking it too seriously and Lynne was keen for me to go back to Bolton, but even she could see that a 50 per cent wage cut made no sense. I wasn't going to have long as a player, and at 26 had to maximise my earning power, even if it didn't look a great move for my career.

● ● ●

I persuaded Lynne to go to London and meet the Millwall chairman Alan Thorne, and if she didn't like it, I'd see if I could strike a better deal with Bolton. The minute we got off the train at Euston, Alan worked his charm, pulling up at the station in his personalised Rolls Royce. He took us off to the Dorchester to meet the player-manager Peter Anderson who told me he'd been watching me and was hoping I would join. He saw me as the new Barry Kitchener, a famous Millwall central defender, who was coming to the end of his career. Lynne and I went for something to eat with Alan and his partner Sharon. He was a local lad made good with his slicked-back hair, a trilby and a crombie coat, which made him look like the old comedian Tommy Trinder. He was a property developer who'd built a number of tower blocks in London and had pictures of them all over his house. Alan had the sales patter with that East End accent when he greeted you, as in 'Alright, Saaaaam?'

He sold Millwall to Lynne more than to me and offered us one of his houses in Sevenoaks to live in rent free. This was no suburban semi; it was a six-bedroom mansion. It had a special booklet all of its own, advertising its sale with gorgeous gardens, a swimming pool, games room, party room and its own bar. The chauffeur's apartment was on the top floor and we were allowed to use his services when he was free. Lynne was putty in Alan's hand. He knew that getting the wife onside was three-quarters of the battle when trying to sign a player. It was funny that after Millwall struck an agreement to buy me from Sunderland for £95,000, every friend we had in Bolton came to stay with us within six months. Sharon and Lynne became good friends, to the point where on occasions when I got home after training Lynne would be out with Sharon lunching on Park Lane.

I hadn't thought too deeply about where my career was going, but it hit me when I ran out for my first game, Chester away, in front of 2,052 fans. I could have counted them all in about ten minutes, and it was easy to pick out Lynne and the kids in the stand. My last game of the previous season had been at Anfield in front of 40,000. What had I done? I was going to have to work hard motivating myself for days like these.

There were a few local heroes at the Den – Dave Martin, Paul Roberts, Andy Massey and Keith 'Rhino' Stevens had the gift of the gab and were always cheating at cards on the team coach. They were good young lads though, who were making their way in the game. We finished the season just above halfway, but Thorne wanted promotion. Striker Trevor Aylott and Willie Carr, the Wolves veteran, joined before the new season kicked off, but we made a terrible start, and by November Peter was sacked. Trevor and I had been left out of the home match against Wrexham and Alan went mad when he found out we were fit. Peter was suspended when he turned up at the Den for the game and complained, 'I thought only criminals and hooligans got banned from football grounds.' Peter was only 33 and it was his first management job, but it all proved too much for him. We were put back in the team and drew 1–1.

Our poor results weren't the only thing exercising Alan's mind. Millwall's hooligan problem had resurfaced. The club did not have a reputation for friendly fans and when we lost 1–0 away to Isthmian League Slough in the FA Cup first round, it all kicked off in the crowd. Alan threatened to close the Den if there was any more trouble and never reopen it again. Older players like me who cost a bit of money were understandably getting the blame for our poor form. I hadn't played in the Third Division before joining Millwall, and although it was easier in that opponents weren't as good, the ball spent so much time in the air that I needed two aspirins before every game to cope with heading away so many balls. We were waiting to see who the new manager would be, when Alan invited me out and hit me with a question which to this day still leaves me in shock.

'Will you be the new manager, Sam?'

I was only 28, it was crazy. I wasn't remotely tempted, I was only interested in playing at that stage and was keen to get my career back on the right track after getting seduced by the money. It would have been the start of the end of my playing career and was way too soon.

Having turned Alan down, he went out and got someone ten years older, George Graham, once a player with Arsenal, Chelsea and Manchester United, who would go on to become a big-name boss with the Gunners. George came from coaching QPR and brought Theo Foley with him. I was looking forward to the change of regime with somebody who had a real pedigree as a player. George's training sessions were based on persistent practice, repeating and repeating drills until we got it right. We worked on being a unit to catch people offside which I was quite comfortable with. It was a strict management style built on discipline, which was ironic because apparently, as a player, George was anything but disciplined.

One day, I was summoned to George's office.

'As captain, it will be your job to tell me everything going on in the dressing room, and I mean everything,' he said.

There was no way I was going to do that, not a chance. What would the lads think?

'I won't grass-up my team-mates, boss. I'm their captain, they look up to me,' I told him, in terms that made it clear this was not for negotiation.

That was the end. I was cast aside to train on my own with Willie Carr who had also been blown out by George, and basically we were just made to run all the time. I think part of it was that George knew I'd been offered the manager's job and he saw me as a threat. He needed me gone. Some of my major influences in the game were called George. There was Pearson for the Dudley town team, Taylor the youth coach at Wanderers and Mulhall the first-team coach. George spoiled the run. That said, although I wasn't best pleased with George at the time, I have used some of his management methods, particularly the repetition practices. You learn something from everyone in a football career, and it all adds to your experience.

It was about getting away now but on my terms, not George's. The transfer deadline was the last Thursday in March, and the day before he told me I could have a free transfer, which gave me little time to fix up a new club. I'd heard Charlton fancied me and I talked to their manager, Lennie Lawrence. It was a good chance to start moving forward again, with Charlton being in the Second Division. The bonus was we wouldn't have to move from our new house in Kent and the kids wouldn't have to change school. Alan had tired of us living rent free at his place so we'd had to find somewhere ourselves, but we loved it in Sevenoaks, which had a community feel to it with a fantastic standard of living. I sat by the phone all the next day waiting for Lennie to ring . . . and waited . . . and waited for the call that never came. Lennie did ring the following day to apologise but it was too late now to get a new club, so I had to grit my teeth through to the end of the season.

It's no fun when you're out of favour. I still had to sit in the stands for home games, and if the team were away I trained on a Saturday morning before going home. I was playing for the reserves, but even that led to trouble when I asked for a new pair of boots. You were only allowed one pair per season, but mine always took a hammering. George told me to look in the skip where all the old boots were kept and fish a pair out of there. I refused, I wanted new ones, but he said, 'If you don't want to wear the second-hand ones, you don't have to play.' He was being pathetic. I made it plain that I wasn't refusing to play which could have got me suspended and allowed Millwall to withhold my wages. In the end, I swallowed it and bought my own in order to get a game.

I wrote to every club in the First and Second Divisions, telling them I was available on a free, or rather Lynne did while I told her what to type. With my dyslexia it would have taken me weeks to do them all, but Lynne was a shorthand typist. George said Chesterfield and Doncaster wanted me and that I should take one of them up on their offers. Bury tried too, but they were in the Fourth Division. It felt like my career was going down the pan. I'd put money first and now it was coming back to savage me. We went off for a family holiday in Florida and when we got back Lynne took a call and said, 'It's Bobby Gould for you.' I thought she was kidding but Lynne wouldn't have known he had just left Bristol Rovers to become the boss of First Division Coventry. It had to be one of my old mates playing a prank, yet sure enough it was the real Bobby Gould. He'd got my letter, seen me playing for Millwall against Bristol Rovers, and thought I could do a job for him as a back-up centre-half. He offered a one-year deal on the same £300 a week and bonuses for appearances. I was more than happy with that. Where was the pen?

Gouldy had a gift for finding players in the lower divisions and non-league. The best of them all was Stuart 'Psycho' Pearce, a full-time electrician and part-timer at Wealdstone who he bought for £25,000 a few months after me and who went on to play 78 times for England. He also found three who went on to play in Coventry's 1987 FA Cup winning side: Micky Gynn from Fourth Division Peterborough, Trevor Peake from Lincoln and Dave Bennett from Cardiff, as well as Dave Bamber, Micky Adams and Terry Gibson. Bobby mixed it up, adding more top-class experience in Ashley Grimes from Manchester United.

● ● ●

The next day, an agent called Dennis Roach asked if I fancied going to the States where some of the greatest players like Bobby Moore and Pele had played in the late '70s. America had exploited the loan system where players could pop over for three months in the summer, as Worthy and Willie Morgan had done, and be back for the start of the English season. But FIFA thought that was abusing the rules and decided transfers had to be permanent, which made it much more difficult to get the best players and was probably why the US League fell apart in the mid-1980s. I'd never spoken to Dennis in my life but he reckoned he had a good deal lined up for me with Tampa Bay Rowdies.

It didn't look possible for me to go. I didn't want it to threaten my move to Coventry but Dennis told me to leave it with him and he'd square it off with Gouldy. The deal was $1,000 a week, flights for the family, apartment paid for, car, private medical insurance and win bonuses on top. What was not to like about that? Gouldy agreed to let me join Coventry when I returned from the States. If Tampa made the play-offs it could be September, but Bobby knew I would be fit and able to go straight into the Coventry team if necessary. This was all too good to be true.

I talked to Roy Greaves, who played for Seattle after leaving Bolton, and he thought it was a great opportunity. Now I had to execute the next stage of my plan. I didn't want George knowing I had two clubs lined up; I wanted him to think I needed paying off so that I could find a club. 'Make me an offer and I'll happily cancel my registration and be out of your hair,' I said. He agreed to speak to Alan, who wasn't talking to me since George had turned up. I think he wanted to put some distance between us and not interfere. Anyway, George came back with a cheque for £15,000 and asked, 'Where are you going then, back to Bolton?'

'No,' I said. 'I'm off to play for Tampa and when I come back I'll be signing for Coventry. See you, George. Thanks for the money!'

5

STATESIDE WITH THE ROWDIES

The American adventure was one which was to shape my future as a manager a great deal more than I realised. I drove home and packed my bags for a flight into the unknown to Seattle, which is where Tampa were playing, but I got stuck in traffic on the way to Heathrow and missed the plane. I eventually reached the twinkling lights of Seattle with about 48 hours to spare and got adjusted to the time difference as best I could. I caught up with the coach, Al Miller, who came through the American college ranks and was briefly the US national boss. His team was an extraordinary mix of South African, South American, Dutch, Brazilian, Argentinian, Canadian, American and me, the Englishman. Such a diversity of cultures was not something I'd encountered before, and we didn't all agree on how to play the game. It was a whirlwind going into that first match in front of 60,000 in a place where they were fanatical about their soccer. Boy was it noisy, not least because this was an indoor arena.

We nominally had players in defence but we didn't know how to defend. There only seemed to be me who was bothered about it, while everyone else went running up to the other end doing tricks. It was difficult for the coach to get his message across too, with all the different languages being spoken. I don't know how I got through the game on the astro-turf which was a surface completely alien to me. What with the travelling and the heat, I was on my arse, absolutely dead. I was cramping everywhere and begging them to take me off. We lost and went straight on to San José afterwards for another game, before I even set foot in Tampa.

I was struggling with the 80-90 per cent humidity in the first few weeks. The coaches were telling me to eat bananas which would help me cope with the conditions. We took supplements and had to drink two to three litres of energy drinks from a barrel every 20 minutes while training. All I usually had was a cup of tea with two sugars.

The family were set up in a condominium on a beautiful bay which was also where they housed players from the Tampa Bay Buccaneers, the American NFL team. They would have laughed their heads off, if they'd known I was nicknamed Big Sam. Teeny Weeny Little Sam would have been nearer the mark when I was around those blokes; they were absolutely enormous. We had access to all the Bucs' backroom staff, their training facilities and played at their home, the Tampa Stadium. The way they prepared during the week opened my eyes and was another one of those life-changing experiences. I learned there was so much more to conditioning than what we did in England where you had a run around in training, a game of five-a-side, steak for a pre-match meal, a shot of whisky from the skip on the way out onto the pitch and a couple of pints in the bar afterwards. Their attention to detail for every player was staggering.

There were physios and doctors available on site and mobile scanners to instantly check on injuries. They also had three masseurs. I'd never been at a club which even had one. We'd only just got a proper physio at Millwall to replace the old-fashioned sponge man but had to go to the hospital to see him. The masseurs were brutal. I had hamstring problems but they identified the scar tissue building up and got right down to work, digging their thumbs and fingers deep into my aching muscles while I squealed like a pig. Over a period of time, my hamstrings improved no end and I hadn't felt so good for years. They explained how work on the scar tissue could extend my stride by three inches, making me more effective on the field. Nobody had ever done this with me and they reckoned I'd be flying when I got back to England. There were half-a-dozen 'strapping' men who would rigorously tape you up for protection against injury. They were especially important when we played on the astro-turf where you got blisters and burns. The Americans and Canadians wouldn't dream of going on the pitch without being totally strapped up. We had a psychiatrist too, which I initially found rather strange, but nobody thought anything of it out there. Football clubs in England have only recently learned of their benefits.

I watched the Bucs lads doing their pre-season and it was scary what they went through. Every day featured an early morning session, breakfast, a late morning session, lunch, then an afternoon session. There were separate programmes for the quick players, and the heavy lads were constantly pounding away on the big weights. There was a head coach, defensive coaches, offensive coaches, kicking coaches, and conditioning coaches along with nutritionists. And they had statistics guys and analysts who planned the plays and monitored everyone's performance in training and games. Nothing was left to chance.

The Rowdies was a fun experience. Home games were 'a blast' as they say out there and the supporters, known as the Fannies, really got behind us. There was a loud organ which played faster when we went on the attack and slower if we were knocking the ball around in defence. The club mottoes were to 'Get up, go out and get Rowdy' and 'Go make a fanny of yourself' which we players often did. We weren't the greatest side and failed to qualify for the play-offs, but I wouldn't have missed it for the world. It was an experience which stood me in good stead for when I became a manager and helped give me an edge in English football, which hadn't caught up with the techniques I learned out there.

● ● ●

Brilliant as Tampa was, it was time to get back to reality. We moved into our new house in Bromley Cross, which is still the family home today, and I headed off to the Midlands to play for Coventry. The guys at the Bucs were dead right about my fitness. With all that conditioning work, I felt like an athlete on drugs. I was as fit as a flea. The challenge was showing everyone that, at the age of 28, and having gone down to the Third Division, I could still do it at the top level. I'd come in as back-up, but within a fortnight of my return I was not only in the team but I was captain too.

Although we lost at Sunderland on my Coventry debut, results picked up as we beat Arsenal away and went on a good run. Stuart Pearce had one of the best debuts I've ever seen in our home win against QPR. He was shy but fearless, without doubt the find of the season, and so began a long and illustrious career. I thought, 'God almighty, Gouldy's found one here.'

We walloped Liverpool 4–0 at Highfield Road just before Christmas, with Terry Gibson getting a hat-trick against a team which read Grobbelaar, Lawrenson, Nicol, Neal, Hansen, Kennedy, Whelan, Souness, Lee, Dalglish, Rush. I shudder to think what mood Souey was in afterwards. Honestly, I thought I was dreaming. Beating Liverpool by such a margin at any time is an achievement, but they went on to win the League, League Cup and European Cup that season. It was the greatest year in their history. We got a bit too excited with ourselves and after that it was all downhill, with Liverpool getting their revenge big style when they beat us 5–0 at Anfield in the return.

We plummetted down the league and Gouldy fell out with half the team. He had a massive bust-up with our keeper Raddy Avramovic over a goal he let in, and Raddy being a tough Serb did not back down. Gouldy told him he would never play for the club again and went with 18-year-old Perry Suckling instead. Perry had played a few games at the start of the season, but now we were in a downward spiral and it was asking a lot of such a young lad. We had to build up his confidence by shooting directly at him in training so he could make a lot of saves. Gouldy went mad if any of us tried to score.

It was while Coventry were playing Birmingham that I committed the only foul I ever intentionally inflicted on anyone. It was on Mick Harford and I felt he thoroughly deserved it. Harford had a reputation as a bruiser of a centre-forward who took no crap from anyone and liked to scare you into submission. Every time you went into an aerial challenge with Mick, you had to be 100 per cent committed because you could guarantee he would be. You also had to protect yourself when he was launching himself through the air, or he would splatter you. As I saw him coming in from the side, he had his elbow out. I could see my nose, which wasn't pretty at the best of times, was at risk. I got the elbow in first, catching him smack in the teeth and splitting his top lip open. Even today you can still see the scar, but there's a war wound on my elbow too. Mick probably spent years trying to get me back. But he never did, and in fairness gave an interview in which he said, 'Sam's elbow caught me a treat. The lights went out. I had 70 stitches and was in hospital for four days. You could see my teeth through my lip. It taught me a lesson – to look after myself. I bore Sam no grudge.'

In that same article about hard men, my old mentor Nat Lofthouse was quoted and recalled, 'In my day, you could get your bollocks kicked off. The difference to then and now is that the defender who did it would walk around the pitch with you afterwards and help you find them.'

I enjoyed the battles with strikers like Harford, they were part of the game and we both understood that. It was the little players I felt less comfortable against, they could break your legs. A small forward would run at you, entice you into the tackle then slide a foot over the ball and stamp on your shin. It's still done now and referees never spot it. The dirtiest player I ever encountered wasn't a forward though, he was a midfielder, Johnny Giles, an Irishman who made his name at Leeds as an enforcer alongside Billy Bremner. He was player-manager at West Brom against Bolton and was someone who could handle himself and wouldn't be intimidated. He was a hugely talented player but had a real dark side. He would go right over the top, you'd feel it on your shin, moan at the ref when you went down in agony then tell you to 'Fucking get up, it's a man's game.'

I don't know how I never had a serious injury in my whole playing career. It was remarkable for a centre-half whose prime job was to battle it out with the opposition centre-forward either in the air or on the ground. I had a few ligament strains through over-stretching for a tackle and rolled my ankle a couple of times but nothing too bad. I never did my cartilage either, which again, in my day, could finish you. Many old players now can barely walk because the whole cartilage was taken out and they were left with bone on bone. They all need knee replacement operations.

We reached the last game of the season at Coventry having to beat Norwich City to avoid relegation. It should never have come to that considering how well we were going up to Christmas. George Curtis, the managing director, was on the prowl, putting the fear of God into everyone. He was the big man at Coventry and something of a burden for a manager because of his legendary status at the club. He was a bit mad and used to grab players and try to bite their noses. Not that he tried that with me, mind. It was a nervous day but we were leading 2–1 when City's big centre-forward Robert Rosario went for a header and everything happened in slow motion. The ball went over me, over Andy Peake and took forever to bounce towards the goal. First I was convinced it was in, then I thought it was wide, before it hit the inside of the post and came back into Perry's hands. We'd done it and a huge roar rang round the stadium. Yet again, I'd been involved in final-day drama. It was getting too much for the old ticker.

Gould and I had a chat at Christmas about a new two-year contract for me starting the next July and we agreed to wait until the end of the season to sort it out. But now that we'd avoided the drop, he suddenly told me I was being released!

'You fucking what?' I said in my finest English. 'You're letting me go now?' I'd been screwed good and proper.

With that I grabbed the bin-liner with my boots in and marched out of his office. Gouldy got the sack the following Christmas but went on to win the FA Cup with Wimbledon in 1988, the year after Coventry won it.

● ● ●

I was totally devastated and headed home wondering, once more, where my next club would be. At the age of 29 I was fast becoming a journeyman. It was time to send the begging letters out again, with Lynne's typing skills in full flow. I was signed up by Mick Buxton for Second Division Huddersfield in July 1984. He had a few of my old Bolton mates in his team including Paul Jones, my former sparring partner at centre-half, Phil Wilson and David Burke. They weren't a bad side, having finished mid-table, and had a clever little striker in Mark Lillis, known throughout football as Bhuna because of his love of a curry. When Bhuna farted, you stood well back! We also had Dale Tempest up front who is now a betting expert on Sky Sports. We were capable of some great stuff on our day, like when we beat Leeds, the big boys from along the road. The fans enjoyed that one.

Bolton, now back in the Third Division, came in for me at the end of the season with a £15,000 bid and offered a three-year contract with the possibility of a coaching role at the end of it. Huddersfield snapped their hands off – their budget was tight and they needed the money, so I was heading back to my spiritual home. Charlie Wright, the goalkeeper when I first played for Bolton, was in charge with Walter Joyce as his coach and, as well as me, he signed Asa Hartford, once famous for failing a medical at Leeds because of a hole in his heart, and striker David Cross. It was good to be back, we were living in Bolton anyway, the kids were thriving and all was right with the world. There's always some bugger who wants to spoil it though – step forward Phil Neal. We hadn't been doing well under Charlie and I suppose a change was inevitable, but when he got the sack I asked for an interview for the job. After all, Bolton said when they signed me that there were coaching possibilities down the line. This was a bit earlier than planned, I got an interview but not the job and in came Neal from Liverpool as player-manager.

You couldn't argue with Neal's pedigree: 500 games for Liverpool, four times European Cup winner, ten First Division titles and 50 England caps. That didn't make him a good manager though. He heard that I'd applied for the job and seemed to be gunning for me from day one. He decided to play centre-half, having spent his entire career as a full-back, and took my place, telling me we needed some stability at the back. I said to him, 'If you don't want me, just tell me.' He kept me hanging around and we got to the final of the 1986 Freight Rover Trophy, a competition for the Third and Fourth Division clubs. It was my first time at Wembley, but I was a sub and I didn't get on. I just sat stewing on the bench, watching us get stuffed 3–0 by Bristol City. Neal got Bolton relegated to the Fourth Division for the first time in their history during his six-and-a-half uneventful years in charge. I couldn't believe it when he became Graham Taylor's assistant for England, but a documentary showing him and Taylor together during the 1994 World Cup qualifying campaign summed him up. He was just a nodding dog.

I asked the directors to pay me up and let me go. I argued it was for the benefit of both Neal and myself because we were never going to resolve our stand-off. More begging letters were dropped in the postbox and first on the phone was Frank Worthington, who was player-manager at Tranmere. I drove over and decided before I got there not to sign. That drive through the Mersey tunnel every day would have done my head in, and when I saw what a rundown ground they had, that confirmed it. John McGrath, the eccentric manager from Preston, got in touch and he sold the club to me in half-an-hour, even though Preston had only stayed in the Football League thanks to the old-style re-election system. 'We'll get the best out of you,' said McGrath. 'You can resurrect your career with me. I'm great at getting teams out of this league. You'll be the backbone of the club, my man in the trenches.' He had total faith in me. The one drawback was that Preston played on artificial turf and I was worried my poor knees wouldn't cope. I wasn't wrong. We trained on it every day and they ached like hell.

I loved McGrath, a former centre-half of the old school for Newcastle and Southampton. He set us up in a 3-5-2 and called the defence the Solicitors because we always had to keep the door closed. He reckoned his solicitor never opened the door to anyone. John did a lot of after-dinner speaking and was a brilliant motivator. But when he tried writing things down on the blackboard, he was more dyslexic than I was, it was complete gobbledegook. He was better just talking to us. His stories always had a motive behind them, even if they went on a while. We had to have the team talk on a Friday, because otherwise he wouldn't have finished it in time for the Saturday afternoon kick-off. And everyone had to be weighed on Fridays in front of the rest of the squad. They were proper butcher's scales too and John would register meticulously on his notepad where the red needle landed. Our little midfielder Ronnie Hildersley used to get a terrible going over. John called him the stuffed turkey because of the way he ran, and was always telling him to get the weight off. Ronnie got paranoid and would run round the track every Friday morning in a bin-liner sweating the weight off, so that John didn't rip into him. To be fair, we all shit ourselves about the scales, because if you were over the weight you either got fined or had to come in on your day off.

John referred to referees as bananas and expected the players to do the same. He would tell us that when we got pissed off with the ref, we should just say, 'Banana, you don't know what you are doing. They're useless, these bananas.' In that way, we wouldn't get booked for dissent or foul and abusive language. After all, how could a ref book you for having a go at a banana? There was logic in the madness. But why did he call them bananas? According to John, when they start out in the game they are green and by the time they finish they are yellow and bent.

We got to the fourth round of the FA Cup against Newcastle who were in the First Division, three divisions above us, and John told us of his counter-attacking plan.

'We're going to be the fishermen today, lads,' he said. 'We're going to get the rod, put the float on, put the hook on, put the weight on the line and get the maggot. Then we're gonna cast it out and wait . . . and wait . . . and wait. The float will start bobbing up and down but you've still got to wait, and eventually it will go under and that's when you strike! Then you reel them in and bash them on the head.'

We didn't catch the fish as it happened, but although we lost we played well, which stood us in good stead for Halifax away the following week.

So on he goes, 'Well lads, last week was like being in the nightclub and seeing Miss Great Britain. You wander over to her and you can't believe your luck, you've pulled her. You've got her home and you've sorted her out. Magnificent night! You can't believe it. The week after, there you are, same place, half past two in the morning, nothing. There's one left, roughest bird in the house but you pull her and you take her back. And you know what? It still wants the same thing.'

I think the point was that Newcastle were Miss Great Britain and Halifax the rough bird. Whatever he was getting at, we thumped Halifax 3–1.

John liked to tell us about soup too. 'You know lads, when you make a soup, it can't all be the same. You've got to have a little bit of carrot, a little bit of swede, a little bit of meat, and a little bit of spice. You've to have a nice mixture. The soup only tastes nice with all the right ingredients. So that is what we are, we are all different. We are a bowl of brilliant soup, we are all mixed in together, with all different ingredients, that's why we are winning.'

I used to use some of John's tales during my early days in management but I gave up in the end. Players started thinking I was as mad as him, and it was all rather lost on the foreigners.

One day, he gave me a pep-talk about my lifestyle. 'You're in your thirties now, Sam, and I know you like a few pints. I used to be like that, no-one could drink me under the table and I drank beer just like you, so I put on a pound or two. I knew I had to change, so I was in this bar one night and saw Vat 69 whisky and I thought, "I had a good year in '69, even got in the England representative team," so I cut out the beer and I've drunk whisky ever since. You should try it.'

It was true I was the wrong side of 30, but I had a few more years left in me. I'd cut down on going out during the week and just had a few pints after matches and the odd cigarette here and there. Loads of players were like that. Ian Greaves would throw me a fag after games if I'd done well, and I used to smoke it in the bath. At most I would have two fags a night after tea during the week if I wasn't going out, and that was it. I only started smoking heavily when I became a manager, and kicking the habit was always difficult for me. I've stopped now but I could smoke one in an instant. My mates detest smoking but I actually like it, which makes the craving even worse, especially as Lynne is partial to the odd one or two. I'm not convinced I will never smoke again.

For all my occasional vices, I was looking after my body pretty well. I'd got into a book called *Eat to Win* by Doctor Robert Haas which provided sports nutrition advice for athletes explaining how, if you had a good diet, you performed better in competition. It told how our bodies used carbohydrates, proteins and fats, and tennis stars like Martina Navratilova and Ivan Lendl swore by his methods. It certainly provided food for thought, and was another little piece of intelligence I filed away for when I became a manager.

We were promoted from the Fourth Division in second place behind Northampton, and the next season we consolidated in the Third Division with Frank Worthington joining us for a while after losing his job at Tranmere. John consulted Worthy after a training session on the artificial turf and asked what he thought the difference was between grass and plastic. 'Dunno, John,' he said, 'I've never smoked plastic.' It was the only time I'd ever known John lost for words.

John thought I was coming to the end and wasn't going to play me any more. I'd done my coaching badges and was thinking of getting into management. An interview came up at Doncaster but I didn't get it, and I went for jobs at York and Notts County and didn't get them either. While I'd been doing my coaching course I ran into Brian Talbot, the former Arsenal and England midfielder, who had not long been in charge at West Brom after Ron Atkinson left for the second time. I knew Brian from him being chairman of the PFA and me being a PFA delegate at most of the clubs I'd played for. He needed a reserve-team coach and asked if I fancied it. Too right I did. He wanted me to stay registered as a player too, which suited me. From being an outcast at Preston, my career was back on the up again.

6

DO YOU KNOW THE WAY TO MONTEREY'S?

Dad died just before I went to West Brom. A double-stroke left him barely able to walk, and over the next four years he deteriorated until he was bed-ridden. It wasn't a shock when the end came, and for Mum it was probably a blessing because it was hard work looking after him. She was embarrassed by the way he verbally abused the nurses and kicked out at them whenever he was in hospital. Even before the stroke, he was getting more and more miserable and his 70th birthday was one I'll never forget. My sister Mary, brother Robert, me, Lynne and all our kids arranged to go down and surprise him on the big day. We took drinks and food with us so that Mum didn't have to do anything, and were there in good time for lunch. We were all waiting for him when he got back in from the social club, but he went straight to bed, ignoring everyone.

Mum was so upset by his behaviour, while the kids couldn't understand what he was playing at. But we all stupidly hung around, waiting for him to wake up so we could celebrate his birthday. A few hours later, we heard five or six loud bangs on the bedroom floor and he shouts, 'Have they gone yet? The snooker final's on.' That was it, it was time to go. I could see the hurt in Mum's eyes and went to give her a big hug, but it was typical of Dad, no-one could disturb his routine. He was who he was, and nobody was going to change him, certainly not his family.

Mum deserved to enjoy the latter years of her life, having spent so long looking after Dad, but sadly she died of a heart attack two-and-a-half years after his death. It was a shock to us all, because she seemed to be in such good health and was an active pensioner who played bingo and went out on day-trips with her friends from the retirement home where she'd moved to. Her passing affected me terribly, I was always her little boy and it took a long time to accept she was gone.

I was still leading a nomadic life with Lynne and the kids in Bolton, and I moved in with our striker John Thomas's mum and dad in Birmingham to begin life as a West Brom coach. John was a team-mate at Preston who was now at the Hawthorns, and I was grateful to him for helping me out.

I was playing for and managing the reserves and was thoroughly enjoying it. We won the Birmingham Senior Cup and I even got a game for the first team. But being a reserve-team boss wasn't an easy job. There were the keen younger players who wanted to get on, and the pissed-off older ones who'd been dropped and weren't interested in lifting a leg. It was a good test of my man-management skills. You had to try and create some harmony, so I'd encourage them saying, 'Do well lads and I'll let the boss know and you'll be back in the first team. But if you're shit, I'll let him know about that too.' One lad really impressed me, Ugo Ehiogu. He'd written asking for a trial, turned up from London on his own with his boots for a practice game, and impressed enough to get taken on. He went from youths to reserves to first team in an instant. After a handful of senior games, Aston Villa signed him. He was an exceptional talent. I felt the same as when Gouldy found Stuart Pearce.

The first team didn't have a great season and Brian decided on a change, promoting me to first-team coach and demoting Stuart Pearson to the reserves. It was an awkward situation and Stuart didn't take it very well. I'm not sure I would have done either. He wanted to go but the board wouldn't pay him off, so he had to accept it and get on with it. I didn't feel inferior to Stuart or Brian despite their great playing careers. Stuart was a striker for Manchester United and England, while Brian was a midfielder for Ipswich, Arsenal and England, but I was happy with the work I'd done in the reserves and didn't fear the step up.

Brian was one of those managers who did everything. He managed the team, went off scouting, took part in training and expected his coaches to put the work in too. He lived in a flat in Edgbaston away from his family, so had nothing to do but concentrate on the club. As I was living away too, I ended up driving all round the country like him looking for players. Brian was a machine, just as he was when he played. And if he took the players for a run, you could bet he would be at the front. No-one could beat him over a long distance and he set the example for the rest to follow. He was ambitious and saw West Brom as his first stepping stone, but his management career was never as good as his playing one.

The season started okay until our star striker, Don Goodman, began suffering with hamstring problems. Gary Robson, brother of my big mate Bryan, broke a leg and we brought in Graham Roberts, who was a top centre-half at Spurs but was now too slow in my opinion. He was playing alongside Gary Strodder who was equally tortoise-like, and we were getting pulled apart. We had a young defender in Daryl Burgess who I thought should have been in the middle of the back-four, but Brian wanted experience. As we stumbled along, we got to FA Cup third round day on 5 January 1991 where we were up against Isthmian League Woking at the Hawthorns. It was one of those FA Cup ties where the TV people turned up smelling blood and it still features on the broadcast reel of FA Cup shocks. We got done by a lad called Tim Buzaglo, who worked in computers, represented Gibraltar at cricket and in his spare time scored a hat-trick against us in a 4–2 win. It was a classic FA Cup fairytale story. Brian was talking about resigning while the game was still going on and the crowd were calling for his head. I talked him out of it afterwards and realised this was something I would have to endure if I became a manager. Inevitably, despite my advice to Brian, it made no difference. We were sacked.

● ● ●

I was 36 years old and wanted to stay in football, but I had to make a living too. Financially, the family was facing a difficult time. You might wonder how that could be after two decades as a professional footballer. Well, firstly players didn't make anything like the money they do today, and secondly the gastro-pub we'd invested in was in danger of going under. We had the house up as security against it and feared our home would be taken away from us. Once you've defaulted on a mortgage you can't get another one and we had no savings. Everything was tied up in the house and the pub.

I'd always had business interests outside the game and worked hard in the summer. In my early twenties, I went into partnership with my brother-in-law Paul, who owned a motor spares firm that delivered car parts all over the North West. I was playing First Division football on a Saturday and on Sundays was in charge of the shop because Paul needed a day off. I had a fast-food business too with my accountant Pete Cowgill, who is now chairman of national leisurewear chain JD Sports and one of my best friends. We tried to do it all-American style and planned to build up a franchise but the locals preferred things more basic, so we flogged it to a guy who specialised in fish and chip shops.

A footballer's natural home after playing was to run a pub, but I wanted to own one and then expand by adding to the portfolio. I paired up with my old team-mate Roy Greaves who owned Northfield Snooker and Social Club at the far end of Bolton where the locals went in for a pint after work, loved their snooker, pool, darts and dominoes and stayed all night. It reminded me of the social club Dad started which became so successful. Roy got his own licence for the place, which was a cute move as it doubled in value overnight. The breweries wanted as many outlets as they could lay their hands on and to get Northfield they would have had to buy the licence as well as the premises. It was a gold mine. I know we should have been advocating responsible drinking but the punters just drank until they physically could not drink any more. Then they would be off to work the next morning and back in the next night. It was also a place where the rogues and scallywags congregated. A lot of them had no bank accounts, so we cashed their unemployment giros for them and then they'd stay and spend it while talking about all the jobs they did on the side. With Northfield going so well, Roy and I branched out further afield. We realised that with the law stating pubs had to shut at 10.30pm, there was a gap in the market for those who wanted to stay out later but didn't fancy going to a nightclub. You could get a licence for a piano bar which ran to midnight on weekdays and 1am at weekends.

We bought a place right in the middle of Farnworth, on the outskirts of Bolton, and called it Brando's as a nod to the actor Marlon Brando. It went down a storm, with a fella called Norman Vernon running it who was a bit of a comedian and an accomplished MC. We'd done it out really nicely and were making good money. It was £3 to get in at weekends, with a capacity of 250, and it was jammed. The Bolton players helped attract the clientele too. It was Norman's life and he was desperate to buy us out, so we took his money and looked for somewhere new.

Roy and I bought a big building off Manchester Road past the grey-hound track which was about 150 yards from Burnden Park. We figured that if we developed it as a pub restaurant we'd get all the crowds in from the football and the dogs but also the families during times when there was no sport going on locally. Monterey's was born and the locals poured in. There wasn't room to breathe on a matchday and we would take more on a day when Bolton were at home than the other six days put together. But while we might take £14,000 in a week, once you took out the costs of staff, beer and food there wasn't as much left as you might imagine.

The pressure was on to keep the volumes coming through the door, because the moment they dropped the overheads were all-consuming. It was essential to be strict on things like portion control on the plates and watching that the staff didn't give their mates free drinks. Everything is computerised nowadays, so it's easy to tell if someone is letting their pals enjoy a night out on the management, but back then it required efficient stock-taking and then trying to trace who was up to no good. It wasn't easy to track when they were queuing five-deep at the bar. Every £1 that was given away would cost you £3 to get back, because to make £1 profit you had to sell £3 worth of stock. Every pub suffered from this problem, but at times we got badly stung. We'd bought the site for about £250,000 between us and, although we made a profit on Brando's, we still had to borrow a lot of money to finance Monterey's. But we had the place valued at £950,000 and planned to sell up in a few years, with a sizeable return on our investment. That was until Margaret Thatcher killed us overnight.

The Prime Minister acted on a report from the Monopolies and Mergers Commission saying the breweries owned too many pubs. The 'Big Six' breweries were told they could keep 2,000 pubs each but had to sell off half the number they owned over that figure. Some of them had six or seven thousand. We weren't owned by a brewery, we had our own licence, but thousands of pubs suddenly went on the market and the value of ours dropped like a stone. It lost three-quarters of its value in no time at all. There wasn't enough equity to cover our borrowings and it was falling in value every day. The more stringent drink-drive laws were hurting us too. Of course drink-driving is dangerous, but for the pub trade the clampdown hit hard, and if people couldn't drive home they didn't bother coming out. Initially customers were prepared to risk it but the police got more vigilant, and for a lot of our punters losing their licence meant no job.

I was working behind the bar and Lynne was serving the food to try and keep things going and cut the staff costs. Meanwhile, I was coaching part-time at Bury for expenses only thanks to my former Bolton teammate Mike Walsh who had taken over as manager and was flying high in the table. I was hopeful that would turn out to be a more permanent arrangement, but after getting to the Third Division play-offs we lost in the semi-finals to Bolton and Walshy didn't have the budget to pay me. I asked Peter Reid, now manager of Manchester City, if there was anything going with the youth team but there wasn't. We still had Northfield Social Club which, despite the troubles in the trade, was surviving okay but Roy had all his savings invested in Monterey's and I was facing ruin.

I had a players' pension but that wasn't going to be enough. To put it in perspective, it is index linked, rises with inflation and only pays £675 a month now. Roy and I didn't see eye to eye on the best course of action and fell out, which I suppose was understandable. It was sad, with us having been friends since I started at Bolton, but I vowed from then on that if I ever got back into football, I would make it a rule never to hire a friend as a coach. It causes too many complications and blurs your judgement.

●　●　●

It felt like only God could help us, and, in a way, he did. That summer, the phone rang one evening.

'Hello Sam, it's Father Joe Young here!'

'Piss off,' I said, and put the receiver down. I couldn't be bothered with any prank calls, I wasn't in the mood.

The phone went again and the voice protested: 'Sam, please, I really am Father Joe Young and I'm the chairman of Limerick. We wonder if you'd be interested in becoming player-manager of our club.'

What did I have to lose? We flew over for the weekend to have a look at the place, and by a strange quirk Reidy was out there with City for a pre-season game and I watched as the match was played on what was the equivalent of a low-grade semi-pro ground in England. There was a social club at one end with the dressing rooms attached, a crumbling wall around the pitch, and a grass bank with some terracing next to it. Limerick was nicknamed Stab City following a spate of knife murders, which didn't exactly encourage me to sign on the dotted line, and the main street seemed to consist entirely of pubs, some of which opened at six in the morning. I don't know what their licensing laws were or whether they just didn't take any notice.

A consortium had taken over the club which had a proud history in Irish football but got caught up in a lot of politics. Limerick had just been relegated from the Premier Division and it was clear Joe was important to the new owners if they were to make a success of it. Joe was the head of the local parish and his church was just round the corner in the poorest area of Limerick. I can't imagine the collection plate raised much on a Sunday morning, but the locals loved him and he knew everyone.

I took the job and the deal was I would fly over on Thursdays and back home after Sunday's game. I trained back in Bolton and the coach Billy Cunan, who I stayed with, took the locals in the team for practice on a Tuesday night. I told Billy we'd be playing three at the back with me in the centre. I couldn't run any more and it was best I sat in the middle, organised everything and used my experience.

Billy proposed that we get some players in from Dublin and clubs like Shamrock Rovers to strengthen the side. I didn't know the scene so trusted in his advice and we had to rely on them being disciplined enough to train at home. I only saw those players on matchdays, while I took training for the rest on a Thursday. On a Friday and Saturday I'd be up and down the street, checking the local lads weren't out on the beer. If the others were out in Dublin, there wasn't much I could do about it.

We started well and were getting attendances of around 300 – not what I was used to but beggars couldn't be choosers. This was my team and my job to make it better and get more punters through the gate. The fans may have been small in number but they were a passionate lot who crowded into the social club afterwards which was the lifeblood of Limerick, where takings at the bar kept the team going. There would be a band on and the hardcore stayed until they were kicked out, then went down the main street for another drink and another one after that. As the comedian Micky Flanagan would say, 'They didn't just go out, they went *out* out.'

The scariest trip was away to Finn Harps as you had to go over the border with Northern Ireland to get there. We were only in a little minibus and the lads are going: 'Don't let anyone hear that English accent, Sam.'

We stopped at a checkpoint and the army came out fully balaclaved up, with handguns and rifles and those mirrors on sticks which check for bombs under vehicles. The Irish troubles were still ongoing and a bunch of blokes coming up from the south crammed into a bus together were an easy target. It wasn't my most enjoyable day out.

On top of our struggles to stay afloat financially, the manager of the social club left. When I flew back to Limerick the following week, I was met by Father Joe who was beside himself.

'Beejesus Sam, you'll never guess, the bloody bar's been burned down.'

It was a shock, especially as I'd only been there a month, but I consoled Joe.

'It'll be okay, Father, don't fret, when we get the insurance money through we'll rebuild the place.'

'Oh beejesus Sam, you don't understand, there's no bloody insurance.'

What with the departure of the manager and the loss of the social club all coming at once, the team couldn't survive, particularly as it needed the income from the social club. The money at the gate was not enough and we needed 1200 punts a week – which were the same monetary value as pounds – to operate. I was on 200 a week alone with my flight and accommodation paid for. The best players were on between 100–150 punts and they would go elsewhere if they weren't being paid. The owners were successful businessmen but didn't have the money to build a new bar, or if they did they weren't going to risk it. At least the one thing still standing was the dressing rooms, which was a small mercy. The rest was flattened.

We had a nice set-up at Limerick University with an office there and training pitch, but that didn't last long because we couldn't pay the rent, so we really were Raggy-Arsed Rovers and the future looked grim. Somehow, we stumbled on, winning most of the time and using what meagre funds were left in the kitty. We won the league by about 16 points but we knew we wouldn't survive in the Premier Division. The club might even go bust before that.

We had a regular meeting with the Limerick directors on a Friday and with two or three games left, the bombshell dropped. The money had run out. There was 500 punts to pay some of the wages that weekend, but after that it was over. We might not have been able to put a team out to fulfil our fixtures, and if wasn't going to be paid I wasn't going to stay on either. To be honest, I couldn't afford it.

Joe was like, 'What are we gonna do, what are we gonna do? We've got to carry on, we've got to find a way.' Off he went and made a few phone calls then returned and pointing his finger in my direction said, 'Sam, you're coming with me.'

'What are we doing Joe?' I asked.

'We're going to get some money, Sam.'

We drove off and pulled up ten minutes later on a street corner.

'He'll be here in a minute,' said Joe.

A young lad came up to the window and passed Joe some money which he threw to me.

'Count it,' said Joe, which I did and it came to about 150 punts. That wasn't enough to get us through the weekend but Joe had only just started. On we went, stopping at petrol stations and shops with various people passing him money. I've no idea who they were or where the cash was coming from, but it was enough to get us to the end of the season. And it meant we could receive the Division One trophy in front of our supporters. If we hadn't finished the season, we might not have got the silverware at all, for failing to complete our fixtures.

Joe was a treasure and I wanted success for him as much as anyone. He deserved it for all his hard work in the community, but he felt the pressure of keeping Limerick and his church going. I could understand why he was a chain-smoker! He had a great knack of getting onside with important people and had a grand plan to build a new national football stadium in Limerick which would be shared with his club. It seemed ludicrous, Limerick was a little speck on the map compared with Dublin, but Joe believed it was possible and there were a lot of influential people who went to Limerick to discuss it. Of course it didn't happen, but Joe did well to get as far with the idea as he did. Had it come off, he wouldn't have had to rely on takings from the bar, that's for sure.

I'd made up my mind to leave Limerick, prompted in part by a journalist telling me there was a dormant PFA fund for players which owed me £330. The alarming thing about the story was the PFA putting out an appeal to find me because they didn't know where I was. 'I'm top of the First Division in Ireland, doesn't anyone bloody know?' I asked the man from the press. 'No, they don't,' he said. I'd become invisible, disappeared off the radar.

Back in Bolton, Roy Greaves wanted me to put more money in to prop up Monterey's but I didn't have it. I felt he hadn't told me the full situation about the finances. We owed more than we did because he hadn't paid the bills on time, but I suppose he was trying to get us out of trouble without me realising. So we came to a resolution whereby I got Northfield Social Club and he got Monterey's. I ran Northfield for a while but escaped at the earliest opportunity, managing to lose only £60,000, which was a result. Of course £60,000 was a huge amount, I'd never earned that in a year, but, although I had no money, I didn't have any debts either and we'd kept the house. I still speak to Roy when I see him but we don't go out for a drink any more. It's a shame but that's life.

7

'I DON'T THINK OWEN'S VERY HAPPY'

I was in danger of being forgotten and had to get back on the football ladder, even if it was on the bottom rung, so I was grateful that Walter Joyce, a coach in my Bolton days, and assistant to Les Chapman at Preston, made me their youth-team coach and centre of excellence director. It sounds grander than it was but I was happy to take it, and I enjoyed finding and developing young players. More importantly I was helping my son Craig to become a pro, as he was already at Preston where he'd been as an apprentice since leaving school. So I had him in my youth team and we sometimes turned out for the reserves together. It was an ambition of ours to play alongside each other in the first team just once, but it never happened.

Les got the sack in October 1992 and I was made caretaker manager, with Walter as my number two. They didn't exactly push the boat out for me though. My club car was the groundsman's old white fiesta van with a knackered old lawnmower in the back which was awaiting repairs! Walter and I won a few games and we were quite pleased with our progress. I played occasionally due to injuries and the need for experience, given we were fighting it out down at the bottom of the third tier – now known as the Second Division, with the Premier League having just been formed. I'd played 23 games for Limerick the previous season so I still knew my way round the field, but I was 38 now and this was a much higher standard.

The players respected me and I felt it wouldn't be long before they offered me the job permanently. Instead, they went through an interview process and invited applications. We all knew who they were talking to because they did it in the boardroom after training. I saw Chris Nicholl in there, then John Beck who had been sacked by Cambridge where he had a reputation for his unorthodox methods. Beck grew the grass longer in the corners at the Abbey Stadium so that the ball would hold up when kicked from the other half, a tactic which was going to be hard to implement on our astro-turf, and he was also known for throwing buckets of cold water over his players to get them prepared for battle.

I didn't get the job, Beck did, and I was right hacked-off about it, so much so that and Lynne and I went to one of our favourite pubs, the Rose and Crown, and quietly drowned our sorrows late into the night. I didn't like Beck and he didn't like me. He wanted me out but the board had guaranteed I'd keep my job as youth coach whatever happened. Beck and his assistant Gary Peters made Craig's life hell. Peters subbed Craig off in the reserves and said the team was better playing with ten men. So I told Craig he was never going to win the battle and was better off out of it than being humiliated by those imbeciles. He left and went to play in China, which didn't exactly please his mum. But he wanted to be a footballer and if it had to be in China, then so be it. He was one of the first Europeans to play there and Channel 4 made a documentary about his experiences.

Beck played brain-dead football and the players hated it. There was a ridiculous set of rules, written up as cartoons on the wall, and if you didn't stick to them you were fined and dropped. If a player had his back to goal when receiving the ball, he had to hook it over his shoulder down what Beck called Paradise Alley which was the area between the 18-yard-box and the touchline. At Christmas, he called it Santa's Grotto. Then there was the Reach, where midfielders or defenders were ordered to target an imaginary rectangle between the edge of the penalty area and the corner flag. If you didn't hit the Reach often enough, you were out of the team. There was no arguing as the stats recorded whether you'd done it, and it didn't matter how good a game you'd played. I liked stats too but not to the exclusion of all else, they're just part of the whole.

Beck's got his analyst to record how far players could head it or kick it. He wanted the opposition forced into taking throw-ins by their own corner flag and worked out that 70 per cent of the time we won the ball back from their throw. The players had to get crosses in as soon as possible and wingers weren't allowed to cut inside, they had to go outside the defender. If they came inside, they were instantly subbed. They weren't allowed to receive the ball at their feet either, they had to be running on to it behind the full-back. And the ballboys, who were usually the apprentices, had to get the ball back within five seconds, if it was a Preston throw. They had hand towels sewn into their sleeves to dry the ball, and he always had a player in the team who could throw it long into the box. It didn't matter if you couldn't play, if you could throw it 50 yards you were in. I've used variations of the long ball in my time and played off the front men, but this was taking it to ludicrous extremes.

The philosophy didn't just apply to the first team, it ran right through the ranks, which meant I had to follow it all as well. We had just won the quarter-final of the FA Youth Cup, beating Everton, which was quite an achievement, when Beck called me in.

'You've got to change the playing style now.'

'But we're playing some great stuff using a back three and the lads are enjoying it,' I said. 'How do you think we beat Everton?'

Beck wasn't interested. 'I don't care, change it.'

I told the lads they had to do what the manager wanted, and I had to placate the parents who threatened to take their sons to other clubs. It was hard defending the indefensible. I was in the dressing room telling them, 'Hit it into the Reach, target those corners, hook it on when you've got your back to goal.' How did I feel? Shit. We had talented youngsters such as Kevin Kilbane who were capable of so much more. Fortunately, it didn't harm Kilbane too much as he went on to play for West Brom, Everton and Sunderland and won 110 caps for Ireland, but I'm sure it destroyed others. There was one young lad who was a tidy player but wasn't enjoying it at all. He said to me, 'Boss, I never really wanted to be a footballer but my Dad wanted me to be and I didn't want to disappoint him.' I asked him what he wanted instead and he replied, 'To be a mechanic.' He'd saved all his money and bought an immaculate VW Golf which was his pride and joy. I called his parents in and said, 'You do realise your son wants to be a mechanic, don't you?' His dad was distraught but his son was happy when I let him go. Being a footballer isn't for everyone, especially when John Beck's in charge.

John McGrath always told me it was much easier to get another job in football if you were already in it than if you were out of it so I stayed, but it was one of the toughest times I had in football. Beck's madness continued unabated. As he couldn't grow the grass in the corners of the astro-turf pitch, he had it heavily sanded until it was like Morecambe beach. He also got the apprentices out there with a big bristle brush to fluff up the fibres and asked Mitre for balls with matt finishes rather than gloss because they stuck to the surface better. As Beck and Peters had taken some big scalps with their tactics at Cambridge, they were not for turning or mixing it up a bit. This was the way it was done and their arrogance was breathtaking.

Beck sent me out scouting on top of my youth-team duties. I was driving thousands of miles and barely getting any sleep. One Saturday, I went to Falkirk to watch a game and then drove back in time for our Sunday Under-16s match at Liverpool. It felt like he was trying to break me. Mind you, he did sign a young David Moyes from Falkirk on my recommendation, so the trip wasn't wasted. Preston went down that season but Beck stayed and got the team winning as they tried to go straight back up again. He ruined it all one Friday when he dropped three players for not achieving enough 'Reaches' in the previous game. None of the lads could believe what he was doing. Preston should have gone up that year, but Beck screwed it up because of his stupid obsession with a stat and they lost in the play-off final to Wycombe.

●　●　●

Preston was doing my head in and a scout I knew, Fred O'Donoghue, tipped me the wink that I might have a chance of the manager's job at Blackpool where he was working. They had just avoided the drop into the fourth tier but had a flamboyant owner, Owen Oyston, who was big in commercial radio. He'd interviewed Reidy, Ray Wilkins and Bryan Robson but none of them fancied it. With so many big names being talked about I didn't think I had a hope, but Fred convinced me to send a CV to the managing director, Gill Bridge. Billy Bingham was Blackpool's director of football, a man who managed Northern Ireland in their famous World Cup campaign in 1982 during which they beat the hosts Spain 1–0. Fred told me Bingham could be difficult to work with but that was part of the challenge. Blackpool wrote back to thank me but said they were considering other people with more experience, so I thought that was the end of it.

A couple of weeks later Fred was in touch again, telling me Gill Bridge wanted to see me. I had to insist the interview was after 4pm so I could get away from Preston in my training kit and change into my suit. They were looking for any excuse to get rid of me and, if they'd found out I was in talks with another club, would have given me my cards in an instant. I walked into the wood-panelled boardroom to meet Gill and Billy, and Owen burst through the door with this big wide-brimmed hat on and took over the room. He turned to Bingham and said, 'Right, Bill, what are we looking for?'

Bingham recalled how they had been searching for a manager for a while but that they all wanted to bring their own staff, while Blackpool expected the new manager to work with those already there. He passed me a list of backroom staff which included Dave Bamber who I knew from Coventry, and, of course, Fred. So I said, 'Okay, what about the contract?' and Bingham replied, 'The job doesn't come with a contract.'

With no guarantees of security, I grabbed the bull by the horns and told them they needed a first-team scout and an assistant manager and I knew a bloke who could do both, Bobby Saxton. Bobby had done it all in football and was well respected in the game. Bingham goes, 'I like that.' So I said, 'When do I start?' They were rather taken aback but I continued: 'Preston will let me go and I can start tomorrow.' They went off into another room, returned with an offer of £18,000 a year on the proviso that I couldn't sign a player without Billy's approval, which I agreed to, and that was that. Blackpool had their new manager.

Blackpool was one of those great traditional old North West clubs, but the golden days of the Stanley Matthews era were long gone. Bloomfield Road was falling to bits and the training ground at Squires Gate was an abomination. Ian Holloway described it as 'a hell hole' when he was in charge. It basically comprised of a bit of grass and a wooden hut, and when it rained water came pouring in down the walls. I told Billy it was unacceptable and that it was hard to create a team spirit when the players were turning up already changed then going home straight after training in filthy gear. It wasn't good for our team of geriatrics, most of whom were over 30. Our keeper Les Sealey was 37 and defender Phil Brown 35. So we got some heating put in and had the roof fixed, which was a start, at least.

We were thumped 4–1 in our first game of the season at home to Huddersfield. I took Bobby into the boardroom to see the directors afterwards and Oyston slaughtered us. 'Rubbish,' he said. 'You'd better get this sorted out.' I hadn't bought a player of my own yet and gave Owen a few home truths back. Bob came out of the meeting and said: 'We're in trouble here, Sam, we'll have to get results quick. He won't wait.' I was only just starting and I felt Owen had to show faith and back me with investment.

In fairness, he did and we brought in Darren Bradshaw from Peterborough, Micky Mellon from West Brom and a horrible in-your-face centre-back from Blackburn called Andy Morrison for a club record fee of £245,000. Andy was a complete nutter, his party-piece was to down a pint in three seconds flat, but he was the right man for the job we needed, and Blackpool fans quickly grew to appreciate him. In fact, he was voted into the club's hall of fame by the Blackpool supporters where his name stands alongside the greats like Matthews, Stan Mortensen, Alan Ball and Jimmy Armfield.

Les Sealey was not the best person to have around. He was ranting in the dressing room after the Huddersfield game and I told him, 'Two of the goals were your fault.' He didn't like that but he was losing it, so I had to get rid of him. Bingham kept tweaking my buttons telling me, 'It isn't going as well as the board would like, Sam. I don't think Owen's very happy.' I knew with a bit of patience it would get better. I managed to get Jack Chapman in, who was the best chief scout ever, and I changed the physio, bringing in Mark Taylor, a former Blackpool player. Mark was more important than any new signing. He was top drawer and I took him to Bolton and Newcastle in later years where he was my head of sports medicine and science. If you haven't got a good physio and medical team, you might as well not bother. They are worth 15 points a season. It doesn't matter how many good players you buy, if they aren't fit it's money down the pan.

Billy was still grumbling and told me, 'You've got to sack Bobby [Sexton], Owen doesn't like him.' I was pretty sure it was Billy who had the issue, not Owen, and demanded to see the owner. But Bobby himself told me not to call it on. 'Keep your job, Sam, don't even thinking about leaving,' he said. 'I'll go and I don't want you following me. I'll find somewhere else.' He did too. He joined Peter Reid who had taken over at Sunderland.

We finished halfway in the table but only won one of our last 11 games to drop out of the promotion race, and, with Bobby gone, I made Phil Brown player-coach. Phil had done all his coaching badges and had this infectious character which cheered everyone up. He was never miserable, ever. He got the nickname 'Sunbed' because he always looked like he'd been in the tanning salon, but he didn't need to, it was a natural pigment in his skin that gave him the bronzed look.

I needed to delegate a bit more to the likes of Phil, and took Bobby's advice about not doing everything myself and to try and calm down. I was volatile in the dressing room and went through all the managerial clichés of throwing cups of tea across the room and upturning plates of sandwiches. I thought that's what you were supposed to do as a manager but it had limited effect, and after a while players looked at you like you were an idiot. I was using the f-word a lot too, especially in training, and realised the expletives sometimes detracted from the message I was getting across.

We had a strong side with strikers Tony Ellis and Andy Preece, another big-money signing for £200,000 from Crystal Palace, winger Rick Holden, and Dave Linighan at the back who'd spent eight years at Ipswich and formed a formidable combination with Morrison. We signed Jason Lydiate from Bolton too, with the fee decided by a tribunal. Their manager Bruce Rioch took his own Bible along to the hearing to swear he was telling the truth about why Jason had only played 30 games in three seasons in order to bump the fee up. I brought my son Craig to the club too. I was confident he could play at that level and was good back-up for us, but I wasn't brave enough to risk him in the team. I was worried about him being slaughtered by the crowd and accusations he was only playing because he was my boy. If you lose and your son is out there, that rela-tionship is always the first target. Steve Bruce would back me up on that one, because he gets it when he picks his lad Alex in his team.

We got a new keeper in, Steve Banks, a deal which was arranged by Mark Curtis, who was to become my own agent and great friend. Unfortunately, Banks got injured with nearly half the season left, so I got Eric Nixon on loan from Tranmere. Nixon was an experienced keeper who had played for Manchester City and another big character around the place. When he and 'Jock' Morrison got into an argument, the walls rattled, and the pair of them had a huge fight one night when they were on the town. The police turned up and somehow a totally innocent Micky Mellon was arrested and carted off. Morrison was a law unto himself. He once nicked a model pig from a hotel after a team bonding session and adopted it as Blackpool's lucky mascot because we went on such a great run afterwards. But it turned out the pig was a valuable sculpture imported from Africa and I told him, 'The pig has to go back.' Morrison was distraught and begged the hotel to let him keep it, but they threatened legal action so eventually he returned it.

Blackpool were going at it with Steve McMahon's Swindon and we were top of the table at the beginning of April, but we got a few injuries, drew two and lost four of our next six and dropped to third. A win at York on the last day wasn't enough to lift us into the top two automatic promotion places and we were condemned to the play-offs. We were absolutely gutted. When you spend most of the season looking odds on to go straight up but you miss out, you take a huge psychological hit.

It didn't help either that during the second half of the season Owen was rather pre-occupied, having been charged with rape and indecent assault. He was cleared of one of the charges but a re-trial was set for April. The focus was on Owen and not the team. It was front-page news in the *Blackpool Gazette* and I couldn't talk to Owen about getting new players because the case was taking up most of his time, and anyway Billy wouldn't let me anywhere near him.

We had to get our heads round being in the play-offs and that we still had the chance of promotion, instead of feeling sorry for ourselves. We were up against Chris Kamara's Bradford in the two-legged semi-final and were absolutely buzzing in the first leg at Valley Parade where we won 2–0 and everyone thought we were on the way to Wembley. Our programme for the return leg gave the fans details of how to get tickets for the final and directions to get there. That was tempting fate. I had a bad feeling about the second leg the day before the game. In practice the team were crapping themselves, they couldn't pass it five yards. I told Brownie, 'We're in the shit here', and even Mr Happy didn't seem as upbeat as usual. I stopped the session and told them to have a five-a-side instead. I couldn't watch any more.

The verdict in Owen's case was looming. We heard it was going to be the following week and in the meantime he would be coming to the game. He'd been on the pitch telling the crowd, 'I'm innocent, I'm innocent,' and that when the whole mess was over he would be building a brand new stadium. It was a surreal situation and I couldn't imagine what his wife Vicki was going through.

We lost the second leg 3–0 at home, folding like a deck of cards, and were out 3–2 on aggregate. The backroom staff stayed the night in Blackpool with our other halves and had a few consoling drinks. But we told each other that next season there would be no mistakes and we would go up as champions. We had taken a team which was nearly relegated to halfway up the table and then on to the brink of promotion. Morrison's view was simple. 'If we hadn't lost the bloody lucky pig, we'd have gone up.'

There was a board meeting scheduled to discuss the season, but before that took place Oyston was found guilty of raping and indecently assaulting a teenager and sentenced to six years. The judge told him: 'You were 58, she was 16. You were rich and powerful with a strong personality. She was young and vulnerable.' The judge said he would have gone down for nine years but for the fact he was now 62, the offences had taken place four years earlier, and he was of previous good character. He was the richest man in Britain ever to be jailed for sex offences. I felt numb. He was so confident of getting off that we'd all been brainwashed into believing he would, although I had a few mates in Manchester CID telling me he would get done. They argued the police would not have gone after someone like him, if they weren't sure of their ground.

I met the board, with Vicki now in charge in place of an indisposed Owen, and explained how we needed to get on planning pre-season and that I was confident we would go up as league champions next time. They listened as I set out my ideas for signings and who we should let go, and all seemed fine. I asked if they could speak to Owen and tell him I needed to talk to him. I wasn't sure what the protocol was with him in prison, but we needed to have a proper conversation about the future.

There appeared no question that my position was safe, it was very much a forward-looking meeting. Mick Miller, a well-known comedian who was a big Blackpool fan and did a few turns in the Tangerine Club at Bloomfield Road, was saying, 'We'll be alright next year, Sam. We're looking good.' Gill Bridge called me back for another meeting, and Lynne and I thought it was to talk about my new contract. I was hoping for a two-year deal and a bit more security as I drove the 45 minutes from our house in Bromley Cross over the hills and down to the coast. Craig was waiting there with the other lads ready to sign his new contract too. But the moment I walked in, I felt like one of those members of the Mafia about to join the fishes.

'We feel you should have got us promoted, so we've decided to look for a new manager,' said Gill.

'You've got to be kidding me,' I replied. 'I stabilised the team in the first year, nearly got us up this time and next year we will go up. But I'm obviously not going to change your mind.'

There was no further discussion. I got a £13,000 pay-off, called Craig into the office and told him to sign his contract straightaway before they rescinded the offer, and left in shock. It was a complete about-turn from the board meeting a few days earlier and it had to be Owen's doing. Every decision went through him, and with his wife now in charge she was doing his bidding. I told the press I'd been sacked by the chairman from his prison cell. This prompted Vicki to write to Lynne, asking her to get me to stop making such an accusation. She said it was the board's decision, not Owen's.

I met up with the backroom staff to deliver the bad news. Brownie wasn't too bothered though, he'd been tapped up by Bolton and was off to join Colin Todd as his assistant. Talk about 'I'm alright, Jack.'

MADNESS AT MEADOW LANE

8

I was on the managerial scrapheap, yet at the back of my mind I felt Blackpool ought to count for something. It wasn't as if we were relegated, we were nearly promoted, and I'd also won the First Division title in Ireland before taking over as caretaker at Preston and getting them up the league. It wasn't the worst CV. Friends in the game were confident that another manager's job would come along soon. But would it? All the other end-of-season sackings had been done and new bosses were already in place. So there was nowhere for me to go. And the cold-hearted side of football meant I needed someone else sacked in order for me to get back on the merry-go-round.

It hurt more knowing I'd done a good job. I wouldn't call it a blow to my ego, more to my self-confidence. Big egos develop when you stop listening to other people and think you've got all the answers. I've always been a good listener and ready to take advice. Self-confidence can be perceived as arrogance but you can still believe in your own ability and listen as well. I'd got to know a few of the more experienced managers like Jim Smith who was always available with his words of wisdom, and I was never afraid to pick up the phone to him and ask for help. It was why I wanted the experience of someone like Bobby Saxton at Blackpool in the first place.

You have to change your entire way of thinking when you move from player to manager – it's a big transition. As a player you are selfish, only interested in your own needs; as a manager you have to put everyone else ahead of yourself and your family. Managing players is the easiest part; managing the owners, the fans and the press is not so straight-forward. Keeping everyone happy is impossible and you have to get used to that. Players can have a good game and even if the team loses they can be happy they performed well and earned praise from the media. There is no refuge for a boss, you're right smack in the firing line. When times are tough, you have to convince the owners you are worth sticking with and investing in, while they are getting it in both ears from the fans.

It was horrible being in limbo. Our friends Graham and Diane had wanted us to go on a cruise with them at the end of the season for their wedding anniversary, but the play-offs meant we couldn't go. So I'd lost the play-offs, lost my job and lost out on a cruise. Ronnie and Gail Wood, another two friends who were on the boat, offered to fly us out to the Caribbean to join them which was a fantastic gesture, but it would have been wasted on me the way I was feeling. I was in a daze. Lynne could have told me the house was being burgled and I'd have gone, 'Yeah, yeah, love.' And that's me who prides himself on being a good listener. Ian Greaves, who knew what it was like to be sacked, offered some helpful words of comfort: 'You feel bad the first day, a bit worse the second day and on the third day you feel suicidal!'

Pat and Dave, our pals from Bolton, had emigrated to Spain five years earlier and had a house in Moraira on the Costa Blanca. So we joined them a few weeks later instead, and fell in love with the place so much that when our fortunes picked up years later, we built our own villa there. The holiday did me the world of good and stopped me feeling sorry for myself. When people say they don't need a break, they are kidding themselves. It recharges the batteries and gives you the energy for a full-on return to work. Brian Clough used to take a holiday once a season and got back just in time for the game, but he was a brilliant manager. He didn't care how much stick he got, the method worked for him and his teams. Countless managers talk about the job being 24/7 and having to be there from morning until night, but with today's communications you can be away in the sunshine and still working. I can think about it 24/7 without being on site. Going away in the old days meant returning to an answerphone full of messages and having to catch up. Now they can be dealt with straightaway on the mobile.

Contacts were important to me staying in football, and Peter Reid and Bobby Saxton threw me a lifeline by appointing me academy director at Sunderland. It wasn't a case of jobs for the boys either, I was qualified for it after what I'd done at Preston. It was also a chance to work in the Premier League. Yes, it was back in Sunderland again, but the circumstances were different from when I played there.

I was involved in the whole set-up, including joining in the head-tennis to start the day which was my favourite training game. The trouble was you had to play until Reidy won, so it could take hours. I headed balls five times a week for 25 years as a player and then probably another 15 years as a coach. No wonder my neck cracks every time I turn from one side to the other; the vertebrae have crumbled. It's painful and I have to exercise the muscles a lot to prevent the neck stiffening up. I couldn't head a ball now, it would be too dangerous. I might end up crippled.

Running a Premier League academy is not a small job. In some ways it's the biggest job of all. It has become a critical part of a football club and there is never a minute's peace. You start early in the morning and don't finish until late in the evening, catering for ages from six to 16, with over a hundred players to look after as well as part-time scouts, physios, parents, and issues such as contracts, health and safety and child protection. We didn't have the flash training complex Sunderland has now, so we worked out of local schools. There was so much to organise, including minutiae like whether we had enough balls for all the different sessions going on in the region and were they blown up to the right pressure. The weather could play havoc too, especially in Sunderland. That dictated whether you did everything in a gym instead of outside which meant facilities being cancelled and others booked at short notice, then contacting everyone to let them know.

Academies should be run in the summer, not the winter, so that the kids train in nice weather and learn their skills in good conditions. What does it matter if they don't follow the same timeline as the seniors? It would also mean getting a lot done with them in the school holidays, and parents wouldn't have to worry about racing home from work, driving their children miles to training two or three times a week, then having to hang around waiting to take them home. In the holidays, they could drop them off in the morning and pick them up at night. It's free child-minding too! Winter conditions mean you might not see how a kid is developing for a couple of months and he might hardly play any games. But in the summer, you will at least get a good look at everyone over a six-week period.

We've talked about this so many times in meetings with the FA, ever since England lost in the quarter-finals of the 2006 World Cup, and they went looking for answers about why we kept failing. Nothing ever changes though. Unfortunately, a single club cannot randomly implement a summer academy, because they are all linked, and games are played from mid-August to May. I thought Lilleshall, which the FA closed down some years back, had a lot of merits. It was a boarding school for the best players where they received top coaching and got an education too. Many of them, Michael Owen being the best example, went on to play professional football. I visited for a couple of days to see how the place operated and it was very impressive, but it was decided clubs should take over responsibility for elite player development rather than having a centralised system.

At Sunderland, I put together a report about how to develop our own players, drawing on all my experiences. Bolton, for instance, had a phenomenal track record of bringing talent through from the youth ranks, and six of my playing group made it into the first team. My idea was to build a support structure for the best young players by joining forces with the local schools and organising a curriculum for them that included training and a formal education. It would have been a mini-Lilleshall. The message came back from the board, via Reidy, that I should get on with it. That was easier said than done, as we had no links with any local schools and no training facilities of our own. We needed a decent budget to get it off the ground, but I was convinced it would work if we were committed to it. Howard Wilkinson made the system work at Leeds, where Paul Hart was academy director, won the FA Youth Cup a couple of times, and brought players through who went on to play for the seniors in the Champions League. Sadly, Sunderland weren't prepared to put the money in to make a real go of it and got left behind.

● ● ●

I was dealing with this frustration when the agent Mark Curtis told me the Notts County manager's job was up for grabs. I'd been interviewed by the chairman, Derek Pavis, a couple of years previously but didn't get it. Pavis had been a director at Nottingham Forest, fell out with Brian Clough and bought the neighbours instead. But they were second bottom of the third tier, having not won a league game since late October, and we were now in January. They were odds on for relegation.

Reidy wanted me to stay but understood why I was eager for another crack at management. He warned me about Derek though, telling me a story about when he was a player there. Apparently as soon as Notts were safe, Reidy was dropped and the rumour was it was because Derek didn't want to pay him appearance fees any more. It put me on my guard but didn't stop me going for the interview.

There is not another city quite like Nottingham for the way its sporting arenas are set out. Notts County's Meadow Lane sits one side of the River Trent straight opposite big brother Nottingham Forest which is right next door to Trent Bridge Cricket Ground, home to many a historic Test match. It's a great city and I was delighted to be offered the job, even though Notts were in a desperate position. The brief from Derek was nothing complicated. 'I want you to keep us up and we'll go from there,' said Pavis.

I emphasised in the local press how I'd taken Limerick up and turned round Blackpool's fortunes. I'd also played in all four divisions, so I knew my way round English football. But I was in for a shock, as everything that worked for me at Blackpool didn't at Notts County. The players would not respond. There were also rumours about the players drinking in town too often. I nailed a few of the lads for being out on Thursday nights in an attempt to get some discipline in the place. They weren't as fit as they should have been. No matter how dedicated footballers claim to be in the lower divisions, they cannot hold a candle to the ones at the top.

Whatever I tried, we just couldn't get a result. We went 15 league games without a win, 18 if you included cups. Had I got the bullet after that run of results, I might never have got another job. The anxiety made me angry and I was lashing out in the dressing room, but it probably had a more negative effect than a positive one. If you just scream at players all the time, they switch off, thinking, 'Here he goes again.' I learned over time to mix it up. We had no luck either. If we were winning you could guarantee our opponents would get a late one to equalise, and if we were drawing we'd be beaten by a last-minute winner. One game we lost 2–1 and scored all three of them, two in our own net.

My assistant Mark Smith and I were both tearing our hair out but not as much as Derek who was going absolutely mental. He rang at all hours and if I didn't answer would leave a message in his distinctive deep voice saying, 'I don't want to speak to a fucking answer phone, I want to speak to my manager.' He watched the pennies too. If I left the light on in the office at some godforsaken hour, he sent a memo about wasting electricity. He would tell me, 'This is my money you're spending, you know.' Pavis was extremely difficult to work with, but you had to take it on the chin. He would call me up to the boardroom and go, 'Well, what went wrong today then, Sam?' then ask why we hadn't done this or that. He thought it would help if he went into the dressing room before games. I told him he would put the players off rather than help them and his answer was, 'Couldn't do any worse than you're doing.' I wasn't in a position of any strength to argue with him.

Inevitably, we went down at the end of the 1996–97 season and the pressure was on to go straight back up again. I didn't have long to prove myself. If I wasn't in the promotion shake-up in the first dozen games, I was out and I couldn't have any complaints. The League Managers' Association will tell you that, once sacked, 80 per cent of managers never get another number one job again. Derek was right to think we should not be in the mess we were. We had some good players in midfielder Shaun Derry, and a young Steve Finnan who went on to be a Champions League winner with Liverpool, while I was also reunited with Gary Strodder from my West Brom days. We signed Mark Robson too, a quality little midfielder from Charlton who years later became Tim Sherwood's assistant at Aston Villa.

We got on with winning promotion. I switched to a back three with Strodder in the middle who, by now, was even slower than before but could read a game. We were quickly into our stride, winning our first two games and, though we had a little sticky patch, we went on a club and Football League record of ten wins in a row from the start of December to the end of January which blew everyone away. It would have been 14 off the belt but for a draw against Shrewsbury. Two lads needed hernia operations, Ian Hendon and Ian Richardson, but they didn't want to stop playing and because we had such a small squad, neither did I. So they hardly trained and we patched them up each week. We couldn't stop scoring. Everything we hit went in and everything our opponents hit seemed to miss. I've never known a time like it as a player or manager. I'm not known for complacency, but I kept expecting to win every game and so did the players. I'm usually nervous on a Saturday morning, but I was waking up every weekend without a care in the world.

We had the best team by far and became the first club since the war to win promotion by March when Robson scored to beat Leyton Orient, a match commemorated by a painting which I have on my office wall at home. Topping it all off, we were confirmed as title winners too. It was my first major honour as a manager and I went into the press conference clutching a glass of champers. 'It'll be a long time before anyone does that again,' I said, 'if they ever do.' We were presented with the trophy on the last day of the season after we beat Rotherham 5–2 at Meadow Lane in front of 12,500 very happy supporters.

Success breeds discontent though, because everybody wants rewarding, including me, and we were dealing with a chairman with extremely long pockets and very short arms. We also needed new recruits but Derek was not keen and it was obvious the following season was going to be hard. I would sometimes bump into Dave 'Harry' Bassett, the manager of Forest, and he was great to talk over my troubles with, and have a laugh as well over a cup of tea or a beer. It's a lonely life being a manager and to have someone so close by who understood was a help. You can talk to your staff and your family but nothing beats a chat with a bloke going through the same experiences.

Smudger Smith left for Sheffield Wednesday to become youth-team coach, and I appointed Gary Brazil, an ex-Preston team-mate, and Dennis Booth to the backroom team. We couldn't buy anyone because Derek wouldn't spend any money and our results back in the Second Division were mixed at best. Derek had zero tolerance of the problems. 'The team's rubbish, what the fuck are you doing? The fans are turning against you.' He wasn't exactly morale-boosting, so I went public and told the local paper exactly what was going on, which was a big gamble on my part. We didn't have any injuries, we were shuffling the players around to try and find a winning formula but still sliding down the table, and that showed we needed reinforcements. I told the press that if we didn't get a goal-scorer, we would be relegated. When he saw the paper, Derek was straight on the phone with an almighty half-hour tirade. 'I'll sell all the players and I'll never buy you another one, do you hear me? Fucking going to the papers, who do you think you are?'

I didn't answer back, I let him have his rant which admittedly was a good one, even by Derek's standards. My gamble paid off though, because we got striker Kevin Rapley in from Brentford. We only met him on the day of his first game at Luton but I played him, and Kevin handled one into the net, got away with it on the ref's blindside and we won 1–0.

One of my biggest problems though was the physio. As I said earlier, a good physio can be your best signing – a bad one gets you sacked. Ours was highly qualified but had no sporting background and no experience of football injuries. The treatment room was packed and the players took the piss out of him and were always pulling the wool over his eyes. Derek agreed to pay him off and I went and got the old physio Roger Cleary back. Roger had gone off into private practice because Derek wouldn't pay him enough, which was a false economy for the club. Roger returned with a nice pay rise and cleared the treatment room in a fortnight. He ruled that anyone injured had to do double rehab sessions and stay from 9am to 6pm. Amazingly, they were suddenly all fit again.

After Rapley's goal, we took maximum points from four games to climb out of the relegation zone and stayed up. Derek also realised his mistake of the previous season and let me spend a bit to try and mount a promotion push, with the result that Craig Ramage arrived from Derby along with former Manchester United defender Clayton Blackmore.

● ● ●

I was on a contract which included a percentage of the profits when we sold anyone. That might sound contradictory to building a successful team, but I knew I could never stop Derek selling a player, so I might as well have a slice of the deal. The decision to flog anyone was never mine, it was always Derek's. Anyway, a manager would not sell someone just for a 5 per cent cut when you are trying to win cups and titles, because results are what get you the real rewards and ultimately more money. It was no different to being a CEO of a company who is paid on a percentage of profits.

Pavis wanted to change my contract and take the 5 per cent clause out. 'You should never have had that clause in the first place,' he said. Yet he'd agreed to it, rather than paying me a bigger wage. Derek kept going on about how the club was costing him money and he didn't need the hassle. But he loved it. He enjoyed sitting on the coach, hob-nobbing in the boardrooms and mixing with the FA blazers, as long as it didn't cost him too much. We could never stay overnight before games. If the journey was too long, the lads had to fund it themselves. The groundsman could never get the right fertiliser for the pitch either, because Derek said it was too expensive. Anywhere he could save a few pence he would try and do it, and my contract was no exception.

He was always ringing me up to find out where I was. The family was still living in Bolton so I got back when I could, but I was travelling here, there and everywhere watching our next opponents and looking at players. You could see reserve games in London in the afternoon and be back to the Midlands in time for another one in the evening. Notts County were renting a house for me but when Pavis rang home to Bolton and found me there, he'd go, 'What's the point of me paying for a house in Nottingham when you live in Bolton? I thought we played in fucking Nottingham.' He would also try to catch me out by asking if I was in the office and when I replied 'Yes' would walk in two minutes later just to check I'd been telling the truth. In the end, I stopped worrying about him. If he was intent on dishing out a ticking off he would, so you took it and got on with the job.

The following season we were second in the table by mid-October, but I continued to be in conflict with the chairman. We beat Bury 3–1 away and always with one eye on the finances he complained about the cost because of the bonuses he paid out if we were in the top three. He was joking, but sometimes I wondered how he could even say such things. After we lost 2–1 at Cardiff, he went nuts because I put Dennis Pearce on as sub.

'Why the hell did you do that?' he asked.

'Er . . . we needed a sub on, chairman,' I replied.

He was fuming. 'Yes, well you still lost and it's cost me £25 in appearance money.'

When you think how much money I generated for him, it was pathetic. Take Jermaine Pennant for instance, the 15-year-old schoolboy we sold to Arsenal for a fee which, with add-ons, was worth close on £2 million. Our youth coach Alan Young had told me how promising Jermaine was but that he had a troubled background. Jermaine came from the tough Meadows Estate and his family life was all over the place. He'd left school barely educated but he would always turn up for training.

What a talent he was. At 14, I got him in training with the apprentices and it was clear to me that if we got him sorted out, we had a

Left: Bob Allardyce, my dad, third from left in the back row, in the Dudley Police team of the 1950s. That's where the discipline came from.

Below: A fun day out with Robert at Dudley swimming baths.

Above: Aged 3, with brother Robert, and I'm behind the wheel already, no doubt preparing for my pride and joy, the Ford Cortina!

Sycamore Green Primary School football team. Can you spot me?

The sporting all-rounder getting a spot of tuition from sis, Mary.

Here we are in happier times with Mum and Dad and my elder siblings Mary and Robert.

Even the Bolton youth team captain could do a professional job of slicing the turkey. Not sure about the checks though.

Back in the 1970s, as a centre-half in the lower divisions you had to know how to look after yourself.

When asked the difference between his experiences on grass and plastic Worthy replied, 'Dunno, I've never smoked plastic.' Legend.

The Bolton team of the mid-1970s, with the likes of manager Ian Greaves and players Peter Reid and Frank Worthington, and of course a youthful looking Allardyce.

Lynne and I were married at St Maxentius' Church when I was 19. Her parents Ted and Vera had been so good to me. By Christmas, sadly, Ted had passed away.

Leaping salmon-like to head just past the Hereford goal in a match at Burnden Park in 1977.

The Player of the Year trophy presented to me in 1978 by the great Nat Lofthouse.

Left: A happy dad with kids Craig and Rachael.

Below: With Craig's first child Harriet.

Celebrating promotion in 1978 with my Bolton team-mates, after 14 years out of the top flight. We were kings of the city.

Our pub restaurant Monterey's was initially a huge success and the locals poured in – but the pub sell-off by the big breweries killed us.

A spell playing for Tampa Bay Rowdies taught me some big lessons for my later managerial career. Here's me and the family holidaying Stateside.

Left: The incident with Mick Harford in the Coventry v Birmingham derby game where I split his lip open. 'The lights went out. . . I had 70 stitches,' recalled Mick later. My elbow was sore too.

Below: I captained Preston to promotion from the Fourth Division in 1986–87.

The call from Father Joe Young to come and manage Limerick was timely. We won the league in my one season there, 1991–92, and those were happy days with the team.

Left: 'I don't want to speak to a fucking answer phone, I want to speak to my manager.' Notts County chairman Derek Pavis and I celebrating being back in the Second Division in 1998.

Below: At ease with a cigar and the Third Division champions trophy, as boss of Notts County.

special player on our hands. He was one of the best I'd seen in many a long year. Jermaine had an awareness and understanding of the game that is so rare in youngsters. He didn't need any coaching, he knew instinctively what to do and where to be at any given moment. There is lots of ability below Premier League level, but what sets the best apart is a football brain and Jermaine had it. He knew how to affect the game and get the best out of those around him, and found space while others ran into brick walls. He could handle it when he trained with the bigger lads in the reserves too. Kids don't always cope with the step up straight away, but Jermaine found it easy. However, the authorities said he couldn't train with us if he wasn't going to school, and that meant we had to find a solution. We approached the local education authority and proposed a training scheme whereby we were responsible for Jermaine's education rather than his parents. We got his mum and dad's approval to move him to a hostel which we looked after and saw that he got an education.

We had an agreement with Jermaine to sign a YTS contract on his 16th birthday, with the promise of a two-year pro contract to follow, and Derek went further than we had ever done for any youngster. I presume he had the pounds signs in his eyes. We would have signed Jermaine earlier, but the regulations said players couldn't do so until their 16th birthday which meant he was vulnerable to being poached. Tottenham were particularly busy trying to tempt him away. His name was getting around and everyone knew who he was. We would have got compensation under the regulations, but it was a pittance compared with the transfer fee he was worth.

For smaller clubs to survive, they have to be properly compensated for developing youngsters, especially when they have done as much as we had There has to be an incentive for the effort the club puts in, and we were putting in a lot with Jermaine. On the grander scale, Sir Alex Ferguson was a master of making the system work at Manchester United. The amount of money he generated from players who didn't quite make the grade at Old Trafford was phenomenal. Yes, he had the famous Class of '92 with David Beckham, the Nevilles, Nicky Butt, Paul Scholes and Ryan Giggs, but he could recoup millions a year in sales from those on the fringes who were good enough to play in other Championship and Premier League sides.

A £2 million fee for Jermaine had the potential to fund the Notts County academy for five years. By contrast, the compensation from a tribunal, which would have been around £250,000, was a drop in the ocean. His development had surged on in the space of a year, helped by the fact he was almost a full-time player anyway compared with kids of a similar age. I warned Derek, who was remarkably naive, that someone might nick him. We had to find a way to sell him, because there was no way Jermaine would be staying on past his 16th birthday and formally signing that contract.

I reckoned if I played Jermaine in the first team that would at least help enhance his value, if the worst came to the worst and we had to go to tribunal. So I named him on the bench for an FA Cup third round tie at Sheffield United. He got on, as we earned a 1–1 draw. I told a journalist friend at the *Daily Express* that he was for sale for £2 million and how I was furious at the behaviour of some clubs in the way they were tapping him up. It was child exploitation, and I said so. Liverpool rang, asking me to make it clear I wasn't talking about them. But I felt some clubs were doing it and were offering him and his family all kinds of incentives.

The chairman realised the danger: 'Let's get the bloody deal done and quick,' he said. Mark Curtis had tipped off Arsenal to go and watch Jermaine at Sheffield United and they were desperate to sign him and scupper Spurs in the process. The very day the 'For Sale: The £2 million Schoolboy' story appeared in the *Express*, Jermaine travelled to Highbury to meet Liam Brady, Arsenal's head of youth, vice-chairman David Dein and manager Arsene Wenger. The deal was done that night, with Arsenal paying £350,000 up front and the rest coming from a pre-season game against the Gunners, and payments depending on first-team appearances all adding up to £2 million.

It didn't happen for Jermaine at Arsenal. In fact, it didn't really happen for him anywhere. I felt sorry for him. He had had such a difficult childhood that he was always up against it. He got into off-the-pitch scrapes and spent time in prison while moving from club to club. He played in Liverpool's 2007 Champions League final defeat against AC Milan, incredibly alongside Steve Finnan, but failed to fulfil his potential and never won the England cap his talent warranted. Then again, given his upbringing, maybe he achieved more than could be reasonably expected. If we hadn't sorted him out at Notts County and looked after him, he wouldn't have made it as a footballer at all. He went from a 16-year-old with nothing to having more money than he knew what to do with at Arsenal where the capital city brought so many distractions and there was no-one to control him. It must have been a total culture shock.

There are a few players with Jermaine's type of background who turned life around and made the most of their careers, Paul Ince being a good example. But sometimes they just can't change. I later took Ravel Morrison to West Ham from Manchester United after Sir Alex lost patience with him. Ravel had even more talent than Pennant but was unsaveable. It's not his fault he had a tough upbringing, but it was his fault that he didn't realise what he was throwing away. Everyone told him he was in danger of blowing a great career, but he wouldn't listen. It didn't seem to bother him. Sir Alex told me he was impossible, and I was also beaten by him. There comes a point where you cannot do any more for a player who won't help himself. It's not enough to be gifted, you have to be dedicated too. Cristiano Ronaldo is the best player in the world but he works hard too, he doesn't take it for granted.

It was a sad day when Jermaine left Meadow Lane. No manager wants to lose his best players. Finnan had already gone to Fulham for £700,000 and Derry for about the same, while Ian Barraclough was sold to QPR for a sizeable fee too. So Derek raked in over £3 million in sales which for a club like Notts County was absolutely phenomenal. That's probably why he wanted to lose my 5 per cent clause! It was hard work though to keep making the team better when the rug was being pulled from under me all the time. Derek loved the money coming in but still had to get results. I knew he would have no hesitation in sacking me if we started losing.

BOLTON, BROWNIE AND A RIGHT KICKING

9

There were stirrings at Bolton where Colin Todd had walked out seven games into the season in protest at the £1.7 million sale of Per Frandsen to Blackburn. Bolton needed the money and were being threatened with closure by the banks, with everything having been spent on the new state-of-the-art Reebok Stadium. Mark Curtis asked vice-chairman Brett Warburton what the situation was and told him that if they were looking for a new manager, I was their man. Brett was a mate, who I'd known since I was 17 and had long been part of the club through their close association with his family's company, Warburtons the bread makers.

I'd always wanted to go back, and a meeting was arranged at Brett's house. I learned there were new people coming in as investors, the main one being Eddie Davies whose company sold the thermostats on electric kettles which were used worldwide and had made him a multi-millionaire. Eddie didn't want to be chairman, and nor did Brett who felt the job was best left to the man he'd brought onto the board, Phil Gartside. Brett wondered if I could get out of Notts County without Bolton having to pay compensation. I figured that with how things stood with Pavis, I had a good chance.

That night there was a function for the winner of the Notts County lottery and I joined the squad for a few beers. I decided to resign the next morning, knowing all the players would be off after their night out and no-one would be around at the training ground or the stadium. None of the staff knew what I was planning, not even Gary Brazil, my assistant. I slipped away at midnight and went back to the house to write my resignation letter which, of course, took a little while given my dyslexia.

I was up at 6am and straight down to the ground where I left the letter on desk of the chief executive, Geoff Davey. I cleared out my office, jumped in the car and headed north. I rang Derek at 9am. 'I can't work for you any more,' I said. 'I've packed my bags and gone back to Bolton. I've had enough of all the stuff you've done to me. Thanks for the opportunity. Bye.' He didn't get a chance to argue. After that I rang Gary, my chief scout Bob Shaw and physio Roger Cleary to let them know. They were shocked and I wasn't surprised by what happened next. Derek got them all into his office and asked each of them: 'Did you fucking know?' 'Did you?' 'Did you?' All could legitimately answer that they didn't have a clue. Pavis refused to accept my resignation and it became a war. I went to the LMA for support and to speak on my behalf. But they said the fact I'd resigned meant they couldn't help.

Phil Brown, my former assistant at Blackpool, had taken over as Bolton caretaker. I knew he wanted the job and when whey beat Huddersfield 1–0 to notch up a third win in four under Brownie, Brett and Phil jokingly asked if I could get the resignation letter back off Pavis. At least, I think they were joking.

●　●　●

I was eventually appointed Bolton manager on 19 October 1999, five days after my resignation on what was my 45th birthday. Notts County had vowed to get heavy at a tribunal, but I didn't care about that, and in the event the tribunal ruled that no compensation was due. It was the most special moment of my career. This was the football club that gave me the opportunity to fulfil my dreams as a player, and now I was going back to fulfil another dream, as manager.

Brownie was a bit huffy. I'd warned him I was coming and that if he didn't like it, he could move on. Gartside was ready to ditch him and go for a fresh start. I wanted Brownie to stay as assistant, but if there was going to be resentment there was no point in him being there. I told him, 'If there's any backlash from you we'll have a problem, so what is it to be?' I wasn't going to fail here. I was going to show everyone what this meant to me and how good a manager I was, and nothing was going to get in the way. If anything, Brownie was the more popular man at Bolton at the time. He'd been associated with the club more recently than me and played during the successful times under Bruce Rioch. I said his time would come but I had management experience and he had none. His argument was, 'How will I get that if they keep overlooking me and I stay as your assistant?' Then I laughed, 'I've got more right to be manager than you, I was here longer.' He laughed too and we got on with it. He was never a moment's trouble. He'd proved himself as my assistant at Blackpool and I trusted he would be even better now.

If my situation with Brownie was awkward, it was worse upstairs, with the new board coming in and the old one still around, while the club was in self-administration and needed money in to satisfy the banks. They wanted to sell players and our young Icelandic striker Eidur Gudjohnsen was attracting a lot of interest, but keeping him was critical to me. The best option was to sell lesser players to pacify the board and keep the cash tills rolling.

For all that we had a lovely new £100 million stadium, beautifully designed with a 28,000 capacity, we couldn't afford a decent training ground. We only played at the Reebok 20 times a year, whereas we needed training facilities every day. We were practising at a decrepit old ordnance factory sports ground next to a working men's club and a bowling green where they would stand around outside having a fag and a pint watching us train. On the other side of the building was a shooting gallery! Bromwich Street had been sold off for housing and we were left with this apology of a facility. It was like a repeat of the horror days at Blackpool and the same thing happened – the players came in already changed and went home straight afterwards for a shower because the water always ran out. There were no catering facilities either. The situation was going to have to be sorted out, even if it took me some time.

As I drove to the Reebok for my first game against Crewe, I felt a great pride. The stadium loomed large against the skyline beckoning me towards it. I thought to myself, 'This is your big chance, make sure you take it.' I told Brownie I'd sit this one out in the stands while he patrolled the touchline. We only managed a 2–2 draw, with goals from Eidur and Dean Holdsworth, but from my vantage point I could see this was a team with great potential. We had an outstanding Finnish goalkeeper in Jussi Jaaskelainen, who I'd promoted from third choice, and an impressive South African centre-back in Mark Fish, who was alongside Icelander Gudni Bergsson. There were a lot of talented Danes in Claus Jensen, Bo Hansen and Michael Johansen, and Ricardo Gardner, a Jamaican winger who made his name at the 1998 World Cup. It was something of a league of nations combined with English grit in Holdsworth, and defenders Mike Whitlow, Jimmy Phillips and Neil Cox.

There were no youngsters coming through like there was in my day though. Phillips was the last of them and was 33 by this time. Maybe the facilities weren't helping but I wasn't convinced about the structure behind the scenes either. However, I told all the backroom staff not to worry about their jobs and that we'd crack on to the end of the season and see how it went. I wanted everyone to show me what they'd got on and off the pitch. There was a lot of negativity about due to the financial problems we were in, with debts totalling £45 million and the acrimony over the sale of Frandsen which had led to Colin Todd quitting. I raised a few quid by selling Cox to Watford as his contract was running out. And I had to get rid of Toddy's son, Andy, after he beat Brownie up and put him in hospital. It was the single worst moment in my entire time at Bolton.

We'd gone on a supposed team-bonding trip to the Mottram Hall Hotel in Cheshire. I'd gone to bed, which was unusual for me, leaving a few of the players and staff chatting, and there was no hint of the explosion to come. Suddenly, Jimmy Phillips is banging on my door.

'Boss, boss, you've got to get down there. Toddy's given Brownie a right kicking. He says he's killed him!'

I went into the toilets and found Brownie who was not a pretty sight. I couldn't see his tan for blood and his face was swollen up like the Elephant Man.

'Get him to hospital, now,' I told physio, Ewan Simpson.

'It's going to be trouble for us if we do,' said Ewan. I knew that but Brownie's welfare was the priority and I couldn't be worrying about the headlines in the papers. I grabbed Toddy.

'What the fuck have you done?'

'He deserved it,' he replied coldly, without a hint of emotion.

I called the chairman. 'Hello, Phil. You know we went on that team-bonding session. Well, I've got a bit of news which might end up in the papers. Andy Todd has beaten Phil Brown to a pulp and he's in hospital in a terrible state. He needs an operation and they will have to rewire his jaw.'

I went straight back to the Reebok where I met up with Phil Gartside and chief executive Des McBain. Toddy arrived and was in a defiant mood. 'He got what he deserved,' he said once more. Andy got angrier as we questioned him then said, 'He had a go at my dad when he left the club so that's why I did it.' We suspended Todd for a fortnight while we wondered what the hell to do. If Brownie pressed charges, Andy was looking at a possible jail sentence. On a more immediate level, Brownie was going to need weeks if not months to recover from what was a broken jaw and cheekbone, and I was without an assistant manager.

Alan Curbishley was on the phone soon afterwards. 'I believe you are interested in selling Andy Todd?' Too bloody right I was. I would have paid Alan to take him but I tried to play it cool and replied, 'Make us an offer.' He went for a really good figure which was a result, and a couple of years later, Charlton put him on their transfer list amid allegations of a training-ground bust-up with keeper Dean Kiely who allegedly suffered a black eye. I could have laughed when I read the comments of Colin Todd who had gone to Derby. 'Anyone who knows Andy knows he is not a bad lad. He has never been in trouble anywhere apart from a football field.' I had to beg to differ. Andy was so lucky that Brownie didn't involve the police.

● ● ●

Brownie was out of action for a couple of months but we ploughed on, going the right way up the league table. The crowd got behind us and we enjoyed an unexpectedly fruitful run in the League Cup which took us through to a two-legged semi-final against Tranmere, although we managed to lose 4–0 on aggregate which wasn't very clever. But we got to the semi-final of the FA Cup too, against Aston Villa at Wembley. There was a real buzz around the town, the financial pressure eased and despite Derby and Chelsea wanting Eidur, I persuaded the board to keep him for the remainder of the season. We were in with an outside chance of making the play-offs, which was a long shot when I took over, and I told them, 'If we go up they'll still want Eidur, and he'll be more valuable then anyway.' Jensen was also attracting attention but this was not the time to be selling. The club had not expected me to win promotion for three or four years, nor did they expect us to challenge for the cups.

By this time I had a great relationship going with Phil Gartside and I was rewarded for our improvement with a ten-year contract which, in truth, wasn't worth the paper it was written on. If I was sacked, I was only entitled to a year's compensation. But it was a public statement that I was the man to take Bolton on for the long term, whatever the outcome to the season, and told other clubs to keep their hands off me. For players considering joining us, they knew if I wanted them I would not be buggering off the moment they arrived. It also meant Phil could remove the clause that gave me a percentage of sales. Like Derek Pavis, he wasn't too happy about that line in the contract. I told the press, 'If I'm lucky enough to manage this club all the way through my contract, I will be 56 and that will be it for me. I will be wanting to do other things in life by then.' I was already well aware of the strain the game put on managers, remembering what John Barnwell, the LMA chief executive had told me: 'You look after everyone else and forget to look after yourself.'

The FA Cup run affected our league form for a while, but it was hard not to get excited about a Wembley day out, and I thought the positives outweighed the negatives. The lads were enjoying themselves and we were playing good football, even if occasionally the results didn't go for us. Walking the team out at Wembley was amazing, especially considering I'd been at Notts County six months earlier. The odds were against us, with Villa going well in the Premier League in sixth place, but we were up for it. Tactically, we were brilliant and dealt well with the threat of dangermen Paul Merson, Julian Joachim and Benito Carbone. They brought Dion Dublin on and we still kept them out, although Dublin hit the woodwork as we went into 30 added minutes with the scores 0–0 before Dean Holdsworth struck the post.

But then came a moment which I replayed over and over in my mind for years afterwards, and I dare say Holdsworth did too. With ten minutes of extra-time left, Gudjohnsen went clear on the left and David James came out of his box to try and tackle him. Eidur skipped round James and cut the ball back for Deano who was ten yards out with the goal gaping. This was it, this was our place in the FA Cup final. 'Hit it, Deano! Fucking get in there!' As the ball left Holdsworth's boot I waited for the bulge in the back of the net, but it never came. Instead, the ball sailed over the bar. 'How the fuck did that happen?' I collapsed onto my knees. If I could have backed one player to stick away a chance like that, it would have been Dean Holdsworth.

To his credit, he was man enough to stick away our first penalty in the shoot-out, but Allan Johnston and Johansen's kicks were saved by James before Dublin stepped up and finished us off. It was gut-wrenching, but I had to drag the lads off the floor. I called them together and told them, 'Be proud of yourselves. Now let's get on with making the play-offs.' We couldn't afford to wallow in the disappointment. I couldn't criticise Deano, he felt bad enough as it was. It happens in football. But they are big moments in a career. If they go for you, they can change your life forever.

We set out our plan for the rest of the season. We weren't going to shrivel up and die. We won five of our last six games to finish sixth and earn a play-off semi-final against Ipswich, our third semi of an eventful season. But those first two semi-finals were nothing compared to this last one. While Holdsworth's miss comes back to my mind from time to time, the name Barry Knight, the referee in the second leg against Ipswich, rarely leaves my consciousness. He was the worst referee in the history of the game.

We were sharp out of the traps against the Tractor Boys at the Reebok and were 2–0 up through Holdsworth and Gudjohnsen inside half an hour, but they pegged us back to 2–2. I still felt we would go through as we headed to Portman Road three days later for the return. Deano put us 1–0 up but then Knight destroyed our dreams. He gave Ipswich three penalties, two of which were a complete joke, dished out seven or eight bookings and sent two off while Ipswich didn't get a single caution, with several blatant fouls by their players going unpunished. We were 3–2 up with a minute left, but Magilton completed his hat-trick with a late equaliser and we went on to lose 5–3 after 30 minutes of extra-time as we tried in vain to plug the gaps with nine men. I can't describe what I wanted to do to Knight. Where did they find these people?

In the tunnel, I went banging on the ref's door screaming, 'Come out. Explain yourself!' I distinctly remember not swearing, which was odd, but I would have done had I got through the door. Knight locked himself inside, which was probably a good thing because the police would have had to take me away. In my after-match press conference, I said, 'Knight's performance was totally unacceptable, he lost control. I don't think one Ipswich player was booked and that shows a distinct bias against my team. That referee shouldn't be allowed to ref another game.'

I knew I would be charged by the FA, but what of it. I told the journalists, 'I don't give a shit what they charge me with and they can fine me whatever they like.' In my view, managers should be allowed to comment on a ref's performance without fear of censure. If he's bad we should be allowed to say so, but the authorities are too sensitive and too keen to protect them even when it is clear they are not up to the job. I never felt as sick as a manager as I did that day. Brownie and I were due at the Football Writers' dinner in London the next night and drove straight there in a complete fuzz. We stayed up until breakfast time, outraged at the injustice. We'd been in three semi-finals and lost the lot.

At my FA hearing, I played a video of every decision Knight made and went through them all with a fine-tooth comb. I said to the panel, 'Is it any wonder I criticised the ref at the end of that?' I could see the embarrassment in their faces. They had to be seen to be doing me, but I only got warned as to my future conduct which was tantamount to being let off. Knight had just been promoted to the Premier League list that season and I was sure he would be dumped. But he stayed on for another eight years, proving his bosses were as clueless as him.

I don't think refs grasp how much their crap decisions affect people's careers. It's no good saying, 'Never mind, you'll get there next year.' You might not. Missing out on promotion meant we had to sell more players. Johansen got fixed up back in Denmark while Eidur was sold to Chelsea for £4 million and Claus Jensen to Charlton. Gartside was going to let

Ipswich have him for £3 million but Mark Curtis got £4 million from Curbishley. It was good business, but I didn't want to lose Claus any more than Eidur.

● ● ●

For all the comings and goings on the playing side, the most important thing for me was to build a backroom team which would lay the foundations for years. I wanted sports scientists, strength-conditioning coaches, nutritionists, psychologists, better scouts and the Prozone system which analysed games by using cameras right round the stadium. I wanted more of the American concept that so inspired me in Tampa. The budget for players was small, but by getting the best backroom team and equipment we could compete with our big-money rivals. I wanted us at the cutting edge and aware of every new innovation. I convinced the board that, in the long run, it would ease the financial burden, and one of the directors, Dave Speakman, provided us with second-hand laptops because he was changing all the computers at his travel agency. Previously, the only computer Bolton owned was in the secretary's office.

When the lease ran out on the ordnance factory, I refused to go back there unless we got permission to turn the social club into our own leisure and eating area. The food was vitally important to me; I wanted the players to get used to eating the right meals. I also brought in my old faithful scout Jack Chapman. The Prozone company gave us an analyst, Dave Fellows, who knew the system, and he turned out to be such a genius we gave him a job and he eventually moved on to Liverpool. His nickname was 'Fingers', as he was always tapping on the computer. He watched all the DVDs on the opposition and cut them into bite-sized chunks so we could study them. He would get in DVDs of possible signings too and analyse them all, so he began assisting on the recruitment side.

The brilliant Mike Forde, who was initially our sports psychologist, oversaw it all as performance director and went on to become head of football operations at Chelsea. He is now based in New York, advising sports teams across the world.

Neil McDonald arrived as our first-team coach and I handed Jimmy Phillips a coaching role while he was seeing out his days as a player. Jimmy was Mr Bolton and I wanted people who were the lifeblood of the club to play their part. I brought physio Mark Taylor, who was with me at Blackpool, in from Blackburn and he was vital to what we were trying to do. I also revamped the youth policy by appointing Chris Sully as academy director and Geoff Davey as head of youth recruitment, both of whom I'd worked with when I was on the development side at Preston. A sports psychology company was hired as well, on the understanding they were only paid if we were successful. I liked it that they had so much confidence in their techniques they were happy to accept the deal.

We got guys in from Liverpool's John Moores University to advise on nutrition, and specialist masseurs who were available to the players before and after training. We started weighing them and testing their body fat while teaching them the benefits of electrolyte drinks which prevented fatigue. Nobody was doing electrolytes in England but I'd learned all about them 15 years earlier. Training damages muscles, which is why they ache, and it can take 48 hours to recover. The key is to get the body to recover in the first 20 minutes using the electrolytes. The players dodged them at first because they didn't like the taste, but I banned tea and coffee so they didn't have an option. We started using fusions too which were vitamin boosts into the bloodstream, although they were eventually banned by the FA, wrongly in my opinion.

Holdsworth and Bergsson were the main sceptics. They still wanted steak for lunch and a cuppa at half-time. I wasn't going to force them to change their ways, I wanted them to do it for themselves and to realise how it could help prolong their careers. They got the message eventually.

Watching us on our pre-season tour to Denmark, I feared we'd be in a relegation battle rather than fighting for promotion again. We were awful, losing by four and five to teams we should have wiped the floor with. We took a squad of 15 away and nine were triallists. We urgently needed players in. We signed Michael Ricketts, who had given us problems in both our games against Walsall, and he was good value at £400,000. We brought in loan-signing Isaiah Rankin from Bradford and we rescued Frandsen back from Blackburn, where he'd failed to settle, for £200,000 less than we sold him for. That was a bonus, as was the acquisition of Ian Marshall from Leicester who could play centre-back or centre-forward. Marshy could come on for 20 minutes and change a game for you wherever you needed him, either by calming it down at the back or by getting you a goal at the other end.

Now Marshy was getting on a bit and wasn't too keen on training. He was, shall we say, old school. He didn't exactly embrace our new methods, like the wearing of a heart monitor to check his fitness levels. All players were required to wear them, but because Marshy lived in Leicester we let him train at home during the week, as long as he wore his monitor. But we couldn't work out why Marshy's was giving such peculiar readings compared to the others. The analysts were worried he might have a heart abnormality so called him in for tests. Marshy confessed he'd been putting the monitor on his dog while it ran around in the hope we'd think he was training when he was actually flat out on the sofa watching TV!

Ricketts adapted quickly as we started way better than I expected. He scored five in our first seven games, six of which we won. Fishy was causing trouble though and wanted a move to Charlton, where all our players seemed to be going. He went through the motions in a draw at Birmingham and I told the chairman, 'Get what you can for him and get him out.' He was letting us down and we were better off without him. We were begging, stealing and borrowing from wherever we could. I got Colin Hendry on loan from Coventry who was 35 but I needed a replacement for Fishy. Hendry was nicknamed 'Braveheart' after the film with Mel Gibson for the way he threw himself into challenges without any fear of the consequences. He had won the title with Blackburn, another one over the border at Rangers and amassed a half century of caps for Scotland. This was a man who loved a battle.

A teenage Kevin Nolan was breaking through and looking the part after I'd converted him from a useless centre-back to an accomplished midfielder, while a strange quirk of the campaign was that we used four goalkeepers. Jussi got injured and so did our number two Steve Banks, so we brought in the Northern Ireland international Tommy Wright on loan from Manchester City, but he was nearly 40 and I knew after three games we needed someone else. I went to Bradford for Matt Clarke, who had been playing in the Premier League up until Christmas, but lost his place to Gary Walsh. The team gelled and it seemed we might go up automatically in second place behind Fulham, who were home and hosed at the top. Instead, we missed out on the runners-up spot to Blackburn and I was plunged into the dreaded play-offs again.

10

THE SHEEP'S TESTICLES

Play-offs – a word I had come to hate. But at Bolton we couldn't complain too much about failing to gain automatic promotion in the 2000–01 season. Fulham, under Jean Tigana, and Blackburn, managed by Graeme Souness, possessed far bigger budgets and far better players than us. We hadn't beaten either of them, and were hammered 4–1 at home by Rovers which was a tough one to take. We were better than the rest of the teams in the play-offs though, as we finished nine points ahead of Preston and Birmingham and 13 clear of West Brom. That said, the play-offs had become a jinx to me, what with Blackpool's semi-final defeat and the previous year's nonsense against Ipswich.

True to form, it was looking like another disaster in store for us as we went 2–0 down in the first leg of the semi-final against Gary Megson's Baggies at the Hawthorns. They played with a back-three and two wing-backs, and we were being pulled apart. Our captain, Colin Hendry, was already in the book and I said to Brownie, 'We need to get him off or he'll be sent off, and then we'll be in deeper shit than we are already if we go down to ten men.' I was sat on the bench already thinking about another summer of selling players and wondering how we were going to get through the following season with more budget cuts.

So I switched to a 4-3-3 and took a chance in the hope that Megson wouldn't change his system. I got booed by the travelling Bolton fans for taking Deano off, but he was slow and I needed quick lads down the flanks in Gardner and Hansen to expose their three central defenders with Ricketts harassing them through the middle. Mego put subs on but didn't change the system and we went for it.

Bergsson's looping header went in off the bar and finally a penalty decision went our way when Hansen was fouled and Frandsen converted. I could see West Brom were crushed by our comeback, which had produced two goals in the last ten minutes. We won the second leg 3–0, although it wasn't as easy as it sounds as West Brom dominated for long periods. Another one from Bergsson, a cracker by Gardner and a third from Ricketts got us through to the final, which was to be staged at Cardiff's Millennium Stadium while Wembley was being rebuilt.

It was a big psychological hurdle to have overcome our semi-final hoodoo and we were ready for David Moyes' Preston. We'd beaten them 2–0 home and away during the season, so there was nothing to fear. It surprised us that they got past Birmingham in the semi-final, scraping through on a penalty shoot-out, and while you're shouldn't admit to a preferred opponent I thought Birmingham were much stronger than Preston. We'd had two tough draws against them in the regular league campaign and I was glad they were out of the equation.

With 11 days before the final, it meant Fordy could be meticulous about our preparation. We had to keep the players ticking over without working them too hard, and quickly deal with the distracting side issues that arise from being in a final. There were tickets to sort out for friends and family and travel arrangements for partners. The club wanted the wives and kids to travel down on the day of the game, but I thought that they should go the night before. We didn't want to be worrying on the day about whether our families had got their tickets or made it safely to Cardiff. These things might sound incidental but it was important the players' minds were focused on the game. Roy Keane once explained how he became so weighed down by ticket requests for United games, it drove him mad.

I asked the Lion himself, Nat Lofthouse, to talk to the lads about his cup final experiences and he did just the job. He was not the most popular man in England when he scored both goals in Bolton's 2–0 FA Cup final win over Manchester United only three months after the 1958 Munich Air Disaster. And his second goal proved controversial as he shoulder-barged goalkeeper Harry Gregg over the line. He was a great man to have around the place and was always saying to the players, 'Do well for Bolton, cocker. You'll be alright, cocker. Don't worry, cocker.' He called everyone cocker because he could never remember their names. He was proud to be the club president and was a delight to listen to.

Once in Cardiff, we suggested to the players that they should go and watch the Second Division final between Reading and Walsall the day before our game to get a feel for the atmosphere and the stadium. Our concern was the pitch which was notorious for cutting up, and as our game would be the third in three days it was unlikely to be in bowling-green condition. On the morning of the game, there was an article in the papers in which Moyesie told how I'd scouted him for Preston and brought him to the club but this was the day he was going to break my heart. No more motivation was required. I saw Moyesie walking into the ground and he looked nervous. 'We'll win this,' I told the team. 'Just play the game, don't get overawed by the occasion and we'll be fine. You're experienced enough to handle this, it's too big for them and they're shitting it. You know what's at stake and the only way to enjoy the day is by winning. Now go and do it.'

We were going with a 4-3-3 with the idea being to outnumber them in midfield. Gareth Farrelly scored early to settle the nerves, but we couldn't get a second even though we were so much on top. I couldn't see Preston scoring, but as long as we only had a one-goal lead we couldn't relax. Marshy was rabbitting away, going, 'Get me on, gaffer, I'll get you a goal, get me on.' But after Clarke pushed one away from David Healy, I put Ricketts on for Holdsworth instead. Ricketts eased the tension when he nipped past their keeper and rolled the ball into an empty net for our second with only a minute left. We rounded it off in style when Gardner collected in his own half, saw off two or three tackles and smashed a shot into the net from 35 yards. What a finish.

'You fucking beauty!' I screamed out.

Marshy was still going at it. 'Put me on gaffer, put me on.'

'Marshy, we've used three subs, I can't put you on.'

'You bastard,' said Marshy.

The final whistle went and it was party time. This was what I'd been working for, the chance to pit my wits as a manager against the best of them in the Premier League. Winning the league in record time at Notts County was good, but this was Bolton, my club, back in the top division far quicker than anyone expected. I was going to enjoy this, and having that medal swinging round my neck meant everything. We had an after-match beano at the Angel Hotel across the road from the Millennium where the families were waiting for us and friends like Steve Bruce had come to cheer us on. Our friends Ronnie and Gail, and Diane and Graham, had come down on a fancy executive coach. The cigars came out, the champagne flowed and when we got back to the Reebok after midnight we continued the celebrations in the boardroom.

● ● ●

I had two weeks off but they were a blur. This was the big league and we had to get it right to make sure we didn't spoil it by being relegated straightaway. Bolton owner Eddie Davies was in full control, having told shareholders that if they didn't give their shares up the club would go under. They were rendered worthless, which was a blow to me as I'd bought a lot of them. But it was important Eddie ended the uncertainty so that we could go forward. He hadn't planned for all this happening so soon, and the reality was now hitting home.

The stats say that teams are far more likely to be relegated in their first year in the Premier League than the second, where it drops by about 15 per cent, and in year three it falls by about 30 per cent. So if you can get to year three, you are well on the way to establishing your club in the Premier League. You should only fail in year four if there is a horrendous financial crisis at your club, or your recruitment is particularly dreadful. There would be more money coming in now that we were in the Premier League but plenty more going out, and we needed to improve the training ground which was one of my bugbears. I applied for help to the Wanderers lottery fund, a hugely successful fundraising scheme which handed out grants to different parts of the club but could not be used to buy players or pay wages. It was started by a man called Alf Davies who was the commercial manager when I played for Bolton and was carried on by lottery manager Andrew Dean. It could pull in £750,000 a season, selling golden goal and lifeline tickets around the town and at the ground on matchdays. I'm still a member of the scheme and pay my £8 a month into the club's funds. I was successful with my application and got a grant to build a gym, which replaced the shooting gallery, and some new offices.

Looking round England I couldn't find many players who justified the fees being asked and the wages they wanted. Newly promoted clubs had been burned in the past by giving new signings lucrative long-term contracts, then being stuck with them when they got relegated. There was a possibility we could go down again, and we were favourites with the bookies, but the extra burden of signings tied to long-term deals would put us in even worse financial trouble than when I took over.

Agents bombarded me with offers to take players from abroad on six- or 12-month loans. It struck me this was a win-win. If they did well we reaped the benefits, and if they failed we could get rid with little damage being done. It was the right way to go for us, but Bolton was not the most attractive destination for a cosmopolitan footballer, even for a short stop-off. The first one we tried, Bruno N'Gotty, was a strapping 6ft 2in defender who had played for Lyon, PSG, AC Milan and Marseille. He'd won the European Cup Winners' Cup and Serie A and was a French international. We got knocked back by Bruno straightaway but we stuck in there and eventually got him. Bruno became one of the rocks which stabilised Bolton in the top division.

We had to give foreign imports a reason to join us other than Premier League football and money. We had to make them feel more at home than other clubs competing with us for the same signature. So we appointed two player liaison officers, Sue Whittle and Matt Hockin, who looked after them from the moment they landed in the country. They would book them into their hotel, sort out an interpreter, go house-hunting with them, arrange their kids' schooling and deal with any problem which might crop up, day or night. It was a personal service that I felt tipped the balance more in our favour. Too often I'd seen players come into the country, get dumped in a hotel and left to their own devices, with the result that no sooner were they here, they were agitating to quit. If a player is unsettled off the field, he cannot perform on it. Occasionally, no matter what you did for the new arrivals, they abused it. Djibril Diawara, who we got from Torino, was a nightmare. He played in Jean Tigana's Monaco side that knocked United out of the Champions League in 1998 but I hadn't done my homework on him properly. I named him in the team at centre-back and he wasn't best pleased.

'No, I only play centre-midfield.'

'No, you're a defender and that's where you're playing,' I told him.

'I will not.'

I told him to fuck off and hoped he'd change but he didn't. It was a lesson that stood me in good stead, and with future signings I gathered all the information possible about them, talking to previous managers, coaches and team-mates to ascertain their character. As technology progressed, we would trawl through their social media accounts. When I occasionally give talks to businesses about the art of management, I explain how meticulous I am. I tell them, 'We want to know if they are womanisers, drinkers or smokers – and if they do all three we sign them up!' That one always gets a laugh.

With the backroom team I'd put together, the tools were there to compete against the bigger clubs without spending money we didn't have. I knew people were sneering at us and there was scepticism in the media.

'A psychologist? What does he need one of them for?'

'He's got a full-time nutritionist? You've got to be kidding.'

'A data analyst? Has he lost his marbles?'

I didn't care, I knew it was right.

We showed the squad the stats about what it took to stay up, which was our sole aim for the season. We told them how many clean sheets it would take, how many goals we had to score, how many needed to come from set-plays and who had to score them. They learned how many we could afford to concede and what the tipping point was. We split the season into three tens and an eight for the 38 games, and worked out how many points were required in each section to be sure of survival. One group might have been mainly fixtures against teams like us or just a little bit better, and we reckoned we could get a bigger points haul from that section than say another one which might have included games against Man United,

Chelsea and Arsenal where we wouldn't get much. If we lost 5–0 to them, we didn't worry as long as we were hitting our targets.

At the training ground, I built the War Room which was off-limits to everyone bar the backroom staff. No players were allowed in. We would have regular meetings in the mornings and afternoons sometimes involving a few staff, other times up to 20. The War Room was where we planned our strategy and analysed our data on a big screen. We could be in there for hours. We even mapped out where the team should be in three and five years' time. It was the Oxford University of football. It took years to get it as I wanted, and I never managed to properly recreate it anywhere else. There was a flow about it which just worked with all the right people in place. We had charts on every player's fitness levels and his statistical performances in matches from distance run, pace over ten metres, to tackles, interceptions, and pass completion. We knew immediately when a player's level dropped. There could be many reasons for that, mental or physical. And the advantage was that the physios got an early warning sign of a possible injury. That was vital, because treating an injury before any serious damage is done can make all the difference between being out for weeks or months. I've left players out knowing an injury was coming, while they are protesting they're perfectly okay to play. We had a small squad and having them available for as many games as possible was crucial. When I hear reports of lengthy injury lists at Premier League clubs, I wonder what on earth they are doing behind the scenes. It shouldn't happen if you get your set-up right, unless you are very unlucky.

I decided to sit in the stands rather than the dugout after a discussion with my coaches. 'Gaffer, you're a pain in the arse on the touchline' was the general view. I was screaming and hollering and it had become a joke. Nobody was listening when I went off on one, and it wasn't very constructive. I knew the players were cocking a deaf 'un where they pretend not to hear you, even when you know they can. I would forever be turning to the coaching staff going, 'What the fuck have you lot been doing all week? He's shit, him. Why did you tell me I should play him?' I just went on and on. Up in the stands, I could take a proper considered look at the game and the players could get on with it, and then at half-time we would show them clips of the action and identify the good and the bad of our performance. Visuals saved a thousand words.

I was in contact with the dugout by radio, although in those early days we didn't have a secure line so when I tried to talk to them there was often interference from outside. I would be shouting, 'Tell fucking Nolan to tuck in!' and they'd be hearing, 'Taxi for Mrs Jones, 3 Poplar Gardens,' or 'Do you want extra toppings and a garlic bread with your order.' We sorted it out in the end.

● ● ●

For all that we tried hard to recruit over the summer, when the big day arrived for the Premier League kick-off on 15 August 2001, the team was pretty much the same as the one which got us up. We were away at Leicester and I couldn't have imagined what was about to happen. Nolan put us in front with a header, Ricketts outmuscled their defence to get our second, Nolan netted again, and Frandsen rifled in a 20-yard free-kick. Leicester had scrappers like Dennis Wise and Robbie Savage in midfield, men who could scare the living daylights out of you, yet here we were 4–0 up at half-time. My big idea of sitting in the stands was paying instant dividends! I didn't have a clue what I was going to say in the dressing room. This was the Premier League and I'd never had an easier 45 minutes as a manager. 'Er . . . keep it going lads, well done,' was the best I could come up with. What more was there to add? Frandsen got another one in the second half and we'd won five bloody nil! Leicester got booed off while we were cheered to the rafters by our 2,000 travelling fans, who were no doubt as incredulous as I was.

This brought into play our novel incentive scheme, which was one of Deano's ideas from his Wimbledon days. If we lost by more than three, the players had to eat sheep's testicles . . . but if we won by more than three, then the backroom staff and I had to eat them. So Phil Gartside organised a delightful meal of sheep's balls for us long before the TV programme *I'm a Celebrity . . . Get Me Out of Here* was invented. You needed plenty of sauce on them to get through it, I can tell you. But it was a fun day out and added to our bonding as a squad, with all of us pulling in the same direction.

It was onto our first home game the next Tuesday, and not surprisingly there was a great atmosphere as we beat Middlesbrough 1–0 thanks to a Ricketts strike. The pundits were fully expecting us to get our comeuppance the following Monday against Liverpool, and so was I. This was a Liverpool team that had won five trophies in six months, the League Cup, the FA Cup, the UEFA Cup, the Charity Shield, topping it off by victory over the mighty Bayern Munich in the European Super Cup. Their team included Carragher, Gerrard, McAllister, Hamann, Owen and Fowler.

A draw was the best we could hope for, and that's where we looked to be heading after sub Emile Heskey cancelled out a Ricketts header.

But in the last minute, Deano tried a shot which keeper Sander Westerveld allowed to skid under his body and we'd won it 2–1. This was ridiculous. We were top of the Premier League with maximum points, having scored eight goals and conceded one. We followed it up with a 0–0 draw at Leeds and, although we lost at home to Southampton, we got further draws at Blackburn and Arsenal to go top again. Arsene Wenger was grumpy as hell about that, but he should have considered himself lucky. We had to play for an hour with ten men after Ricardo Gardner was sent off for a supposed foul on Dennis Bergkamp on the edge of the area. If Ricardo touched Bergkamp at all, the contact was minimal .The ref was going to let it go too, until the linesman intervened and Ricardo was red-carded. I was furious. The Gunners peppered our goal and it was no surprise when Thierry Henry and Robert Pires combined to set up Franny Jeffers to score. I threw Ricketts on and after our new signing Rod Wallace pulled the ball back, Ricketts flicked it up, turned 180 and volleyed over David Seaman. It was a goal worthy of Worthy in his pomp.

A slump followed and we went on a run of six games without a win. We had a shocker at home to Sunderland and followed it up with a 4–0 home defeat by Newcastle. The pundits who had tipped us for relegation were in that 'told you' sort of vein. So when we travelled to face the champions, Manchester United, in October there was not much cause for optimism, especially as they took the lead through a Juan Sebastian Veron free-kick. But Nolan hit a blinding volley from a Ricketts knockdown to equalise and, after Jussi made a double save from Scholes and Cole, Ricketts got the winner, capitalising on Wes Brown's mistake and lifting the ball over Barthez. There was talk that United were not the team they once were, and with Fergie having announced his impending retirement the first time round at the end of the season there was a feeling United were losing their edge. That didn't lessen our achievement – any time you win at United it's a big deal.

Ricketts was a right handful. No defence had a strategy for him. He was rewarded with an England call-up the following February and made his debut against Holland. But he had an awful 45 minutes, got subbed and never played for England again. His dad apparently got there late and missed the first-half, so he never saw his son kick a ball for his country. Michael didn't score for us again for the rest of the season and we started having trouble with him as he went Billy Big-time. His body fat was too high as he pigged out on takeaways and he would sneak bags of sweets onto the bus. One day I spotted him with more sweets and ripped them out of his hand.

'Stop scoffing sweets, will you. I never want to see a bag of those things on this bus again.'

'You know what, Michael?' I continued. 'You are the only person I know to play for England twice in one game, the first time and the last time. The way you are going, you'll be at fucking Walsall in a couple of years.'

He was only 23 but I could sense his career was already on the wane. As it happens, it took five years before he was back at Walsall but there was Middlesbrough, Leeds, Stoke, Cardiff, Burnley, Southend, Preston and Oldham in between.

● ● ●

All was not going smoothly, either on or off the field. I had to squeeze whatever money I could out of the board and did a presentation to persuade them to release more cash to help us survive the drop. I knew it would take us over the wage budget, but I believed it was worth the gamble. I brought in Danish international hard-man Stig Tofting, and German striker Fredi Bobic on loan from Borussia Dortmund. Bobic was a shock capture but nothing compared with the one which I still consider my greatest transfer coup of all time which saved us from relegation, the signing of French international attacking midfielder Youri Djorkaeff. Youri was no ordinary footballer; he starred for France in their 1998 World Cup triumph over Brazil and won Euro 2000. But I'd been tipped off by agent Mike Morris that he was out of favour at Kaiserslautern and was told he wouldn't be selected for the 2002 World Cup finals if he wasn't playing regular football.

I flew out with Mike to meet Youri in Germany, while Gartside was convinced I wouldn't be able pull it off.

'We aren't one of the biggest or most fashionable clubs in England,' I told Youri, 'but we are a group of battlers fighting to stay up, and with you in the team getting the regular football you need we can only improve, so it works for everyone.'

My French is not the best but I heard 'Je comprends' before the interpreter sprang into action.

'If I can help you, you can help me,' he added. 'If you can work it out with Kaiserslautern, I'll come.'

That was all the encouragement I needed. We had to get this done. Youri didn't come cheap but in the context of keeping us in the Premier League which, at the time was worth around £20 million, he was a steal. It wasn't a simple deal because there was an image rights contract to wrestle with too, but we found the solution and I was proud of myself for having got him. Youri's arrival showed we were serious about the Premier League and not content to meekly surrender and become a yo-yo club. He wasn't just class, he was world class, and listening to him talk football was an education for us all. I was dealing with someone with an extraordinary drive to succeed. He didn't suffer fools gladly, which had brought him into conflict with the Dortmund coach, and if he thought anyone was slacking he let them know. How could the players argue with someone of his pedigree? He wasn't at Bolton for an easy time. He took as much pride in his performance for us as he did for France in the World Cup final. The higher the calibre of player the less motivation they need, in my experience, and it rubs off on the others. He had hardly been playing when he arrived in February 2002, but he slotted in seamlessly straightaway.

Youri got us a much-needed 2–1 win at Charlton, scoring both, and threw his shirt into the crowd as our supporters chanted, '*We are staying up!*'. Not yet, we weren't, but we followed that with a 3–2 defeat of Aston Villa where Bobic opened his account. The result that sealed our survival was the one for which Bobic will always be remembered with affection by the fans, a home drubbing of Ipswich in what was billed as a relegation showdown. Bobic rattled in a first-half hat-trick and Youri got the other. It was the second time that season we'd been four up at half-time, which was a rather remarkable stat. We were safe, and frankly it felt like winning a title. Sheep's testicles were back on the menu but they tasted like caviar.

11

JAY-JAY, YOURI AND THE WIG

The big test now was whether Bolton could kick on, show we were more than one-season wonders in the Premier League, and attract world-class talent like Youri Djorkaeff. After France endured a terrible 2002 World Cup, getting knocked out without winning a game amid stories of behind-the-scenes bust-ups, I assumed Youri would retire. He was 34 with nothing left to prove, but it was a huge surprise hearing he wanted to come back to Bolton and sign on a permanent basis. This was unbelievable news and a real boost for us.

Despite his age, we gave him a three-year contract without any haggling from Phil. His name was going to attract other better players to the club; he was like our worldwide ambassador. Youri wasn't coming back to sit around and pick up a last pay cheque; world-class players don't do that, it's not in their make-up, they'd rather pack it in. Youri explained how when he won the World Cup and then the Euros he reset his goals each time, because you always have to be more determined than before, otherwise you fail.

I had my eye on another man from the 2002 World Cup, the Nigerian captain Jay-Jay Okocha, who had produced some eye-catching performances, including against England. Jay-Jay had been around the European scene for a while at Frankfurt, Fenerbahce and PSG who paid around £14 million for him. But he was out of contract and on the market. We had to move quickly, if we were to get him ahead of others who were bound to be interested, so I arranged to meet him at Charles de Gaulle airport.

Jay-Jay pulled up outside the terminal building all alone, driving his own car. There was not even an agent with him, but he knew what he was worth. I started the usual spiel.

'We're not the most fashionable club . . . dah dee dah . . . but we have got Youri Djorkaeff . . . dah dee dah.'

'I know I want to come to Bolton,' he said in perfect English.

I thought it was going to take weeks to sort it out, but we did a deal at the airport and I flew home while he promised to follow the next day to complete the paperwork. Would he really turn up? If he did I thought he would fly in, but not Jay-Jay. He drove all the way from Paris to Bolton, a journey which must have taken eight or nine hours, parked up, got straight out of his car, marched into the Reebok and signed. Quality.

The fans took to him instantly and coined the song, *'Jay-Jay Okocha, so good they named him twice.'* We had acquired a world star on a free at the age of 28 and he brought with him entertainment too. Thierry Henry said, 'Jay-Jay is so good even I'd pay to go and watch him.' That was some tribute from a player regarded by many as the best the Premier League has ever seen.

I loved Jay-Jay's tricks on the ball, I could watch him all day. There's no point to a trick if it doesn't get you anywhere and you don't come out of it with the ball, but Jay-Jay always performed his with a purpose. And he did it against the best: Manchester United, Arsenal, he had them in knots. He could do drag-backs, flick-overs, double step-overs, there's been no-one else like him, not even Cristiano Ronaldo. He got people off their seats, even opposition fans loved him. He was a cool African who collected watches and big cars.

'How much are they paying you?' the Bolton lads would joke with him.

'Boys, when you're as good as me, you can have cars like these your-selves.' That would shut them up.

I was getting bolder in the transfer market. Ivan Campo, a shaggy-haired centre-back/defensive midfielder and La Liga and Champions League winner at Real Madrid, was available for loan and I was going to have him as well. There was no stopping me. I was warned Campo was too much to handle and was on tablets to calm himself down, but I was confident I could sort him out. If I could liken him to anyone today, it would be David Luiz. He looked like him and played like him, not always reliable as a centre-back but accomplished on the ball in midfield, and you had to accept he would make the odd mistake in exchange for the benefits he gave you in launching attacks. Campo wigs flew off the shelves in the club shop.

Bernard Mendy, a right wing-back and team-mate of Okocha's, came on loan too. Now Bernard was a fiery lad who took no nonsense and in particular was no fan of Akin Bulent, a Turkish-born Belgian we signed from Galatasaray. Bulent turned out to be hopeless but he was hard as nails, and the pair had the most violent fight I ever saw in my career. During training, Akin and Bernard went in for a 50–50 tackle, fists started flailing and the scrap continued all the way into the changing rooms. Neither of them were going to back down. There were expletives flying in five different languages, with the occasional 'Fuck you' thrown in, in English, at regular intervals. The lads managed to split them up, but the minute they thought it had calmed down it went off again. I shouted for Faz, our big masseur, who made extra money on the side as a doorman in Manchester. Faz was our go-to man in times like this, and he dragged the two of them apart again. I hauled Bernard into my little office in the training-ground portakabin and sat him on the desk.

'Stay there and don't move till we get him out of the place,' I said. 'We'll deal with the two of you tomorrow.'

'But it's him, gaffer,' said Bernard in his broken English. 'He kicked me and then fronted me up, and when that happens you've got to get the first punch in.'

Akin was snorting like a bull outside and wasn't going anywhere. He wanted blood. Suddenly, the office door flies open and Bulent comes through the air Eric Cantona style, his right leg fully extended, and *bosh!* he takes Bernard out at the neck, sending him flying clean off the desk and onto the floor with a smack. Bernard took a couple of seconds to get himself together and was off chasing Akin into the car park. But Faz blocked him and Akin drove away.

Next day, I had them both in and was raging. 'You don't have to like each other, but one more incident like that and you're out of here. I know there are fights in training sometimes, but that was unacceptable. Now fuck off, the pair of you.'

Nowadays, a fight like that would find its way onto Twitter and make all the papers, but we managed to limit the fallout. A Sunday tabloid picked it up but a club spokesman was quoted saying, 'We have nothing to say on the matter.' I didn't mind a dressing-room scuffle as a rule. It means there's a bit of passion and feeling about the place. Players who come in, sit down and just put their heads to the floor all the time annoy me. I want to hear voices and I welcome opinions as long as they don't go too far, but Mendy v Bulent crossed the line.

While we successfully neutered the papers over the Bulent assault, we found it harder to counter accusations in the press that we were a team of mercenaries comprising short-term hired hands. I understood the point but I was acting within the regulations, and it was the best way to go while we got the finances in order. We took loads of players on trial. In one period, we must have looked at about 75 players from abroad and didn't sign one. It was hard work. You had to take chances sometimes which didn't always come off.

● ● ●

I was doing everything at Bolton, from organising the team to sorting out the contracts. I was a proper old-fashioned boss. The board meanwhile were finding it difficult coping with our status as a Premier League club, which meant we were now a worldwide brand, and the demands being put on us. I helped them set out a business plan so that we could secure a 25-year loan with the bank while Ray Ranson, the former Manchester City player who was big in the financial game by this time, was lending us money based on the valuation of our squad to help strengthen the playing side. With our debt, cash-flow was a big problem and through Ray we borrowed another £5–£6 million, but I'm not sure how much I saw of it to spend on players.

We struggled on the pitch through to Christmas of 2002 after a poor start, although Ricketts came back to life at Leeds where we won 4–2. He was on fire that day. We should have won the next one at home to Chelsea too but conceded an equaliser to Jimmy Floyd Hasselbaink in the 90th minute. If there's one goal which stands out as the worst ever conceded in my time as manager it was that one, and it was such a kick in the knackers because it meant we stayed in the relegation zone. They rolled it out from the back into midfield, out wide, back again, up to midfield, went forward, kept going right through the middle, crossed and scored. I went absolutely potty in the dressing room and I still hadn't got over it by Monday. I showed it on the big screen at training time and again.

'Listen to me. There's a minute to go and they've gone right through our team without anyone doing a thing about it. What were you thinking? Can't anyone tackle?' I was boiling.

We got to the game at West Ham just before Christmas sitting in the bottom three. In the team meeting that week, we'd gone through the stats and reckoned if we lost we would be more likely to be relegated because no team had avoided the drop from that position. We got a draw, with Ricketts scoring again, and followed up with an amazing 4–3 win over Newcastle where Ricketts got two. We'd been cruising at 4–1 but Shola Ameobi scored and then Alan Shearer smacked one in and I was bricking it as we hung on. After that Michael started playing up, wanting a move and chucked it in for us. It was rumoured Spurs were in for him, the same rumours we'd heard back in the summer, but there were no actual bids. As usual they left it until the last minute, but I needed replacements if he went, and I found out that if we sold him there wouldn't be much money left because of the agreement we had to pay back Ray Ranson.

So I lined up two men, Florent Laville from Lyon and Pierre-Yves André from Nantes, who were major players I knew could help us secure our Premiership status. They signed ten minutes before the transfer deadline and we accepted Middlesbrough's bid of £3.5 million for Michael five minutes earlier. I'd gambled that Ricketts was incapable of carving out a long career and I was right, as Boro quickly found out. His best days were behind him. It was a criminal waste of talent. He was a natural goal-scorer, had pace and was left- and right-footed, but he had no discipline.

We were grinding our way to the finish, doing enough to stay out of the bottom three and losing only two out of 11 but five of them were draws. We went into the penultimate game knowing if West Ham lost to Chelsea and we at least drew at Southampton, we were safe. What happens? West Ham beat Chelsea and we run out for our 5.30 game against the Saints feeling sick as pigs having dropped into the bottom three. The wait before our kick-off was excruciating but I told the lads, 'Don't worry about West Ham. Our fate is in our own hands. Try and win the game but make sure we don't lose.'

We were awful in the first half and I went at them at the break. I picked out Djorkaeff, Okocha and Campo for the treatment.

'You've won the World Cup, and you've played at two World Cups and you've been to a World Cup and won the Champions League. What the fuck's the matter with you all?'

We were much better in the second half and got a point to climb out of the relegation zone again. So we faced a final match eight days later against Middlesbrough, still needing a win to be sure of staying up. If West Ham won at Birmingham, a draw would not be good enough for us. I gave everyone four days off to relieve the tension. There was no more training we could do, no more fitness work and no more drills. They needed some brain space but the press were wondering what I was doing. I had to trust my instincts were right and even had a day out at Chester races with Brownie, Phil, Ed and the girls. It was the longest week of my life. I rang Steve Bruce, the manager of Birmingham.

'You will be taking this seriously, won't you? Are your players up for it? We might need you to win.'

Brucie was quite indignant. 'What are you on about? Of course we'll try to win.'

On the Friday, we went through some team play and I strolled out in shorts and sunglasses with a cap on and whistle in hand.

'Let's have a game,' I said.

I thought back to that day before the second leg of the play-offs with Blackpool and how they had all bricked it. This time I wanted everyone to relax.

It was going to be an edgy day against Boro but goals from Frandsen and a gorgeous free-kick from Okocha in the first 20 minutes put us in control. Nothing was going to be easy though and Ricketts came off the bench to pull one back for Boro on the hour with his first goal since his transfer. As it happens it was offside, but the flag stayed down and we had half-an-hour to hold out. Our player liaison, Matt Hockin, then runs round to our dugout, informing us West Ham have taken the lead. What a brilliant five minutes this was turning out to be.

But Birmingham recovered and shared the points and we won, which meant we were safe at last. I was dancing on the pitch with Jay-Jay with moves as smooth as his, and the fans refused to go home until we'd done two laps of honour. This was what survival meant to them. I was shredded and admitted afterwards: 'I feel completely drained and emotionally unstable but absolutely delighted and so relieved. It feels like the weight of the world has been lifted from my shoulders and I'm floating six feet off the ground.

'We're talking history here. You'd have to go through the archives and wipe the cobwebs off the books to find the last Bolton team comparable with this one.'

We had four more points than the previous season but finished one place lower and it felt like a much harder slog. The good start we made in the first season up meant we had never felt under the same pressure as in the second season.

'We can never be left in this position again,' I told Phil Gartside. 'We've got to spend some money or there's nothing more I can do for this club. We can't just keep surviving on loan players. This has to stop.'

● ● ●

We were still scouring the free transfer market but at least we were allowed to do permanent deals. Brazilian defender Emerson Thome came on a free, and we scouted Stelios Giannakopoulus from Olympiakos which wasn't the most straightforward signing. The agent Mike Morris tipped me off about his contract being up and how he wanted to come to England, so I went to watch Stelios at a very lively derby against AEK Athens in which the fans seemed to spend most of their time firing rockets at each other while police and their dogs went piling in to try and stop them. At half-time, Mike and I were having a drink in the executive lounge when five security guards came flying across the room, jumped on this bloke and smashed a plate glass window. The Greek agent with us explained that they had just taken down the former club president who had pulled out a gun! He obviously wasn't very happy but the agent just said, 'That's Greek football.'

So Stelios arrived after ten highly successful years in Greece which got the club shop excited about potential sales of the 14 letters needed for the back of his shirt. Extra orders were in the pipeline for 'n', 'o', 'u', and 'a', until he decided he wanted to be known as Stelios.

I took a punt that I could revive the career of Kevin Davies, a striker who had made a name for himself as a youngster at Chesterfield but lost his way after spells at Southampton, twice, and Blackburn who paid £7.5 million for him. Davies had been released by Saints, but he was only 26 and I couldn't understand what had gone wrong. I remembered him from when I was at Blackpool and he played for Chesterfield. He was trim but strong with a good touch and could run and run. We had become the masters of resurrecting careers and it was not a big risk to take him, because if it didn't work out he wasn't costing much.

Kevin admitted Blackburn was too big and overwhelming for him and he had lost his confidence. He was essentially a happy-go-lucky lad who wanted to enjoy his football. We took him to Ireland pre-season and I sat him down and said, 'Look, this is your last chance. If you blow this you've got nowhere to go. Are you going to do this, or are you going to totally fuck up your career?' We battered him with sports science and got his body fat down to less than 10 per cent by threatening him with fines.

We'd never had a target man to play off. Deano was alright but got too old and Ricketts wasn't interested in doing anything he was told. Kevin was an instant success. He wasn't a prolific goal-scorer but that didn't matter: he was great to work off, held the ball up well and won free-kicks around the penalty area. Djorkaeff picked up the pieces from him and Stelios provided the crosses. Stelios enjoyed his season so much he went off to Euro 2004 and won the thing with Greece, which was probably the biggest shock in international football for years. I was laughing when he received his winner's medal and his little lad who he was carrying round the pitch was wearing a Bolton shirt. We had made it on the international stage. Stelios loved Bolton so much that he still has a house there.

I wanted some competition for Jussi in goal so we agreed a deal for

Tomasz Kuszczak from Hertha Berlin. But our secretary Simon cocked up and allowed him to go back to the hotel after Tomasz said, 'I'll sign in the morning.' At breakfast time he wasn't there, he'd gone to West Brom. We told our goalkeeping coach Fred Barber it was his fault, because he was part-time with the Baggies as well as us. Fred was beside himself. So we asked him where his loyalties were and he said, 'To you, Sam,' and we made him full-time at Bolton. If we couldn't have Kuszczak, we were having their coach. Simon didn't get off lightly though. I gave him an absolute monstering.

We made a dodgy start, losing our first game 4–0 at Manchester United where Cristiano Ronaldo came off the bench and absolutely fried us on his debut. David Beckham had just left for Real Madrid and United had a new hero. We also lost 4–0 at Portsmouth but we beat Spurs, Leeds and Everton in November and never had to worry about a relegation battle. We also got to the Carling Cup final, beating Liverpool and Aston Villa along the way. Our first goal against Liverpool was scored by Mario Jardel, a striker who was once the talk of European football with his goals for Sporting Lisbon, Porto and Galatasaray. His record was amazing, 264 goals in 380 games, even though he had a reputation as a party animal. He told Gartside, 'Put two goalkeepers in and I'll still score you lots of goals, chairman.' Phil goes, 'I love this man,' and paid him what he wanted. But this was one career I couldn't salvage. We nicknamed him 'Lardel' because he was so overweight. By Christmas, we got shot of him. English players get some stick for enjoying a night out, but nobody did it quite like Mario.

Jay-Jay scored two against Villa, as we won the first leg of the Carling

Cup semi-final 5–2, and his second was a rocket round the wall with the outside of his boot from a free-kick. I was pretty elated by that one and remarked afterwards, 'I've been with this club as a player and manager for 17 years and I've never seen a better player. People talk about Nat Lofthouse and the like, but I honestly believe Okocha is the best we've ever had.' It was no disrespect to Nat.

Jay-Jay had to leave for the African Cup of Nations before the second leg. We nearly bottled it when Villa beat us 2–0 despite them playing with only ten men in the second half following Gavin McCann's dismissal after a clash with Thome. It was my first major cup final as manager or player and I drove straight home to Lynne and poured us glasses of champagne, while I treated myself to my favourite sandwich of fish fingers and cheese!

Our cup final opponents were Steve McClaren's Middlesbrough. It wasn't like we were playing Arsenal, Chelsea or Man United so we had a chance, but I dare say Boro were thinking the same about us. I was taking in the atmosphere at the Millennium Stadium in Cardiff and remembering how we had won our play-off there against Preston when Phil Gartside stopped for a chat. It was clear he was worried about money.

'Do you know what, Sam? It's been a great journey but if we win this we are going to get into Europe and I'm not sure we can afford it.'

I couldn't believe it. Phil was cautious whereas I firmly believed getting into Europe, though expensive, was a sound financial investment.

My relationship with Phil went downhill from then on. I couldn't get my head round what he'd said. I was disgusted.

We conceded a goal inside two minutes from Joseph-Désiré Job and Boudewijn Zenden converted a penalty with only seven minutes gone.

The penalty-kick should have been ruled out as Zenden fell over and connected with both feet, which is illegal, but the goal stood. Davies got one back, beating Mark Schwarzer at his near post and we were denied a last-minute penalty of our own when Ugo Ehiogu, the young man we'd discovered when I was at West Brom 15 years before, handled Stelios's shot. It was a clear penalty but referee Mike Riley missed it. I publicly criticised the decision, calling it 'a disgrace' and landed myself with yet another FA charge. Punished again for speaking the truth. Riley told me afterwards that if he'd realised Zenden had connected with both feet for his penalty, he'd still have given a goal because Zenden's action was unintentional.

We finished the season strongly. I tried an experiment before our away game at Wolves on the Easter Monday, letting the players know that if they won they could be off until the Thursday. The sports science team were going ballistic, telling me how they would all come back stiff as boards and it would be an almighty job to get them fit for Saturday's home game against Spurs. Anyway, we won and I stuck to my promise. Ten minutes before we went out against Spurs I said, 'Okay lads, if you win you can be off till next Thursday.' Again the medical staff were screaming but we bagged three points again. 'You can't keep doing this Sam, it's not good for them,' they said. But we looked at the stats and the players were performing even better in all aspects. We were at the part of the season where they didn't need to be trained hard and I didn't want them mentally fatigued either. We kept going, taking four days off each week and won five in a row before losing the last game of the season at home to Fulham. I couldn't offer the same incentive for that one, because they all knew they were off for the summer anyway. It was a good job we didn't win any more or we might have qualified for Europe via the league and that would have given Phil a coronary.

● ● ●

We were now an established Premier League club and it was time to start acting like one.

I thought we should be looking up the table, not looking down and having to base our plans around survival. But I was still forced to shop at Tesco rather than Harrods, not that you couldn't pick up some great bargains at Tesco. We snapped up Gary Speed, unwanted by Newcastle because he was nearly 35, but all the reports told me Speedo was one of the fittest players in the Premier League. Gartside didn't want to fork out for him, because he thought he was too old. If he was £5 million I might have seen Phil's point, but this was a drop in the ocean and Speedo's stats were those of a 25-year-old. Newcastle had signed Nicky Butt so thought they could do without Gary, but Freddy Shepherd said to me while we were negotiating, 'Don't tell Bobby Robson about this till it's done. He won't be very happy.'

We brought in an even older player, 36-year-old Spanish legend Fernando Hierro, winner of five La Ligas and three Champions Leagues. I didn't worry about their legs, I wanted their brains. Hierro had been playing in Qatar but wanted to experience the Premier League before retirement. Agent Franny Martin said he wanted his kids to learn English and as long as we paid their school fees we could pay Fernando what we liked. Campo was a former team-mate of Hierro and said, 'Oh hell, here we go, he comes in and I'm out.' He wasn't exactly putting out the welcome mat. We played Fernando at centre-back and he struggled. But when he switched to midfield, in place of Campo as he correctly predicted, he was unbelievable. There wasn't a better passer in the Premier League, and I include Paul Scholes who was the master. His accuracy was laser-like and the others only had to make their run and Fernando could find them. He was intercepting 15 balls per game. Nobody in the league was doing that. He'd win 20 headers every match; no midfielder was doing that either.

Radhi Jaidi, a man mountain of a centre-back from Tunisia, came on a free transfer too, which was the deal of a lifetime. Two years later we sold him to Birmingham for £2 million without so much as a 'well done' from Gartside for a cracking piece of business. I also got El Hadji Diouf on loan from Liverpool, who we signed permanently a year later for £3 million. I'd never met anyone quite like Dioufy. He used to call me 'Dad' for the way I looked after him. Liverpool paid £10 million for him, but he had gone off the rails and needed an arm round the shoulder. He told me, 'Liverpool never liked me, so I didn't like them. They never helped me.' He was a young man with a reputation for trouble, but he was a pussycat. If there was a fight going on, he ran away. And if you treated him the right way, he delivered for you. I loved him and was prepared to give him a bit of licence to get the best out of him. Every player is different and the key is to find what makes them tick. Dioufy was off the wall, I'll say that. Every one of his suits had his initials stitched into them.

As we continued our recruitment, my son Craig, who had become an agent, spotted a talented young Israeli defender Tal Ben Haim and he was another through the entrance door. Sadly, one passing him the other way was Youri following an argument over a contract extension. He went to our arch-rivals Blackburn, of all places, but didn't stay long before heading off to America.

Newcastle made an approach for me at the end of August after they'd sacked Bobby Robson. We'd won three out of our first four and were sitting third in the table with Newcastle lying 16th. It was a shock that Bobby had gone; he was an institution and it was early days in the season but the chairman, Freddy Shepherd, felt it was time for a change, contacted Mark Curtis and told him they wanted me. There was a compensation clause in my contract of £1.5 million and Freddy was going to pay it. Newcastle were the bigger club but their team was nowhere near as good as mine. I wrote down the squads on two separate sheets of paper, laid them side by side and there was no comparison. But Newcastle was a massive football town, still buzzing from the Kevin Keegan era and the re-birth John Hall's investment had provided, which Freddy was carrying on in the chairman's office as the club's second biggest shareholder. They got double the crowds Bolton did, 52,000 every week, and the attention they attracted was huge if strangely disproportionate to what they had achieved, which was nothing at all in terms of silverware. Alan Shearer, the Premier League's leading scorer, was approaching retirement which worried me. He guaranteed you 20 goals a season and if he was in his prime I might have jumped at the job, but not when he was coming to the end. Where would I find another Shearer? I got permission from a reluctant Gartside to speak to Newcastle but he begged me not to go, and as Mark drove up the motorway to meet Shepherd,

Phil was phoning us both to try and stop it. In spite of my relationship with Gartside deteriorating since that episode at the Millennium Stadium and feeling that Shepherd was my type of chairman, I couldn't go through with it. I told Freddy I was staying at Bolton.

'I'm sorry,' I said. 'You've offered me a fantastic opportunity and I thank you very much for that, but I can't leave.'

It wasn't over. John Hall's son, Douglas, asked if he could see me during the international break in early September while I was taking a break in Marbella.

'Why? I've made my decision,' I said.

'Just let me come and have a talk,' said Douglas.

So he turned up and goes, 'Have you ever had £25 million to spend on a player? No you haven't, and you never will as long as you stay at Bolton. But you'll get it at Newcastle.'

It spelled out the difference in size of the two clubs. But I said, 'I appreciate you coming and I'm flattered how much Newcastle want me, but I'm not changing my mind.'

I got a new improved five-year contract from Bolton, having been five years into my ten-year deal. Even though I'd rejected a massive opportunity, Bolton were the club I'd built, we were the fairytale story of the Premier League, and I was not ready to walk away. Little did I know then that it was far from the end of me and Newcastle.

Turning down Newcastle did not represent a lack of ambition; on the contrary I was very ambitious. So I laid out my terms for staying to Phil. 'I want more money for players, I want to fight for a place in the top four, I want to win a cup, I want this club to go as far as it possibly can.'

Although Phil promised to deliver, it never properly materialised. He still wanted us to work miracles on a relative shoestring.

But I felt vindicated by my decision as we beat Spurs at White Hart Lane. However, as I was preparing the team to face Spurs again in a Carling Cup tie at the Reebok my ambitions took a back seat when our Senagalese midfielder Khalilou Fadiga collapsed during a warm-up shuttle run. There was an immediate panic. Fadiga had undergone major heart-surgery back in May and come through all the tests, but I feared the worst when I saw him unconscious. Nolan and Pedersen raced off to get medical assistance as our player lay motionless on the pitch, and it was an enormous relief when he came round in the dressing room thanks to the expertise of our doctor Richard Freeman and head of sports science Mark Taylor. Khalilou got a defibrillator fitted and did play for us again, but I never felt relaxed when he was on the field. It was remarkable that another Bolton player, Fabrice Muamba, also collapsed against Spurs with a heart problem eight years later. It brought all the memories of Khalilou flooding back, but thankfully due to brilliant medical staff both players survived.

The great Bill Shankly might have said, 'Football is not a matter of life and death, it's much more important than that,' but as both the Muamba and Khalilou incidents demonstrated, there were times when I couldn't have disagreed more.

ALLERDICI 1 ARSENE 0

12

History was beckoning for my boyhood club. Bolton, yes little old Bolton, qualified for Europe for the first time by finishing sixth at the end of 2004–05. We confirmed our place by virtue of a draw at Portsmouth with one game to spare.

I always felt we could to do it, but actually achieving it was a real testament to the magnificent job done by everyone at the Reebok. We had beaten Liverpool at home and Spurs twice, while taking four points off Arsenal, and our stadium was packed to capacity when we beat Everton 3–2 in our last game of the season. I took Hierro off with 20 minutes to go and he received a standing ovation, with hugs all round from his team-mates. We wanted Fernando to stay for another season, but he knew his own mind. It was his final game in professional football.

I firmly believed we had one of the most advanced backroom staffs in the world. We were getting requests from European and American sports teams to come and visit us to find out our secrets, although strangely none from England apart from the national rugby team. The big question was, could we go any further? With investment it was possible. We had acquired such a reputation that we feared no-one. In those days, investment gave smaller clubs a chance to compete but it's much harder now. I doubt a club the size of Bolton will ever again finish in the top six. The Financial Fair Play regulations have had a detrimental effect on clubs which previously might have attracted a big-money investor who fancied some fun. We saw it with Jack Walker and Blackburn in the mid-90s, Mohammed Al-Fayed and Fulham, Steve Gibson at Middlesbrough and on a grander scale Roman Abramovich at Chelsea and Sheikh Mansour at Man City. FFP means investment in the game has all but disappeared, which I think is dangerous for football's health. The dream of a club rising from non league to the top division has gone. And I don't think other countries are playing it fair the way we do. We always seem to abide by the regulations, while over in continental Europe at places like Real Madrid and Barcelona they drive a bus through the middle of them with nothing more than a slapped wrist.

The best players are all in Spain – Messi, Ronaldo, Suarez, Neymar, Bale – when they should be in England because we have the biggest and best brand in the world. Beyond Real and Barça, and maybe Atletico Madrid, Spain has nothing. I watch teams lower down in La Liga and it's woeful stuff. They play it forward, lose the ball and can't keep possession. For all that, I would have liked to manage in Spain. I love the country which is why we built our beautiful villa in Moraira. But I don't speak the language and I'm too long in the tooth to try now. It's my own fault. I've been going to Spain for 30 years so I've had plenty of opportunity to learn, but there are so many people out there who speak English that you get lazy. When I saw Pep Guardiola doing his first press conference at Bayern Munich, and speaking German like he was a native, I couldn't help but be impressed when I heard he'd picked it up during his holidays. I could never do that.

I would have been a success abroad if I'd cracked the language barrier. I had a mate, Fred Shawcross, who was a famous racing journalist and a Bolton lad. He wrote to me as Bolton started taking the Premier League by storm and said, 'If you'd been called Allerdici, you'd be hailed as a coaching genius.' I used the line in a press conference and it stuck. Some people thought it was arrogance on my part, but Fred had a point. I was no longer some big lump from the Black Country, and a clogger of a centre-half. My staff and I were presiding over the best coaching set-up in the Premier League. Our performance director, Mike Forde, would research sports teams across the world, learning how they prepared and cherry picking the best bits. The Milan lab was lauded as being the secret behind Italian football success, but I will happily bet we were better than them and better than Real or Barça. Yet the top clubs in England would not risk taking on me and my team. Nowadays they are rarely managed by anyone from Britain. They've got to get a fancy-dan foreigner in, it's almost compulsory. Are they really any better than the coaches we produce in this country? Do they have more knowledge than we do? I doubt it. The idea that foreign coaches have a more in-depth approach to football is rubbish.

I was loving being in charge of a team that consistently over-achieved and upset the establishment by giving the elite a bloody nose. The more they slagged us off, the more we enjoyed getting under their skin. There is nothing more satisfying than punching above your weight against the bigger guys, knocking them out. We got tagged as a long-ball team because they were so embarrassed when they couldn't beat us. When they hit a 50-yard ball it was a cultured pass; when we did, it was a hopeful hoof. I got used to it; they were having to find excuses for their own deficiencies.

Of course the likes of Arsenal beat us sometimes, but we drew with or beat them more often than expected and Arsene Wenger couldn't handle it. He tried to influence refs through the media and create a perception that we were bullies committing all the fouls, while his team just wanted to play. It seemed he wanted a rule where Arsenal should be allowed to do what they wanted with the ball, without us being allowed to tackle them. That was his ideal and there were more than a few refs and members of the media who bought into it. The game has become too clean now. You cannot make a tackle. Even if you get the ball, if you do it with a snarl on your face, it's a free-kick to them and a yellow card. The rules have changed so much that a ref doesn't even know what a bookable offence is any more.

I was always getting questions like, 'Arsene said you kicked them off the park, what have you got to say about that?' or 'Arsene says you weren't interested in playing football, how do you respond?' There was no credit for the fact we'd spent all week studying how to nullify their skilful players and not let them have a second on the ball. It was a skill finding their weaknesses and how to exploit them. When we succeeded, the press was usually on about Arsenal having an off day and the ref being soft. There was one time Wenger wouldn't shake hands with me at Highbury because we got a draw. I saw him ripping his tie off and throwing it on the floor in anger. He takes it all very personally and has an air of arrogance. He's not one for inviting you into the office for a drink after games. He's a fantastic manager, I cannot deny that, but the more I could wind him up, the more I liked it.

Rafa Benitez was another one. When we beat him he would complain, 'They don't play my type of football.' What was that then? Winning football? He didn't like me and he thought he was superior. Here was a trendy foreign manager with all his smart ideas getting beat by some oik from the Midlands. I put his comments on the wall of the changing room but Campo and Jay-Jay said, 'We don't need those gaffer, we'll beat him anyway.' Benitez wouldn't talk to me at all and that just made it all the better when we won. I can't stand people who disrespect me the way he did. I didn't create any of the conflict between us, it was all down to him. Of course, he can say he won the Champions League at Liverpool, which is something I've never done, but it was nowt to do with him. It was just an extraordinary second half when Steven Gerrard took the game by the scruff of the neck and dragged Liverpool back from 3–0 down against AC Milan to win on penalties. I don't blame Benitez for claiming credit but as managers we know the truth. It's like when you make a substitution in desperation and it comes off. You get all the credit for your tactical brilliance, when often it's just luck.

Fergie was totally different. If you beat United, he'd still invite you in and open a bottle of red. That is class. I'm sure in the dressing room though he gave his players the famous hairdryer, as in, 'How can you let a poxy little team like Bolton beat you?' Fergie became a genuine friend but he stitched me up royally when we played at Old Trafford on his birthday one New Year's Eve. I went to see Gordon Seymour, a director at Wanderers who owned a vintage wine merchants. I bought a special bottle as a present to mark Sir Alex's big day and got Matt Hockin to put the fine Bordeaux in his office for after the game. As Fergie didn't do any after-match press, he was back in his room long before me.

'Come on then, get the wine out,' I said when I arrived.

'We might as well open the one you've bought me,' he said, pointing to the corner.

I proudly handed it over, but when he opened the box I was horrified.

'Are you taking the piss?' he said.

'What? I thought a Bordeaux was good?'

'Well, this isn't Bordeaux,' observed Fergie, brandishing a bottle of Ribena in his hand.

I went redder than the wine I thought was in the bottle and went looking for Matt shouting, 'What the hell have you done?'

Matt didn't know what I was talking about. 'It's nothing to do with me gaffer, honest.'

I went back into Fergie's den to find their goalkeeping coach Tony Coton absolutely creased up laughing and Fergie struggling to keep a straight face. They'd swapped it themselves and got the Ribena from the canteen. They had done me like a kipper – and we lost 4–1.

The tradition of going into the opposing manager's office for a glass or two is dying out now. The foreign bosses aren't keen on it, and there are so many duties after the match that there isn't the time. It is more likely we have a cup of tea together before the game, when it's all nice and friendly and there is no winner or loser. The younger managers are paranoid about giving anything away though, so it's only airy-fairy chit-chat unless you really know the other bloke.

● ● ●

While we were on a mission to embarrass the powerhouses of English football, I thought referees were involved in a conspiracy against us and wanted us put in our place. I was constantly dragging refs' chief Keith Hackett to Bolton to complain that his men were being conned and he couldn't see it. Jussi got booked for time wasting once at a goal-kick and using Prozone I proved that the kick was the quickest one taken in the whole match. The refs didn't have Prozone and Keith went out and bought it after that. I kept getting in his ear because I wanted the standard of refereeing to be better.

Despite the odds being stacked against us, I had to pinch myself to believe what we had accomplished in such a short space of time. The rest of the business side at Bolton couldn't keep pace with the advances we were making on the pitch. We kitted out the dressing rooms so they were American Football style, giving the players a feeling of their own space, and they had their individual names on their lockers. It might not sound much, but it gave them a sense of belonging to a club that was going places. There were screens which told each player their programme for the day, be it rehab or a specific training programme. We built a hydrotherapy pool and brought in free weights as opposed to static weights which were the norm. Rugby players were using them and it meant you had to be more responsible when lifting.

We went to look at Nike, who had become one of the best player recruitment sports companies in the game, and how they treated their clients. They got players young in the hope that eventually they would make it big. They were able to hold onto the best ones, not just by paying good money but also planning a strategy for their development for five and ten years' time and helping them plot a course through their careers. They did the same for their admin staff. When I was a player, Nike were nobodies in football. Now they are enormous and it's been achieved through a careful strategy. They used to send us boots from their factory in Huddersfield asking us to trial them, but they were a small company in football terms; they were only dabbling with it and weren't taken that seriously. They were trying things at the time that no-one else was doing – coloured boots, laces on the side, different innovations. We were grateful for them because we only got one pair of boots a season. Now players wear a new pair of boots every game and parents get fleeced because kids want all the latest designs and colours which is a right scam. Kids don't need new ones every five minutes, they are being exploited. Another con is the ball. We played with white ones all the time in the old days and only occasionally got the orange one out if there was six inches of snow. Now we are told yellow ones are better visually in the winter and you need a pink one for the FA Cup. What a load of rot. It's just a marketing ploy.

I don't think the modern boot, which is made of synthetic material, hugs the player's foot like a natural skin did. I don't like blades in the soles of boots either. A stud is far better and you will never convince me otherwise. There are way more cruciate ligament injuries today and I'm sure they are partly related to bladed boots, because players change direction much more quickly and pitches are harder. But the structure of the boot is better in the way it protects the Achilles tendon which, at one time when it went, could potentially finish a player's career.

We were evolving at Bolton in that while we were still bringing in experienced older players we were also finding plenty of quality under 30s, often with flaws but flaws we could iron out. They weren't just coming for an easy life and a pay-day. To get Davies at 26 and turn his career around was exactly what we were about. Diouf was only 23, with a direct attacking style which the fans loved, and Stelios, Campo and Jay-Jay, who had achieved so much in their careers, brought some of their best days to Bolton by joining us before their 30th birthdays.

● ● ●

Before the 2005–06 season started, I had to return from my holidays to finish my professional coaching licence at Warwick University with my mates Bryan Robson and Peter Reid, along with René Meulensteen, Kenny Jackett, Kevin Bond and Sammy Lee, who was a full-time England coach. It was a good old drinking school, if truth be told. We were sitting around chatting when my first-team coach Neil McDonald rang.

'I've been offered the assistant manager's job at Crystal Palace and I'm going to take it.'

'Are you mad?' I said. 'You're telling me you'd rather be an assistant manager in the Championship than a first-team coach in the Premier League with a team that's going into Europe for the first time in history? Can you tell me why that's a better job? I think you're stupid, but if you're stupid enough then do it.'

Palace had gone down under Iain Dowie, and if they started badly, Dowie and Macca were going to be under huge pressure. But there was no changing Macca's mind.

'I'll never be assistant at Bolton with Brownie there,' he said.

The next phone call was from Scott McGarvey, a former Manchester United player and agent.

'Is it alright if Brownie speaks to Derby about the manager's job?'

'Does Brownie know?' I asked.

'Yeah, he's flying over from Portugal.'

I wasn't going to stand in Brownie's way, even though two of the main men on my backroom team were quitting at the same time. I thought it was right Brownie should get his chance, especially as he'd been getting the piss taken out of him for having reached the age of 45 without ever being a manager.

I waited for Brownie to get in touch. We had a share in a horse called European Dream with Jussi and Kevin Nolan, and when Brownie called he had some news.

'I'm going to the races to watch the horse.'

'Anything else?' I said.

'Er . . . yeah. I think Derby have shown an interest in me.'

'Come off it, Brownie, I know they've shown an interest. If you want to go then go, but you can tell them we want compensation.'

We let him go and the compensation came in the form of a friendly against Derby with us keeping the gate money.

If Macca had hung on he'd have got Brownie's job, and I found out subsequently his wife Joanne begged him to ditch Palace and ask me for it, but he was too scared to do a U-turn. Macca would be my coach and assistant again in the future, but I never let him forget how he deserted me.

I was wondering what to do next, when Reidy suggested, 'You should take Sammy. He's not involved enough at the FA and it's driving him potty. He's hyperactive and he hasn't got enough to do after being coach at Liverpool for ten years.' So I called Sammy to my room and said to him, 'Fancy joining us? You can still do England, which will please Bolton because it will keep your wages down, but I want you to be assistant manager.'

Sammy was keen, and with Gartside on the FA he was the obvious man to sort it all out. It took a little while but eventually Sammy joined. Of course, the fact he was only 5ft 7in meant he was nicknamed 'Little Sam'. For first-team coach, Mike Morris proposed Ricky Sbragia who I'd worked with at Sunderland. Ricky was reserve-team boss at Man United which meant asking Fergie for one of his men. Again that took a while to organise but Fergie let him go in the end. I liked the combination of Sammy and Ricky, it was fresh and interesting and they brought new ideas from having worked at such big clubs.

We were proud to be in Europe, even if Gartside was not so happy. We were well in credit on transfers in and out, but all we kept hearing was that there was no money in Europe, even though it was a status symbol which showed how far we'd come. In the War Room, we had plotted to get into Europe in five years and were well ahead of schedule, but Gartside preached one thing and one thing only: 'We've got to stay in the Premier League. That is all that matters.' He always thought down first rather than up.

I understood that for Manchester United, Chelsea, Arsenal or Liverpool, getting into the UEFA Cup was not an ambition, it was probably a sign of failure, but for Bolton it represented a great achievement. It was going to stretch the squad though. We looked at Middlesbrough's experience the year before. They played ten games in Europe but only won four matches in the Premier League after the turn of the year. That meant we needed finance for more players and enough for two teams, so that some would play in the cups and others the league. We were working miracles. Phil blocked me from talking to Eddie Davies presumably because he was worried about me having too much influence on him.

Eddie was a clever man who collared the market and made a name for himself with those kettle thermostats. Every time you click your electric kettle on, there's a fair chance Eddie sold that switch to the manufacturer and he made millions. He had a big farm in Cheshire where he and his wife kept horses and entered them in international events. They even got one into the Olympics. He also had an eventing course and a pheasant-shoot area, and another big house in the Isle of Man. You had to be careful with him. He was a tough, ruthless businessman who invested heavily in Bolton, and didn't do so to lose money. He wanted a return, even if it meant waiting years for it. But he didn't want to be involved in the day-to-day running of the club; he left that to Phil and relied on his advice. If Phil told him not to deal directly with me, then he wouldn't.

We prepared for the new season by taking part in the Premier League Asia Trophy in Bangkok, and won the competition by beating Manchester City on penalties in the semi-final and the Thai national team in the final thanks to a penalty by Dioufy. But I remember that trip so well for a very different reason. We took a day out to visit Phuket and witnessed the terrible devastation cause by the Indian Ocean tsunami which struck on 26 December 2004. Nothing prepares you for such scenes, even though seven months had passed. Houses were destroyed and trees were still lying on their sides across ripped-up roads. It seemed to me the government was more intent on rebuilding the hotels which had been wrecked rather than people's homes, but I dare say they had to get the tourist trade moving again to give the locals jobs. We organised a coaching course for the kids who had been orphaned in the disaster, and there were a lot of orphans which was so sad. But to see those kids' faces when we got the footballs out and started a kick around was a joy. It was an incredibly moving day.

We didn't get the most attractive first round draw in Europe – Lokomotiv Plovdiv of Bulgaria – but we won both legs 2–1 and were rewarded with a group made up of Besiktas, Seville, the eventual winners of the tournament, Zenit St Petersburg and Guimares of Portugal. Now that was European football. We needed a point from our last game, at home against already qualified Seville, to get through to the last 32 but it was the strangest game. Seville kept the ball for the whole first half apart from one shot which hit our post. With the score 0–0 at the break it suited us, but then N'Gotty smashed one in and Seville didn't take it well. Adriano, their Brazilian who went on to play for Barcelona, came off the bench and slotted the ball home after a rapier-like attack. We kept the ball, Seville stayed in their own half, and we shared the points. So we made it into the last 32 where we were narrowly knocked out 2–1 by Marseille.

I was proud of the fight we put up. We might have gone out of the competition, but we had done so with honour. Bolton's first experience of European football had given me a taste of managing at another level. Little did I realise that the call would come so soon.

ENGLAND AND SWEET FA

13

I certainly never expected to be in with a chance of getting the England job.

In January 2006, the FA announced that England boss Sven-Goran Eriksson would be leaving after the summer's World Cup finals. I didn't take too much notice, after all the FA would surely go out there and get another foreigner. But it became apparent over the next couple of months that they were considering English candidates. In fact, they were positively encouraging them to throw their hats into the ring.

There were some articles appearing that suggested I might be the right man for the job, but I wasn't falling for those. Yet the longer I thought about it, the more I felt I should get it. There was also a man I knew who could give me the inside track, Phil Gartside, who was on the FA board. But would he support me, or try to undermine me? Phil reported to Eddie Davies, so would Ed take kindly to Phil trying to get me the England job?

'I'll do everything I can to help you, Sam,' said Phil in a manner which didn't infuse me with confidence. He had promised me after the Newcastle approach that if a big job came up he would let me go, but I wasn't convinced. His first loyalty was to Eddie, and if Ed wanted me to stay there was no way the chairman would push my case with the FA. I spent a lot of time telling Phil it would be an honour for a Bolton manager to get the England job, but was he listening or was it just going over his head?

Lynne was torn. The profile which went with being England manager, and the fact she and the rest of the family would be in the public eye, scared her. But she wasn't going to stop me.

'This is the chance of a lifetime. I've got to go for it,' I told her. 'It's bigger than a club, with better players than I have ever worked with.'

From then on she was totally supportive. So when Phil allowed the FA chief executive Brian Barwick to ring and ask if we could have an informal chat, it became serious. Brian and his legal man, Simon Johnson, met me at a house in Whitefield just off the M62. It was a farcical start because the electronic gates refused to open. I had to drive around waiting for the all clear to go in because the FA didn't want me standing outside, so paranoid were they that anyone would see us. It was supposed to be a big secret who they were talking to, even though the press revealed the shortlist was me, Martin O'Neill, Alan Curbishley and Steve McClaren. Now Martin didn't qualify as an Englishman, but the general view seemed to be that although he came from Northern Ireland, he'd been in the Premier League so long he was home grown.

Over our chat, Brian said that if I was given a formal interview I would have to put forward a plan setting out my approach to two matches in the qualifying rounds of a World Cup or European Championships, one at home, the other away. I would also have to spell out how I would deal with the media and how I would cope with the pressure that came with the role. We didn't talk cash, I wasn't bothered, but I was excited. I couldn't imagine anyone who would do the job better than me. It wasn't arrogance, it was confidence in my own ability.

I sought out Howard Wilkinson, an ally from the League Managers' Association, who was twice caretaker England boss and knew all the characters on the FA and their idiosyncratic ways. Howard was also the man who came up with the concept of the FA's St George's Park training centre long before it was eventually built. It is a fantastic facility which gets some stick for being in the middle of nowhere, but if the FA had dumped Wembley and built the national stadium in the Midlands, next to Birmingham's NEC, as it should have done, the complex would have been on the doorstep and the stadium would probably have been half the price. Howard gave me a rundown of the person- alities likely to interview me, such as Trevor Brooking, the FA's director of development and a former international who I knew reasonably well, David Dein of Arsenal, and Dave Richards, the Premier League chairman who I'd bumped into at dinners. Richards had even gone on the record saying: 'It's time for a British manager.' I didn't know the chairman Geoff Thompson but he had a reputation for keeping out of the way and not saying much.

David Beckham, the England captain, came out with his opinion on the criteria for the job, and they weren't in my favour. Beckham said, 'The next manager needs to have a certain amount of experience to handle Champions League and World Cup games.' I didn't agree. I argued that it was the same when people said you had to be an international footballer to manage a national team. 'Was Sven an international?' I asked. 'No, he was not, nor was Mourinho, Wenger or Benitez. Nobody seems to question their coaching qualifications. All that matters is you are a great manager. Everyone knows I would love to be interviewed for the England job. If that happens, it would be fantastic.'

I got on the front foot and asked David to lunch in Madrid. I'd got to know him over the years through Bryan Robson, who as a Manchester United legend went to charity functions with Becks. Also Ronnie Wood, the owner of the Birthdays chain of card shops, was a pal of Bryan and me and would invite David and his wife Victoria to his parties. I'd always found Becks approachable and he was happy to meet me at a restaurant noted for being discreet. I wanted to change David's mind and pick his brains about the England set-up. He had enormous influence and Sven worshipped him. David believed England had a team capable of challenging the best and so did I. The ages and level the players were performing at were ideal. There was this fuss about Steven Gerrard and Frank Lampard being unable to play together, but I couldn't see the problem. Why couldn't two outstanding midfield goal-scorers play in a three with a sitting midfielder behind them and take it in turns to go forwards? It wasn't asking them to do anything they weren't doing at club level.

I wanted an insight from Becks into what the players needed and how to improve their lot. We talked about getting the fans onside and stopping the players getting so much criticism. At the time, Lampard was getting way more than he deserved and I wanted to change that. I proposed setting up a foundation too, so the players would donate their England fees to charity. The aim was to get a positive feeling around the squad and David felt some players didn't get enough protection from the media, although he didn't have a problem himself. We agreed it was important to take as much pressure off the players as possible.

Becks and the rest of the squad were warned by the FA's media department not to talk publicly about individuals in the running for the job, but David could see I was serious and I think I left having convinced him I could do it. He said if anybody at the FA asked him about me he wouldn't have a problem, but he didn't expect to have any say on the choice. I didn't bother consulting Fergie. He didn't like England, or the FA for that matter, but I did chat to Graham Taylor and Bobby Robson. Both were fiercely attacked in the press during their time in charge but said I should have no hesitation, if it was offered. Bobby said, 'It's the greatest job, and the greatest honour in football.'

I wanted to do a real knock-your-socks-off interview, so I put together a PowerPoint presentation with the help of Mike Forde which looked at every single detail. Nobody but nobody was going to beat it. We covered everything from breakfast to bedtime and all points in between, for wherever we were, whatever the weather, and taking into account both winning and losing. There was nothing missing. But then Brian

Barwick told me there were no PowerPoint facilities at the interview venue, so I had to print off hard copies for the panel. So much for the progressive FA.

You obviously had to be doing well with your club, which I was, though it was bad timing as we notched up five losses in a row from the end of March through April, including a 4–3 defeat at McClaren's Middlesbrough. There was much frenzy when Curbishley was photographed meeting Barwick and speculation he was the favoured candidate. But I was relaxed, knowing this was the informal meeting like mine in Whitefield. I duly got my invite to the formal interview and was told to be at the Marriott Hotel near Heathrow airport where I would be driven to the rendezvous point so as to avoid the press. It was like being in the secret service as a Mercedes van with blacked-out windows pulled up to collect me. An hour later, I was still in it. The interview was in Oxfordshire, a good 30 miles up the road. As we arrived at the gates of an enormous mansion after about 90 minutes, there were photographers everywhere. It was hardly a secret venue. The driver reversed and we went round the back to an entrance which was paparazzi-free and drove in.

I entered the drawing room of the country house where sitting round a table was the panel consisting of Thompson, Brooking, Richards, Barwick, Johnson and Dein. I gave them all a copy of my PowerPoint presentation but after an hour of going through it, they wanted to ask questions.

'How would you cope with the difference between managing in the Premier League and internationally?' asked Dein.

This is a common question for international managers, but I didn't see it as a problem. You have no time between Premier League games to think, but with England you do. I proposed a secure communications system so that the players could download their programme for the international get-together. It was very much based on the info screens at Bolton. We wanted them to know all about who we were playing, the standard of the opposition, when we were travelling, what the facilities were like, and so on. The idea was that when they arrived, they were familiar with what they had to do and there would be no surprises. I also wanted input into the entire structure, from the senior team through the Under-21s and down the age-groups. That earned me wholehearted nods of approval.

Then Richards piped up, 'If a player came walking into the dressing room talking away on his mobile, what would you do?'

My reply was instant. 'I'd take it off him and throw it in the bin, even if it was Wayne Rooney.'

I got bigger nods for that one. I wanted to curb the use of video games when players got bored, because I felt they were addictive, deprived players of sleep and prevented them enjoying proper relaxation. I wasn't advocating the return of the card schools, but I thought there should be a greater variety of activities during downtime. More nods. Card schools were just as destructive as video games in my playing era. If you lost a lot of money it preyed on your mind, and there was lots of time to lose plenty during international weeks. In my experience, if someone is losing they want to play on and on until they get it back, while everyone else wants to go to bed but can't because they feel obliged to give the loser a chance. That's not healthy for anyone involved.

Thompson wondered if I understood the responsibilities of being England manager and the behaviour expected of the staff and players.

'With every football club I've managed,' I said, 'there has always been a disciplined structure which is paramount to any success.'

It was going well.

Trevor wasn't saying a lot but was making plenty of notes and wanted to know what I thought of the coaching set-up in the country and whether it benefited the national team. I'd got all my coaching badges but I felt the biggest obstacle to success was the Premier League.

'The League is becoming more important than England,' I said. I wasn't sure if this was a wise thing to say, given that the Arsenal vice-chairman and the chairman of the Premier League were on the panel, but it had to be addressed.

'The number of players available for selection is diminishing rapidly because of the influx of foreign players, and this has to change,' I continued.

Fabio Capello and Roy Hodgson made the same points when they got the job. I'd calculated the group to pick from was just under 100 and that around 60 per cent of all squads were made up of foreign imports. It's probably even more now. But I told the panel we had enough with Champions League experience for a team capable of winning a tourna-ment. I didn't think we were far away at all.

With that I left in the Mercedes van, pursued by the paparazzi who were desperate to find out the occupant. The driver was like Lewis Hamilton, dodging cars, whizzing through red lights and going back down roads he'd just come from, in order to shake them off before we got back to the hotel. I knew I'd done well. Indeed Gartside confirmed the general view that I interviewed the best. I still didn't trust him though – did he want me to get the job or not?

'Don't stand in my way, I want this,' I told him.

I flew off to Barcelona to watch the Champions League semi-final second leg against AC Milan and met Martin O'Neill there, who told me he was out of the running for the job. Then a load of press lads came up and asked, 'Have you heard? The FA are flying out to meet Scolari!' After all that time, all that disruption to my life, and all that hope, they'd gone for a foreigner. Yes, he was a World Cup winner, but if that's what they wanted they could have saved me a lot of trouble.

The rumour was that Dein pushed the panel into going for the man who won the 2002 World Cup for Brazil. Was it David's way of stopping them from nicking Arsene Wenger? Whatever the reason, it was a crushing blow. Martin said, 'Typical FA'. But there was another twist. Barwick went to get his new manager but didn't come back with him, because Scolari decided to stay as boss of Portugal. Barwick was on the phone to me.

'Sam, you're still in the frame. It's between you and Steve McClaren and we are going to make the decision by Thursday. Don't worry about that Scolari thing, it wasn't how it looked.'

I wasn't sure I believed that, but I was delighted to be back in with a chance. It was game on again.

I pointed out to Brian that, as fate would have it, we were playing McClaren's Middlesbrough on the Wednesday, so it would be nice to know the decision either way before then. The dice was loaded more in Steve's favour than mine. He was a former England coach under Sven, while the FA's head of communications, Adrian Bevington, was a well-known Boro fan. Boro had also made it through to the UEFA Cup final. On the other hand, we were eighth in the league and they were 15th. I quizzed Gartside if he knew what was going on and he claimed not to have been told anything, insisting he didn't even know it was between me and Steve. I found that hard to swallow. Barwick would have told both chairmen concerned what was going on. I sensed Phil wasn't helping me. He fought to keep me at Bolton when Newcastle tried to get me, and he was hardly going to sit passively by and tell Ed Davies he was powerless when the England job came up. As we approached Wednesday and there was no call from Barwick, I got the sickening feeling it wasn't going my way.

We played Boro, drew 1–1 and afterwards I went up to Steve McClaren.

'Well done, mate, congratulations on getting the job,' I told him.

'What do you mean? I don't know anything.'

'Come off it,' I said, 'it's Wednesday night and I ain't had the call, so if it ain't me it must be you.'

He wouldn't budge, even though I knew he knew. I told the after-match press conference, 'I'm going to be disappointed, Steve's got it.'

Steve dodged the press and sent his assistant Steve Round in. 'Steve's not said anything to us,' said Roundy. Yeah, of course he hadn't.

On Thursday 4 May 2006, McClaren was confirmed as Sven-Goran Eriksson's successor to take over England duties after the World Cup.

Barwick offered me his commiserations saying, 'Thanks very much, Sam, you were close. Sorry you didn't get it.' Then Gartside rang. 'Sam, I'm really sorry, I did everything I could for you. I tried my best.'

'I'm sure you did, Phil.'

● ● ●

The more time Phil Gartside spent on the FA, the more I detected the influence of his blazer-wearing mates on him. He was interfering more and more and wanted to play an increasingly active role in transfer negotiations even though he was hopeless at it. He'd given Youri more than I would have offered when we signed him on a contract, yet on other occasions he wouldn't cough up a fiver for a player we desperately needed. Then he would say to me, 'You're on too much money anyway. I could do your job.' So I told him, 'If you think you can do it, why don't you get rid of me and try it?' I was frustrated beyond belief and my relationship with the chairman was becoming ever more strained.

Newcastle came back in for me again towards the end of the season, unbeknown to Gartside. They had sacked Graeme Souness who they appointed after I turned them down and, while Glenn Roeder was installed as caretaker, Freddy Shepherd wanted another chat, sensing I might be more interested this time round. He'd tried to set up a meeting at the Dorchester a few months earlier for a 'chin-wag' but cancelled when he saw Souey having his haircut at the hotel barbers. The deal was I would take over at the end of the season and Shepherd would fly out to Dubai, where I was on holiday, to finalise the details. This time I was ready to do it and sign on the dotted line, but at the last moment Freddy cancelled his flight. He rang and said, 'Sorry, but I'm sticking with Glenn for next season. You turned me down once and now I'm turning you down, so we'll call that 1–1!'

I'd lost the Newcastle and England jobs within a month of each other, when I had built myself up to leave. I needed a new challenge, even though on the field we were doing fine and I'd taken great delight in knocking Arsenal out of the FA Cup. Wenger's reaction was complimentary as usual. 'I feel we should have won by three goals. Bolton didn't create anything the whole game and won with one chance and one goal.' Our European exertions did catch up with as we staggered through to the end of the season, losing to West Ham in the cup and winning only two of our last ten in the league to finish eighth. It might have been different if I'd managed to get Roy Keane. Roy had left Old Trafford back in November and I tried to persuade him to join us. He came round to my house and we had a really good chat about our ambitions and where the club was heading, but unfortunately the pull of Celtic proved too strong for him and he went to Scotland. It was a shame because I think Keane, with all his experience, would have been great for Bolton, in the same way Youri Djorkaeff was when he joined us. Keane didn't last long with Celtic and at the end of the season took over at Sunderland who were in the Championship. Funnily enough, their chairman Niall Quinn, who I knew from my days with Reidy as a Sunderland coach, had asked me to take over before Roy, but I turned him down.

Working for ITV at the World Cup in Germany was the perfect antidote to my disappointments about Newcastle and England, as I travelled round the country by luxury coach in the company of Terry Venables, Ally McCoist,

Ruud Gullit, Stuart Pearce and Andy Townsend. Terry can't stop talking football, he finds it impossible. He was always grabbing bottles on the table and moving them round in formations to explain some tactic or other. And if Ruud disagreed, Terry stared at him like he'd come from Mars. I'm sure Ruud did it to wind up Terry. Pearce couldn't get on with Ruud either. I heard Man City, where Stuart was manager, contacted ITV on his behalf, demanding he was not seated next to Ruud when the three-man panel worked on games. The presenter, Steve Rider, was obviously under orders to bow to Stuart's wishes and started arranging where we should sit before one of the matches. 'You go in the middle Sam, Stuart sits there and Ruud over there.' I thought I'd have a bit of fun so I've gone, 'Ooh, I can't do that, Steve, I'll have to be on the end, that's where I'm supposed to be.' The look on Stuart's face was a picture, until I let him stay where he was. It turns out Pearce hates Gullit because he dumped him from the team when he was manager of Newcastle.

If I was going to stay at Bolton, I had to make a bid for a top four spot, which I thought was within our capabilities. I needed about £20 million to mount a realistic charge, but I couldn't free up the purse strings sufficiently. I did manage to get £8 million to buy French striker Nicolas Anelka, which broke the club's transfer record. He wanted out of Fenerbahce and a return to the Premier League where he'd first burst onto the scene as a teenager at Arsenal, before leaving for Real Madrid and PSG, and had a loan spell at Liverpool before joining Manchester City. Nobody else was prepared to take another chance on him, because of his bad-boy reputation. I was, though; Nic was just what we needed. We had a few with questionable reputations, so I wasn't afraid to add another one. I told Nic, 'You can get your career back on track with us, and if you take it bigger clubs will want you. But right now we're the best you're gonna get.' He was an angel with me, so quiet you wouldn't know he'd arrived for training but for his Rolls Royce in the car park. When he did speak, it was usually a question about training methods which were new to him, like why he had to drink Nutri shakes or fill in psychoanalysis tests. Once you explained why they worked he was happy.

I bought centre-back Abdoulaye Meite, a big Ivorian from Marseille, but there was no further buying allowed. Bolton didn't have the guts to take it further, the £8 million spent on Anelka having spooked them enough. Yet, it wasn't like we risked the foundations we had built. We were a well-established Premier League club with a structure that was the envy of our rivals. It wasn't suddenly going to go up in smoke if we spent a bit of money; and if Anelka did well, his re-sale value would go up. If he didn't, we'd at least get back what we paid.

The club even made £400,000 on a player who never kicked a ball for us. We'd been interested in Liverpool's German international Didi Hamann for a long time and he'd turned us down twice before, but that summer he agreed to join us. He wanted to move from Merseyside to Bolton, which struck me as odd considering it wasn't a long drive. Anyway, Matt Hockin took him round various houses but said to me: 'He didn't look too keen, gaffer. There was a lot of "I'm not sure" and "I'll have to think about it."' Didi decided he couldn't live round Bolton but I thought he'd just stay living where he was.

'It's too far to travel,' Didi claimed.

'No, it's not,' I said. 'We've got a few who live over your way, you can car-share.'

'No, I don't want to travel.'

Then Man City made an official approach to us for Didi and we told them, 'Right, it will cost you £2 million,' as we plucked a figure out of the air. In the end, we settled for £500,000 and had to give Liverpool £100,000 because we'd promised them 20 per cent if he was ever sold on. Still, it wasn't bad money for a player who never set foot in our stadium and didn't do a day's training with us.

While the Hamann issue was acrimonious, the harmony I'd enjoyed with Phil Gartside in the early days wasn't there either. The first four years with Phil were excellent, until he got right in at the FA and became a different person. Until that point, I'd never had such a good relationship with a chairman and haven't had one since. We had parties in the boardroom after games, socialised together, and the atmosphere was brilliant. It was one big happy family, from chairman to tea lady. As a manager I felt responsible for everyone who worked at Bolton. There were those who worked behind the scenes in the ticket office, the club shop, or at the training ground for whom Wanderers was their life. They weren't earning much but loved it, and they were so important to the club. I knew each and every one of them and I hope I made them all feel involved in our success. We had part-time scouts working for us, for expenses only. Even two or three of the full-time ones were only on £20,000 a year and they were picking out players who would earn more than them in a week. They covered thousands of miles for Bolton to find that hidden gem who could make the club millions.

Phil would return from Premier League meetings asking, 'How do you do it? How have we done what we've done?' We were all proud of our achievements. There was a table in the paper evaluating every manager and equating his salary with the points accrued, and I came out on top. I told Gartside,

'See, you're not paying me enough!' We were in the top half of the league but our budget was nothing like top half. Making money was becoming more important with the income from Sky. It never seemed so vital when I played, when there was more focus on football than cash. But now it was the over-riding priority at Bolton like everywhere else, and I didn't like it one bit.

The issue of making money then cropped up again in the new season via a letter from the BBC – but this time with more serious implications.

14

'FA Investigates Bung Claims,' ran the headline on the sports page of the BBC website on 20 September 2006.

As we kicked off that new season, there had been gossip going round about a soon to be screened BBC *Panorama* programme conducting an investigation into the behaviour of football managers in the transfer market. It didn't concern me, why would it? I had nothing to hide. Being a manager involved talking to agents, discussing deals with the secretary, chief executive and chairman, and seeking the advice of contacts in the game, all in the interests of getting the best deals for the club. We had a democratic process at Bolton which required me to set the ball rolling and Phil to finish off the deal. It was a tried and tested formula, although sometimes it resulted in frustration for me if Phil wouldn't pay the transfer fee or the wages.

Then I received a letter delivered by registered post to the training ground which had BBC in very large letters at the top. They demanded answers to questions about transfers and gave me a deadline to answer them by. Phil got one too. The implication seemed to be that various people, including my son Craig, had been filmed doing something or other which threw up a few questions for me.

We'd made a really good start to the season and were knocking on the door of a top four place but this was a serious cloud hanging over the club; there was no getting away from it. My conscience was clear, but that wasn't stopping the BBC from investigating.

On the night the *Panorama* programme entitled 'Uncovered: Football's Dirty Secrets' was broadcast, 19 September, we were playing Walsall away in the Carling Cup and there was a lot of attention on me. Ordinarily, this was a game which would have made, at most, six paragraphs in the national papers, but not on this occasion. We won 3–1 but that wasn't what the reporters wanted to ask about afterwards. They wanted answers to accusations made on *Panorama*. How could I give any answers? We'd been playing and I hadn't seen an advance viewing. I told the press I would make a statement once I'd watched it. I drove back to Bolton, which took around an hour and a half, and Lynne was waiting up for me when I got home. She hadn't watched it, so we decided we'd do it together.

The BBC had hired a former coach who was posing as an agent interested in buying out other agents and he was secretly filming their conversations. There were a couple of big mouths who were connected to some of our signings. They claimed they paid my son Craig to get special access to me which was absolute nonsense. My footballing decisions were always my own, and were never influenced by anyone else. The big hole in the programme was that some of the agents, and I include Craig, were clearly exaggerating in order to sell their business. Bragging they had a special relationship with me was obviously going to put the price of their agency up. Craig talked up his abilities in a secret recording and admitted knowing me well, which stood to reason as I was his dad! But Craig felt what he was trying to say, in answer to their questions, hadn't come across. The only person at Bolton they duped into a secret recording was Phil Gartside who was shown trying to get the best price he could for Jay-Jay Okocha, which was a chairman's job. There was no covert filming of me at all.

It was true I had used Craig to sign Tal Ben Haim, but there was nothing unusual in that. He'd found Tal, who was a very good player, and he wasn't the only son of a manager who worked in the agency business. Plenty of chairmen's sons had jobs at football clubs too. I won't pretend I didn't talk to Craig about players who might be available, of course I did. But I wouldn't sign anyone who I didn't think was beneficial to the team, and Craig hardly made any money at all from Bolton. He only brought in two players in the entire time I was there, Ben Haim and Idan Tal.

There were others in the firing line – Harry Redknapp, who was then boss of Portsmouth, Kevin Bond, Harry's first-team coach who had become coach at Newcastle, and Frank Arnesen, Chelsea's director of youth development. When you looked behind what they had and got to the bottom of it all, there was no real proof of anything inappropriate having happened.

The daftest part of all was when they filmed a suitcase full of money in a gloomy low-lit room. A greedy manager apparently couldn't wait to get his hands on the cash and was coming to get it. But guess what?

No manager turned up to collect it. The BBC claimed he'd been scared off at the last minute.

Craig decided to quit football altogether to find a new venture in life. He was hugely depressed and felt he'd let me down. I told him, 'Don't ever feel that way. I'm big enough to get through this and we have to move on. It's not your fault.' I was more worried about him than me. He was my son and he was hurting a great deal.

I made a statement the following day: 'Obviously I'm denying all allegations against me. The matter is in the lawyers' hands and will be resolved by due process. I have instructed them to take the appropriate action.

'If there is any real evidence – and there won't be, as I am utterly innocent of any wrongdoing – I would expect the BBC to give that evidence to both the FA and the Premier League's Quest inquiry.'

Every bone in my body wanted to sue the BBC. The programme screamed injustice. But the legal advice was, 'Sam, you either have to be very, very foolish or very, very rich to do this. It costs far too much money, takes far too long and the damages will be minimal.' It actually cost me £30,000 just to get that advice! The programme hadn't cost me my job. Nor did it land me with a criminal charge or a charge from the FA. So I would be suing for damage to reputation and that was hard to quantify. I decided it was best to look to the future without dwelling on the past. It was a chapter in my life I could well have done without, but it happened. I vowed never again to put myself in a position where I could be accused of taking money. You make as many enemies of agents as you do friends. I was known for driving a hard bargain and some of them didn't like it.

Maybe my reputation prompted some to blacken my name. I took less of a part in transfer activity, and once a player was identified it was up to the club to talk to the agents and strike a deal. That has been my policy wherever I've worked ever since. A lot of managers operate that way today.

For the record, I've never taken a bung in my life. I might have enjoyed a meal and a bottle of wine on an agent or two, but that is it. I was earning £1.5 million a year, so I didn't need a little bit extra from an agent. It would have been madness.

The lawyers advised me not to talk to the press. But that didn't do me any favours. The perception was that I was guilty of something, but no-one could put their finger on quite what that was. The longer I stayed silent the more the programme was analysed and the innuendo about my transfer dealings grew. So I hired the celebrity publicist Max Clifford. At the time, he had major influence in Fleet Street and I needed to get some positive publicity. He cost me £20,000 a month but I ended up doing interviews with journalists I knew anyway and could have rung them up myself at a moment's notice. I'd nearly hired Clifford to help push my case for the England job, but Gartside advised me not to. McClaren did use Clifford so either it worked for him or it was just coincidence.

I had enormous support from friends in the game who thought the programme was a load of rubbish, and both Harry Redknapp and I refused to talk to the BBC. I didn't see why I should give them any of my time after what they'd done. To think I'd helped pay for that bloody programme with my licence fee!

There was a danger that by not speaking to the BBC it kept the issue in the public eye because people would keep wondering why I wasn't doing interviews, but I didn't care about that. My assistant did them all instead. We were fulfilling our obligations by putting a member of staff up, but it pissed the Premier League off and they made a rule change saying if the manager didn't turn up to the pre-or post-match press conferences, he would be fined. The positive side to putting my assistant in front of the camera was that the press talked about the actual game rather than anything else. Too often, when the manager is interviewed it's about stirring up controversy, but when it's his assistant the discussion is much more sensible.

I was concerned the hullabaloo might affect the players so I told them what I thought of it. 'You probably all recorded *Panorama* and I'm sure you've watched it, but don't let it affect us. We've got a great team with a great spirit and we want to go and do good things.' Nolan spoke for them all and said, 'Don't worry, gaffer, we'll go out there and get on with winning. Fuck the BBC.' The following Monday we beat second-placed Portsmouth 1–0 thanks to a Nolan special. He came racing to the touchline and jumped on me in celebration. 'That one was for the gaffer,' Nolan said afterwards. 'It just shows the unity we've got at this club.'

The following week it was announced that Lord Stevens' Quest Inquiry into football corruption would investigate 39 transfers, having spent the previous six months trawling through over 350 deals conducted in the Premier League over a period of two years. There were all sorts of gloomy predictions about how football would come crashing down and illegal payments would be uncovered left, right and centre. Lord Stevens was a former commissioner of the Met Police and, according to the broadsheet newspapers, if anyone could uncover a scandal this was the man. I didn't get the feeling they were after me particularly, but they were desperate to pin something on someone.

As well as myself, Phil and our secretary Simon Marland were interviewed by Nigel Layton, the managing director of Quest and his team. Layton was interested in a couple of large payments to agents, but if you were getting players on free transfers, the agent's fee tended to be larger because there was no payment to a selling club. That was common at Bolton where we relied a lot on free transfers. But these were not football people; they just didn't understand how it worked.

Quest demanded all my bank statements for the previous three years which is something not even the police can ask for unless they arrest you. I refused but Richard Scudamore, the chief executive of the Premier League, said if I didn't cooperate it might look like I was guilty. I reluctantly handed them over, but I thought it was a liberty. My bank statements only recorded the size of the payments coming in or going out, they didn't state who they were from or to. I had to go to the bank about every payment and ask where it went or where it came from. I was a wealthy bloke by this time, so there were some big sums going around. I might have bought a car or a holiday or helped the kids out. But I had to make sure that whatever sum they picked out, I could account for it. Mark Curtis was interviewed too and he told them he had never paid a manager in his life and nor had a manager asked him for money.

Quest was a complete waste of time and money. It ticked the right boxes so that the Premier League and Scudamore were seen to be taking action. It was a PR exercise and Quest basically admitted in the end that they hadn't found anything. A statement said: 'There is no evidence of any irregular payments to club officials or players.' It was then said the inquiry remained concerned 'at the conflict of interest it believes existed between Craig Allardyce, his father Sam, and the club itself'. It didn't say why or how. It also said there remained concerns over four Bolton transfers, but didn't say why. It was more innuendo, without any facts.

● ● ●

While all this was going on, we were doing remarkably well on the pitch, getting up to third in the table as Anelka, Davies, Diouf and Speed hit the goal trail. We beat Arsenal again, 3–1 in November, the third time we'd beaten them at home in four seasons. Nicolas opened his account with two against his old club, the first of which was a dipping swerving effort from 30 yards into the top corner.

In my after-match interview I said, 'They always get irate when you upset them and that is why other teams have copied what we do. You know that they will lose their cool and composure and, when they do that, you know you have a chance. Wenger makes disparaging remarks about us all the time – it's about time he ate some humble pie.'

I enjoyed beating Arsenal more than anyone. We'd really got to them and Wenger hated us. This season was the best chance we ever had of reaching the Champions League. After 21 games through to the turn of the year, we had 39 points and were bang on course as we sat in third place. But we didn't have the strength in depth. I emphasised to Phil that the free transfer days were over and we had to buy quality, but he wasn't listening. Nic was proving a bargain at £8 million and would have repaid his fee four times over if we'd made the Champions League. Previously, if we created five chances we may or may not have converted one. Now we were creating five and finishing off one or two. Kevin Davies would always get a few but Nic would guarantee you double figures. Kevin had a big bonus written into his contract if he hit ten in the league and kept getting eight or nine. But he was invaluable to us for the amount of chances he created. If he never scored again, I still wanted him as our centre-forward.

We only needed a little tweak and we'd have pulled off the miracle. It was purring along and for 18 months I hadn't done a team-talk before kick-off. We put a camera in the dressing room to see what those team-talks looked like and reasoned that if we had to rely on them we hadn't done our job properly during the week. In the early days, when we played the big teams it was, 'Come on lads, nobody thinks you're going to win anyway so let's show them what we're about.' Those were the glory games where every point was a bonus. Then when we played the teams around us, I would stress how vital it was to get something from the game because these were our rivals in the relegation scrap. But now we were competing at the top everyone knew the score, there was nothing to say on the day. We pinned up sheets with reminders on them about what to do at, say, corners and free-kicks, and if the players were unsure they just consulted them. Otherwise, they got on with their warm-up and out they went. Giving the pre-match talk a miss was only meant to be an experiment, but we weren't losing any games so I stuck with it.

At Christmas, I asked Phil for some more money. 'Look,' I said, 'we can do this, we can get into the Champions League, us, Bolton. But we need to add to the squad because if we get any injuries at the wrong time, it will kill us. You know the minimum payment we will get from the Premier League, because we won't drop below eighth even if we have a bad run, so let's spend it.'

I wanted Phil to show some balls, to go for it, to be part of that dream which we had in the early days. But the courage wasn't there.

'I'm not sure I can get you it,' he said. 'I'll have a word with Ed but it's doubtful.'

I was fuming and hit back. 'If you aren't going to buy anyone, you're going to have to go and tell the players why not. Anelka came because I told him we could do this.'

Phil got back to me and it was then I knew for sure it was over for me at Bolton. 'We've got no money,' he said. 'You can loan a player, but that's it.'

'What the fuck are you talking about?' I said.

Now I was spitting. 'If we lose in the qualifying round, it won't have cost you anything and if we get through we'll make plenty of money.'

'Let's just stick with what we're doing,' said Phil.

The only player we got in January was David Thompson on a short-term deal from Portsmouth who we signed two hours before the transfer window closed. I was thoroughly pissed off with the club's attitude. I told

Lynne, 'Sorry love, but I'm out of there. I can't stand it any more.' This was hard for Lynne and the family. Bolton was our home and we'd had such a good time in the early days of my management there. But it had changed. I had to think of me for once.

I handed in my letter of resignation and left, but within 24 hours Phil and Mark had talked and it was agreed I would stay until the end of the season. However, if the news leaked out I would have to go immediately. We did a deal. It hurt knowing I was leaving, but I had to shut off what I felt in my heart. That could not be part of the process. It would have been easy to carry on and finish mid-table every year, but that wasn't me. Gartside was virtually saying, 'Can we just tick along and be mediocre?' But where's the fun in that?

Around the end of April or beginning of May, Manchester City were onto me. Pete Cowgill, my accountant, had orchestrated the flotation of JD Sports, which was owned by John Wardle and Dave Makin, who also ran Manchester City. They were going to axe Stuart Pearce and wanted to know if I'd take the job. I didn't mind having a chat, what was there to lose? They asked if there would be any compensation and I said it was no problem although I didn't let on I'd already resigned. They told me, 'Stuart has done a good job, but we're not sure he's experienced enough to handle a club the size of City, whereas we think you are.' We left it and agreed to meet again at the end of the season.

Injuries kicked in, as I expected, and by the time we played Chelsea away at the end of April we could barely get a team out. Unfortunately, we got a draw. I say unfortunately because that probably confirmed Phil's view that we could always get by. News filtered out I was quitting and so I had to go before our final two matches. We were fifth when I went, so, even after some mediocre results, that proved to me that had we got in some top players in January, we would have made the top four.

My statement said, 'After nearly eight privileged years with Bolton Wanderers Football Club, I would like to announce that, after careful consideration and dialogue with my close family and senior officials, I will be resigning as manager with immediate effect.

'It was mutually decided that I step down now rather than at the end of the season, to give my successor the ideal opportunity to experience the preparation and build-up of matchday in readiness of next season. The decision to leave the club, which has been my spiritual home for over 18 years, as both player and manager, is one of the hardest I have had to make in my life.

'However, after guiding the team into a position where the club is on the verge of qualification for European football for the second time in three years, which has been the accumulation of almost seven years of strategic building and hard work across all areas of the football club, I feel it is the right moment to step down from my duties and welcome a new exciting era under different leadership.

'I feel the club is in a great position to continue its upward trajectory with a talented internationally-recognised squad, supported by an excellent academy programme across all ages working under the guidance of a highly-skilled football management team.

'I believe the foundation for the next development stage of the club is well and truly in place. It is with this knowledge that I feel confident that I am moving on with my life, content with a legacy that I have tried to create for this special club and I wish the owner, chairman, staff, players and above all the fans every success in the future.'

Gartside said his bit too. 'I have reluctantly accepted the resignation of Sam Allardyce after eight years of unprecedented success. I would like to thank Sam for his enormous contribution to Bolton Wanderers, both as a player, but more importantly as a manager. Since joining as manager in October 1999, he has helped lead a fantastic transformation of this famous Lancashire club and has helped design and build an infrastructure that will enable the club to continue the progress that we have undoubtedly made in his period of office. He has given his reasons for wanting to leave, which are private and we respect that privacy. I would like to wish Sam and his family every success in the future.'

It was weird waking up and not going into the training ground. It was automatic, something I did without even thinking, but no more. The fans couldn't understand it, but I couldn't say more as we had agreed a set statement at the time. As a manager you get used to making big decisions and this was the biggest one of all, but I'd done it to give myself better opportunities and was proud of what I'd achieved.

There was nothing signed with City and no guarantees but I expected to get the job. Meanwhile I'd recommended Sammy Lee as my replacement and within two days he was appointed. Sammy had earned it, he and Ricky had given the backroom team a shot in the arm after the departures of Brownie and Macca. I was happy that we could split on what appeared cordial terms, but already Gartside's tone was changing and he went public saying, 'We will sit down and look at what Sammy wants and he can write the contract he wants. It was not my choice for Sam to go now. I am surprised and disappointed.

'From the media's eyes and the fans' eyes it might have been more sensible to do it at the end of the season. Maybe I think that as well. That is for me to know. Sam says he hasn't got a job lined up. But if he ends up at Manchester City, I would not be happy with that.

'We would have to look at the circumstances if that situation did evolve.'

Phil had another dig: 'Nicolas Anelka came here and knew Sammy Lee but didn't know Sam Allardyce, so you can take a key man out and replace him with someone better.' He also implied I wouldn't have got the job if I'd been applying for it that day. He was sad and bitter already. Lynne warned me it would be like a divorce which quickly degenerates into a slanging match.

John Wardle contacted me with an update from Man City which added to the fun. 'I'm sorry, Sam, but we're not going to be able to proceed with our plans. Someone's buying the club and although we talked about you, they want to bring in their own man.' That was the end of that. Phil couldn't accuse me of going to City now.

I was invited back to the Reebok for the final game against Aston Villa and stupidly I agreed. It was a big mistake. Phil was already chipping away at me and I wasn't allowed to see the lads in the dressing room. It was a sad end. I would like it to have finished differently but it was my choice to go, and once I was out for good Gartside wouldn't allow my name to be mentioned around the Reebok.

There was speculation I was going to Newcastle when I left Bolton, but there was nothing lined up. However, when Glenn Roeder resigned a week before the end of the season, I was the hot tip to step in. Not for the first time in my career, Freddy Shepherd wanted a meeting. We set a date for Gordon Ramsey's restaurant at Claridge's in London and agreed a deal. Four days later, I was announced as the new manager of Newcastle United.

15

ST JAMES' FARCE

If ever there was a right club at the wrong time it was Newcastle United. I had all the qualifications to be a success there and as I flew to the North East on that May afternoon in 2007 in a helicopter provided by Freddy Shepherd for my grand unveiling, I felt enormous excitement. The pilot was hilarious. He didn't have a clue about football and asked why I was heading north.

'For work,' I said.

'What line are you in then?' he asked.

'Football. I'm going to be the manager of Newcastle United.'

'Oh, are you?' he said. 'That'll be nice.'

It was more than nice, it was bloody fantastic. We swooped over St James' Park twice so I could take a good look at the imposing stadium which stands like a cathedral overlooking the city. This was the big-time. Many managers had spoken over the years about Newcastle being a sleeping giant. I was convinced I was the man to wake them up again.

The questions as I was presented to the media were exactly as I expected: Why was I the right choice for Newcastle? Did I realise what a big club it was? Could I make them better? Bobby Robson and Graeme Souness both warned me I would find relations with the local press difficult. Bobby found it the hardest part of his job at Newcastle. Gary Speed spent six years there before joining Bolton and said the players had to be strong characters, because the fans were unforgiving and so passionate about the club they would crush the weak-minded. Speedo struggled when he first arrived but eventually won them over. It was vital to go out and buy good players with strong character. I remembered what former director Douglas Hall said: 'If you want £25 million to spend on a player, you'll get it.' Newcastle had finished the season poorly in 13th and there was plenty of work to do. Another bottom-half finish would not be tolerated, and Freddy saw it as his last throw of the dice to get the team back to the level it was under Kevin Keegan, Kenny Dalglish and Bobby Robson.

I'd been in place about ten days when stories emerged that businessman Mike Ashley was buying Sir John Hall's stake in the club. I knew nothing about Ashley and tried to get hold of Freddy to see what was going on. Freddy was in hospital with pneumonia and was feeling bad enough as it was without the rug having been pulled from under him by Sir John. He had little warning of what was being planned and vowed to fight the takeover. However, under law Ashley was obliged to make an offer for the remaining shares and it wasn't long before he had over 50 per cent, meaning he was in charge and Freddy had no option but to sell too. It was initially announced Freddy would remain as chairman but, by July, he was out. Freddy was devastated and felt let down.

I didn't know Ashley but Pete Cowgill did. Ashley was in the same field, being the owner of Sports Direct. 'He's a successful bloke, Sam, and he says what he thinks,' said Pete. Mike came up to see me, all very jolly.

'Come on, Sam, we'll have a bit of fun. I've made a lot of money because we've just floated the company,' he said.

'Good. Can we buy some players then? Freddy promised me £30 million.'

'Okay,' he said. 'Go and sign some.'

I liked Ashley. He said he wouldn't be too involved and wanted to enjoy himself. There was no threat to my job.

I went to the Lowry Hotel in Manchester to meet up with two of our players, Michael Owen and Nicky Butt, who were preparing for a couple of England games. Owen had missed virtually the whole of the previous season after damaging the cruciate ligament in his right knee at the World Cup. He'd missed a large chunk of the season before that too through injury, and there was a feeling among the fans that he was more interested in England than Newcastle. Freddy thought his agent was working on a move for him, but I didn't see how that was possible. Michael had barely played for two years and was on big wages. My initial impression was that Michael seemed keen to get his club career going again. Scott Parker wasn't for hanging around though, he wanted a move and got one to West Ham. Kieron Dyer was so keen to go he was in my office crying, begging me to sell him, so when West Ham came on the phone asking about him, we made sure they paid top price for Kieron, who had a bad injury record, and it was good business to sell him for £6 million. Albert Luque, a big lump from Spain, left for Ajax which allowed me to sign Alan Smith for around £6 million from Manchester United and his former Leeds team-mate Mark Viduka from Middlesbrough. I was on the way to getting Luka Modric too from Dinamo Zagreb but, by then, Mike saw the full scale of the debt and put the clamps on, so I had to make do with Geremi from Chelsea instead.

Getting my backroom team in place was important as usual. I wanted to build one like Bolton but needed to do it quickly. It had taken six years to establish it at Bolton and I was trying to do it here in six weeks. I was desperate to get Fordy but he blew me out to join Chelsea. I had promised not to poach Bolton's staff but they were all ringing me asking to come. I couldn't take them unless they got the chairman's permission but Gartside started booting everyone out anyway, and physio Mark Taylor joined me along with chief scout Steve Walsh and Jack Chapman.

I kept Nigel Pearson on as coach after Bryan Robson recommended him. Robbo had total faith in Nigel, who was his captain at Middlesbrough and assistant at West Brom, while I got Steve Round in too. There was already a scouting team of Bobby Saxton, David Mills and a lad called Paul Montgomery, who was a no-nonsense type. Ask him his verdict on a player and it was instant. 'Nah, he's shite' or 'He's fucking brilliant.' I liked that, it was decisive. We tried for Leighton Baines at Wigan and Phil Jagielka at Sheffield United but I got in José Enrique from Villareal and eventually Habib Beye from Marseille and Abdoulaye Faye from Bolton on transfer deadline. I also signed Joey Barton from Man City who I thought would liven things up, which he did, though not in a good way.

Joey had a 3 amp fuse in a 13 amp plug and could blow anytime anywhere. You couldn't read him. He got injured not long after joining and went into a decline and was then arrested for assault at Christmas, having asked permission to go home to Liverpool because his nan was ill. He was subsequently sentenced to six months in prison. Barton was the loosest of loose cannons. A few years later, Kevin Nolan reckoned he tamed him once he joined Newcastle, and tried to get me to take him to West Ham, but I wasn't interested. I won't have anyone tell me Barton is a character; he's a bloody liability.

When the fixtures came out we were given Bolton away on the first day. What were the odds on that? It had to be a fix. I'd never wanted to win a match more than that one, especially with Sammy and Phil claiming they had a winning formula using a more attractive brand of football. It was so strange arriving on the coach at the Reebok. I was programmed into going through the main entrance where the home dressing room was and now I was heading down the side entrance for the away side. I got a great welcome from the ticket girls and staff on reception, with lots of hugs and kisses, but it all went sour when Phil wouldn't allow my family into the directors' box, claiming it was for their own safety.

I couldn't have wished for a better start. We were 3–0 up after 27 minutes with strikes from Charles N'Zogbia and a double from Obafemi Martins. The Nigerian was a scorer of great goals if not a great goal-scorer. He was stocky, strong and quick and when he was on song was unstoppable. But he was a strange lad and it was rumoured he was never at ease until he'd been back home to see his witch doctor.

Anelka got one back in the second half but it was a great win. I didn't feel sorry for Bolton, I was ecstatic, especially as I'd been booed by some of the crowd. We went out for a party and enjoyed a very good night. As it turned out, Bolton never did play that winning brand of attractive football. Sammy was sacked after winning only one of nine Premier League games and his replacement Gary Megson just about kept them up.

Newcastle made their best start in years, taking 17 points from the first nine games, but then Michael got injured, and so did Viduka and later on Alan Smith. I loved Smudger Smith. He was a quirky character with trophies for riding BMX and Quad bikes and was totally committed on the pitch. I wondered though whether we would ever see the best of Owen again. He was a lot quieter and a deeper thinker about the game than I imagined him to be, with more of a dry sense of humour. He was no longer the young gazelle who sprang on the scene at the 1998 World Cup and scored that incredible goal against Argentina. I think it was the legacy of playing at such a young age and I don't think the scar tissue around his hamstrings had been removed properly. In America, I'd experienced how hard the physios worked to get rid of it, but I don't think Michael enjoyed that same care and attention. He became more and more vulnerable to hamstring injuries to the point where he looked scared to push off on a run. All the same, if he was fit, I wanted him on the field, and if he was playing he would score goals even if he was no longer the quickest. I felt he should do more rehab work to prevent himself getting injured again. But there were days when he was nipping off back home to Cheshire by helicopter and didn't have the time to stay. He didn't like doing the core strength exercises I'd introduced, even though I explained how it would keep him fitter for longer.

Meanwhile Damien Duff had a serious ankle problem which the club failed to resolve the season before I arrived. When he went to seek his own specialist treatment, it was discovered he'd fractured the ankle.

We were going along okay and were in 10th place after winning at Fulham with a late penalty by Barton, but there were rumours that Terry Venables was being brought in as director of football. I went for a meal with Ashley at a casino in London and wondered if he was going to mention it. He didn't. I wanted to talk about plans for the January transfer window and stressed how we needed to improve the squad. The fans were grumpy but no more so than with Robson and Souness. With a bit of investment, I felt we would climb the table again. The defence was shaky with Stephen Carr getting injured, young Steven Taylor proving rather erratic and Czech centre-back David Rozehnal not really cutting it. Mike was rather non-committal and I left none the wiser about his thoughts.

More rumours emerged that Harry Redknapp was being lined up for my job. I rang Harry who said, of course, it was rubbish, but I have it on very good authority that it probably wasn't. Supposedly all that stopped him moving was his missus not wanting to leave their home in Dorset. We lost three games over Christmas at Wigan, Chelsea and at home to Man City, and the jungle drums were beating loudly. But we got a good draw at Stoke in the FA Cup third round before Ashley's man on the ground, the chairman Chris Mort, called me into the office. I thought I might be getting a player, but I recognised the body language. Mort couldn't look me in the eye and his head was facing straight down into the table as he muttered, 'I think we need a change.' I was only eight months into a four-year deal and was a bit shell-shocked and all I could think of was to say, 'Well, if you just pay my contract up, I'll be on my way.' Mort asked to sort it out later, but I wasn't budging. 'I'd rather not, Chris, let's do it now.' He was flustered, not knowing his next move. I was content to sit there for as long as it took, even if I had to bed down for the night. What was Mort going to do? Call security and have me marched out of St James' Park? My lawyer's office was right next to where Mort's company worked in London, so I suggested they met up that afternoon. 'You can send my agreement up and we can sign here and now,' I said. Mort was sweating, clearly wondering how Mike would expect him to handle the situation.

Sky Sports were on to me. 'We hear you're being sacked, Sam, is that right?'

'No,' I said. 'I'm in the boardroom talking about new players.'

Then I switched my phone off. I was still there five hours later while Mort was in his office working out what to do. I rang Lynne and told her, 'I could be here all night. I'm not leaving till they do a deal.' I can't say she was too bothered, she couldn't wait to get out of our rented house in Durham and get back to Bolton. To be fair, Mike did the honourable thing and gave the okay for a sensible deal to be made and I left at 8pm. I'd rather have kept the job, but the settlement softened the blow. I felt more sorry for those who had sold up in Bolton to come and join me. They all eventually left too.

I met the staff and some of the players and said, 'I'm sorry it didn't work out. I'd love to have had more time to have done better and think I would have done. But it's not to be and somebody else will be coming in.' I wasn't emotional; I hadn't been there long enough. Anyway I don't really do emotion where football's concerned, that's more for family stuff. I drove back to Durham and Sky were waiting for a word. I made a brief statement before going inside where Lynne was already doing the packing. Freddy was up and about again after his health troubles and said, 'I can't believe what's happened. Now get your arse over to my house in Barbados.' It was a great offer and we booked our flights straight away. We had a hell of a time out there. It had been a traumatic eight months and it was good to get away from it all.

While I couldn't have escaped to a nicer place with its beautiful blue seas, my career had been holed below the water-line. I never had a chance once Mike Ashley took over. I wasn't his man and he just listened to the more vocal fans who demanded change. You can accept the sack when you know you deserve it and you've been on a terrible run, but, like at Blackpool, I felt badly done by. Who knows how successful I would have been with Freddy? He was passionate about the club and wanted to spend to make Newcastle great, but I'm not bitter towards Ashley, even though I've not spoken to him since.

I'm sure Mike expected Harry to take over but he stayed put and instead fans' hero Kevin Keegan returned to appease them.

● ● ●

England didn't make it to Euro 2000 but I was there as a TV pundit for Al Jazeera with Souey, Reidy, Trevor Francis, Gus Poyet and Ray Wilkins. McClaren had been sacked after his failure to qualify and now we were both out of work. What a contrast to two years earlier when we were fighting it out for the number one job in the country. McClaren's dismissal was such a big blow to English coaches. It meant the FA went foreign again by appointing Fabio Capello, and the progress we'd made to further the lot of English coaches counted for nothing. I was shocked at England's failure. We had a good side, with the right age range, and I'd have been hugely disappointed if I couldn't have taken that team into the finals.

During the finals tournament John Williams, the chairman of Blackburn, was in touch. Mark Hughes had gone to Man City and they needed a new manager. I went for an interview and discovered there was at least one other candidate in the running, Steve 'bloody' McClaren. It seemed our careers were inextricably linked. John asked if I'd hang on for a few days, but in the meantime I found out they were going for Paul Ince and I was second choice. I told John, 'I'm not going to be back-up to Paul Ince, so whether you get Paul or not, I don't want to be considered.' Ince didn't even have his coaching badges, which was causing the hold-up while they waited for special dispensation from the Premier League. I thought that was an insult to those of us who were properly qualified.

In the meantime I was doing some hospitality work at Man United, where you get invited into the posh lounges for a Q&A and mix with the punters. We were also refurbishing our family home in Bromley Cross while building a new villa in Spain. We were ready for a Christmas in Dubai too, when Blackburn sacked Ince. They had won only three of their first 17 league games and lost six off the belt to lie 19th, firmly in the relegation zone and one off the bottom of the table. Williams wanted me now. There were plenty of plus sides to this. I didn't have to move house and they had a team which was a lot better than its league position. The downside was I was a Bolton man and they weren't popular around Ewood Park. It was an easy conversation with John though.

'Do you want to come?' he asked.

'Yes, of course I want to come,' I replied.

Blackburn had two basic problems: they were conceding too many goals, and not scoring enough, which is a perfect recipe for relegation. Our England keeper Paul Robinson was saving an average 22 shots per match. Meanwhile, there was lots of speculation that we would sell Roque Santa Cruz to City because Hughes wanted him. But if we were to have any chance of staying up, we had to keep our best players and Williams agreed. We turned down a huge bid from City. I would have let him go for £25 million if we could have got a replacement in, but I couldn't get the man I wanted, Peter Crouch from Portsmouth. Annoyingly, Roque was injury-prone while one of our other strikers, the South African Beni McCarthy, may never have been injured but he never looked fit either. Jason Roberts on the other hand was strong, ran around a lot, could hustle opponents, but was not the most adept at sticking it in the net.

There was a fine passer of a ball in the Turkish midfielder Tugay, a quality centre-back in New Zealander Ryan Nelson, an industrious winger Brett Emerton from Australia, a midfielder with an eye for goal in Norwegian Morten Gamst Pedersen, a busy Irishman Keith Andrews and crowd favourite David Dunn, as well as Robinson who was a class keeper. We sold Matt Derbyshire though in a phenomenal deal to Olympiakos when we had planned to free him at the end of the season anyway.

Macca came in as coach from Leeds but I kept on Karl Robinson, who struck me as a bright young man and who went on to great success as manager of MK Dons. But I let our defensive coach Nigel Winterburn go and terminated the contract of Robbie Fowler, who was only on a three-month agreement and was well past his best. I got a great reception when I was introduced to the fans before my first game at home to Stoke and it never let up, as we did exactly the same thing as in my first game for Newcastle – we went 3–0 up by the 27th minute, remarkable for a team which had just lost six on the spin. Roberts and McCarthy both scored and in the first few games came up with the goods. In fact, we didn't lose until early February when Villa beat us at Ewood, but we were still stuck in the relegation zone. I bought Dioufy from Sunderland when I got word of him being in a training ground bust-up. Sunderland didn't suit him and he didn't suit them either, so after only six months on Wearside we snapped him up for a bargain. Gael Givet came from Marseille to strengthen the defence and I felt we had enough to get us out of trouble.

Our results were up and down and when we lost a couple in April I took the squad away for an activity break at Gleneagles in Scotland. When you're in relegation trouble, a break like that attracts a lot of comment. You get all the usual crap: 'What is he doing? They should be working their arses off in training, not swanning around hunting, shooting and fishing.' But I'd learned from experience it was vital to take the

Right: One of my best signings. The incomparable Jay-Jay Okocha, so good they named him twice.

Below: The football world lost an outstanding footballer and person with the sad death of Gary Speed. He was at Bolton with me for three years and was a manager's dream.

Above: World Cup winner Youri Djorkaeff was my biggest transfer coup of all time, and showed Bolton were serious players in the Premier League.

Left: Craig celebrates with our 2000–01 Division One play-off trophy, alongside wife Nikki and their kids Harriet and Sam.

Left: I was warned off Ivan Campo but our loan-signing from Real Madrid proved his worth. And his wigs flew off the shelves at the Bolton club shop.

Above: My 50th birthday celebration party, with Lynne and a sore head.

Left: With grandson Keaton in May 2006.

Taking to the floor at the Christmas Cancer Research Ball. It's a fabulous event that has been going 25 years.

Above: El Hadji Diouf powers in a header against Lokomotiv Plovdiv during our short-lived UEFA Cup campaign in 2005–06.

Right: End of season walkabout, with my grandson Ollie and I taking in the atmosphere.

Below: Not long before the pressures of the Newcastle job wiped that smile off my face...

Above: Blackburn chairman John Williams welcomes me as manager in 2008. Two years later I was sacked, a decision Alex Ferguson called 'absolutely ridiculous'.

'How do you do, ma'am.' Meeting Her Majesty the Queen at a Red Cross event in Manchester.

Big Sam and Little Sam – I've always been a proud granddad.

Manager of England against the Rest of the World in the 2012 Soccer Aid Charity match organised by Robbie Williams and Jonathan Wilkes that raised millions for UNICEF.

Left: The Vaz Te play-off final winner against Blackpool in 2012 was worth £100 million to West Ham. Without that, who knows if the Olympic Stadium move would have happened.

Left: Sharing a joke with the two Davids, Gold and Sullivan, in more relaxed times at Upton Park.

Below: Happy now, Karren? The bubbly's out for West Ham at Wembley as we win promotion to the Premier League. I did all that I was asked.

I hope Fergie and I ain't having a laugh at Steve McClaren's expense!

Kevin Nolan and Andy Carroll – a brilliant combo and two of my go-to men when they were fit and firing.

Left: And the award for play-acting goes to . . . Chico Flores. It was laughable, except Andy Carroll got a three-match ban for a mystery swinging arm.

Below: Alex Song, our midfield general on loan from Barcelona, gives David Silva the runaround. We got some good results against the millionaires of Man City.

If you can't take it out on the fourth official, who can you fire off a barrel at? Long-term, it didn't do my heart any good.

Daughter Rachael with my smashing grandkids Ollie and Keaton.

tension out of the situation. Of course, if you don't win on your return you get absolutely pelted, but it worked a treat. We beat both Wigan and Portsmouth to virtually confirm our safety, which was rubber-stamped before we played Chelsea the following Sunday as other results went our way.

Our achievement was portrayed as 'The Great Escape' as if we'd fluked it, but I said to the papers: 'This has not been a great escape, it is a survival, we worked hard for over several games.' Williams congratulated me on keeping the club up, but the sting in the tail was that Blackburn were seriously overspent and had to sell. We finally let Roque go to City for a reported £17.5 million, which was still a good trade considering his injury record and the fact he was bought for £3.5 million. I was surprised he passed the medical to be honest, but his problems may not have been apparent on the scans. Roque's knee had been non-active for a while, meaning the hot-spot highlighting his injury would not have shown up. It's only when a player starts training again that the problem comes to light.

That wasn't enough for John. 'We'll have to sell Stephen Warnock,' he said. 'Martin O'Neill's been on and he's offered £4 million.' I knew how much Martin liked Stephen so I told John, 'He's better than that, he's worth double.' Villa paid a lot more than that first offer. I was king at generating cash and I hadn't lost the eye for a bargain either. I found a cracking central midfielder in Steven N'Zonzi, a tall rangy player from Amiens in France who we picked up for around £500,000, so all in all I managed to keep John happy. It was a masterful juggling act.

I was looking forward to a summer break and putting a revamped Blackburn side to the test in 2009–10. Compared with the relegation battles of my first season, things could only get less stressful, surely.

HEART-STOPPING 16

Lazing on a sun-lounger on a beach in sunny Doha, I was feeling perfectly relaxed and anxiety-free for a change. It was the November 2009 international break, with Blackburn just below halfway in the table and life was going pretty well.

I did, however, notice one thing. I had this niggling discomfort in my chest.

It felt like indigestion so thought I'd have a word with the club doctor when I got back. As soon as we landed the doctor, Phil Batty, was otherwise occupied after news that our chief scout, Jack Chapman, had collapsed after a heart attack caused by two blocked arteries while working abroad. I rang Jack's wife, Jean, to let her know we'd fly her out and ensure Jack had the best possible care. Rather matter-of-factly, I then said to Phil, 'By the way, I've got this indigestion I can't get rid of. Can you have a look at it for me when you get some time?' Phil listened to my chest and didn't like what he heard so recommended a visit to the Alexandra

Bolton where I was due to receive an honorary doctorate in recognition of my 'outstanding contribution to football and Bolton'. I eventually collected the scroll the following summer and became Dr Sam Allardyce, which sounded rather grand although I have to say nobody calls me Doctor Sam unless they're taking the mickey.

While I was convalescing we faced Chelsea in the Carling Cup quarter-final. I'd been ordered not to watch it on TV to avoid stress and it wasn't such bad advice seeing as the game finished 3–3 and we won on penalties. That meant a semi-final against Villa who I seemed to face in every cup semi. At Bolton, I lost to them in the last four of the FA Cup and won in the League Cup semi, and here we were again.

We lost the first-leg 1–0 at home with James Milner scoring and were up against it. But in the second leg we came roaring out of the blocks and went two-up in 15 minutes thanks to our Croatian striker Nikola Kalinic. I was thinking, 'Come on lads, this is it.' Then who goes and scores to put Villa right back in it? None other than Stephen Warnock, who averaged, roughly, a goal every 50 games. He needed the help of dozy referee Martin Atkinson too, because it was plain as the nose on the end of his face that Nelsen was pushed by Gabby Agbonlahor before Stephen scored. We then had big Chris Samba sent off for a foul on Agbonlahor, Milner scored the penalty, N'Zonzi added an own goal and Agbonlahor handled one in off Milner's drive which was another blatant offence Atkinson failed to spot. Emile Heskey scored to make it 5–2 and although we somehow got two back, Ashley Young finished us off to make it 6–4. I was not going to spare Atkinson. This was another wholly incompetent performance by an official which had cost me. 'The major reason for us not getting through is the referee, no doubt about it,' I said in my TV interview.

We were much improved in the league, finishing 10th and ending with victories over my old mate Arsene and Villa, which was a form of revenge for the semi-final. Predictably, Arsene moaned that we'd targeted his keeper Lukasz Fabianski. We certainly did, along with his dodgy back four. They were there for the taking and didn't like it. I always felt knackered at the end of the season, but I was ready for a break more than ever after the heart scare. I felt perfectly well though, apart from any time there was a twitch or a tingle in my arm and I'd think, 'What's that?' Anyone who's had a heart scare will recognise the feeling. The worry never goes.

It wasn't the first time I'd been concerned about my heart. During my Bolton days, I agreed to an experiment with my old mate and at that time Leicester boss Dave 'Harry' Bassett for ITV's *Tonight with Trevor McDonald*. We each wore a big vest with electrodes wired to a monitor to check how stress affected us during a match. We were miked-up too and the bleep machine was in overdrive as the TV producers struck gold. They'd hit on the most stress-filled game of the entire season. The referee, Mike Riley, was completely useless and allowed events to spiral out of control. We had two men, Paul Warhurst and Dean Holdsworth, sent off in the first 20 minutes, for innocuous fouls on that paragon of virtue, Robbie Savage, as we went 2–0 down. Savage, who lost it completely, was subbed by Harry within half an hour, other-wise he would have been red-carded too. His replacement Muzzy Izzet was dismissed after the break and we equalised in the 94th minute to get a 2–2 draw.

The evidence produced by the TV show was extraordinary, even frightening. At times my heart rate was almost off the scale, at one point reaching 160 beats per minute which is apparently almost four times the normal resting pulse. I was going, 'Ref, what's going on . . . this is a disgrace . . . why haven't you sent him off too . . . Savage is a disgrace . . .' When we equalised, I was jumping around like an idiot and my emotions were going through the roof, with my heart rate heading for 200 bpm. Meanwhile, Harry's blood pressure was at bursting point too. It was discovered he suffered from an irregular heartbeat which required correcting in hospital. As a result of our experiment, the LMA brought in a health programme and fitness checks for managers which has proved invaluable to us all.

The programme consultant Dr Dorian Dugmore said those levels of heart rate were extremely dangerous. 'Week-in, week-out these guys could be putting their hearts on the line . . . There could be a serious risk involved and the result could be a heart attack, a cardiac arrest or severe angina.'

According to Dugmore, when stress caused the response, it was far more dangerous because the adrenaline narrowed the arteries. 'Your heart needs to be fit to withstand those surges of pressure. Many managers are former players and if they don't take care of themselves, they will be at significant risk.'

I'm glad I did the TV show, not just because it made me more aware of the dangers but because it helped other managers too. It made me calmer and it taught me I had to get away from the job and chill out. Don't hang around at the training ground all day thinking there's more work to be done, get off home. The art of good management is delegation and I learned to do that better over the years. In my fledgling days, I started at eight, left the training ground late afternoon and went off to a game before getting home at midnight and repeating the routine the next day. It was madness. I changed, so that, although I still watched games on TV, I only went to other matches if it was vitally important, otherwise someone else did it and reported back. I trusted my backroom team.

I never slept any better but that was nothing to do with stress, I was like that as a kid. Mum could never get me to bed and I wouldn't fall asleep until 4 am, then I'd be up three hours later. I don't like sleeping, it's a waste of your life. I'd rather watch TV. I'm a box-set man, any drama will do me, and I also like catching up on the soaps, *Coronation Street, Emmerdale* and *EastEnders*. I don't mind *The X Factor* either or *Britain's Got Talent*. When you've lived your dream, as I have, you enjoy seeing others trying to turn their dreams into reality.

The older you get the less you fret about what's going on day to day. If you can go home and tell yourself, 'I've achieved everything I can today' you can be at peace. As a manager, I've always hated matchdays though. I love the build-up but not the morning of game-day. I obsess about everything that can go wrong, even though all week I've enjoyed preparing us to make sure it goes right. I wander round the house or the hotel, praying the phone doesn't ring with news that somebody's ill or injured, or there's something in the papers and one of our players has run off with somebody else's wife. Only at Notts County, when we romped through the division, did I feel at ease getting out of bed for a game. Weirdly, the minute the game kicks off, I'm fine.

● ● ●

John Williams had warned me Blackburn was up for sale. The Jack Walker Trust, set up by the former owner, no longer wanted to keep the club. I thought Jack would have been pissed off with that, but the rest of the family weren't interested in his passion for Rovers. So when Ian Bell, who had been part of the Bolton regime, asked if I fancied becoming manager of Al-Ahli, his new club in Dubai, I was very interested. So was Lynne; she loves Dubai. Al-Ahli didn't draw many fans, only a few thousand, but they were a major club in the UAE. Dubai has a different view on sporting events which takes a bit of getting used to. They host a golf tournament which features the best players in the world but hardly any spectators. They will organise major gigs with stars like Ed Sheeran but you can get a ticket on the day, no problem. The only place you struggle to get in is for the Gold Cup horse race.

We flew out for a chat with the sheikhs who owned the club and there was a white Rolls Royce waiting on the tarmac to whisk us off to a luxury suite at the Mina A Salam Hotel. The salary was two million dollars a year tax free, free flights for the kids, an apartment on the Palm, medical insurance, everything we wanted. There was one stipulation: Al Ahli would not pay compensation to get me out of Blackburn. That was going to be difficult because John always wanted a return on his assets, even if it was the second-hand kettle in the canteen.

It was time for some pleading. 'I want you do me a favour please, John,' I said. 'You told me the club was for sale and that means my job is in doubt, so you have to understand my position. After my experience at Newcastle, I know I can be sacked by new owners any time, so I'd rather go now and take up a new position in Dubai. But I need you to give it the okay and release me from my contract.' I'd done a great job for him and he'd got me for nothing, so it wasn't too much to ask.

'We can't do that, Sam,' said John.

'Yes you can,' I argued. 'Go and tell the Trust committee it's the right thing to do and they'll back you. If you say "Yes" they'll all say "Yes."'

So he comes back: 'We want compensation.' I thought John was driving this, but I was stuck. I was pissed off beyond belief – I felt it was petty and small-minded. Al-Ahli offered to up my salary so that I could pay the compensation, but Blackburn wanted a huge figure and even I wasn't that keen to go to Dubai!

I wasn't happy but there was nothing I could do, so now it was about preparing for the new season. I had to get my head straight and put thoughts of Dubai out of my mind. The blow was softened with a fantastic pre-season trip to Australia where we played Rangers and had some great nights out with Ally McCoist, Walter Smith and Ian Durrant who had us in stitches with the best Fabio Capello impression you will ever hear. I saw we had some good youngsters who had come through from our academy, such as Phil Jones who could operate across the back-four or in midfield. When Alex Ferguson bought him for Manchester United, he said Phil could play anywhere and it's true. Fergie thought he could be the greatest player in United's history and, while he has yet to live up to the billing, he could still get there. Phil lost his way when he first joined United, but he's a good lad with a strong character and extremely talented. He makes a few rash decisions, but they will always get high-lighted more when you're at United or playing for England, whereas you get away with them more at Blackburn.

An Indian chicken-processing company called Venky's was rumoured to be buying Blackburn, but John claimed that even if they took over, nothing would change. I didn't believe that for a second. Nobody spends £30 million on a football club and doesn't change anything. I wanted to know what their plans were for me, and I was feeling even sicker about the Dubai opportunity because it was no longer available, with David O'Leary having been appointed instead.

After the Venky's takeover, it was clear that agent Jerome Anderson was going to have a big say in the running of the club, and he called me down to London for a meeting. He gets one of the owners on the phone, Madam Anuradha Desai, who tells me how wonderful it's all going to be, then Jerome presents me with a list of players he wants me to sign.

'You know there are some good players in here, Sam,' he said. Yes there were, but we had our own list and I wasn't going to have an agent telling me who I should sign.

'I want to go for these ones,' I said, as I presented him with my own list.

'I'm not sure they'll want those ones,' replied Jerome.

Now how in hell would the chicken people from India know which players were best? Only if Jerome was telling them, was my guess. This was not going to end well.

We lost 7–1 to Man United at the end of November, which wasn't great, but we were down to the bare bones due to injuries. Madam Desai wanted to know what had gone wrong. It was easy to explain. The squad was depleted, we'd sold players and we needed new ones, and ones I wanted, not Jerome's.

'If you sell off your assets and don't replace them, it is very hard in this league,' I told her. 'If you want to compete you need to invest.'

We beat Wolves 3–0 at home in the next match, but after we lost 2–1 at Bolton, I was called in by John the following day. I knew what was coming.

'I'm getting sacked,' I said to Lynne.

'You don't know that,' she said.

'Yes, I do. I'll bet you a million pounds.'

I contacted Richard Bevan, the chief executive of the LMA, asking him to get his legal team ready for negotiations. We were 13th in the league and weren't going to go down, but the Venkys felt it was time to get rid of me. On my arrival, John was there with Tom Finn, the financial director. John delivered the message from Madam Desai.

'Sorry Sam, they've told us we've got to sack you . . . oh and by the way, Macca's got to go as well.'

'Who are you putting in charge then?' I asked.

'Steve Kean,' said John.

'Steve Kean. Are you having a laugh?'

Kean came to us after a recommendation from Chris Coleman who worked with him at Fulham. Kean was a good coach but he wasn't management material, far from it. He did, however, have a rather influential agent

— Jerome Anderson! Of course, Jerome vehemently denied he had engineered the appointment of Kean or that of the Venkys as owners. I told John that the club would turn on him as well which eventually they did. It was a shame for John because Blackburn was a well-run club under his chairmanship with great facilities, an outstanding structure, and in general it was a first-class organisation. Fergie was on the phone when he heard I'd gone. 'What's going on with that lot over there?' he asked. 'The game's gone potty. I'm glad I'm not starting off now, it would be a nightmare, I'd never have lasted.' I rang Kean about three days after my dismissal.

'You knew, didn't you.'

Kean was on the back foot squealing. 'I didn't, Sam, honest, I really didn't.'

'Yes you did, don't tell lies,' I said.

Kean was caught on a camera-phone in a Hong Kong bar slagging me off, and claiming all the credit for Phil Jones' development. The recording showed Kean up for what he was and I sued him. We settled out of court and I've never spoken to him since. I gave him a chance, got him off the dole and this was how he paid me back. It put me off 'Cookie' Coleman's recommendations for life. He was very embarrassed and apologetic.

It was the second time I'd been done by new owners coming in. I didn't hold any grudges against John Williams, he was just doing his job, but I felt like I'd trod on a witch. Lynne was happy though, as it meant we went on that Christmas trip to Dubai she'd always wanted. We saw in the New Year out there at a fabulous party. Life had its compensations.

17

SECRETS FOR SUCCESS

In terms of my coaching ability, my man-management skills and knowing how to assemble the right backroom team, I felt I belonged at the top. Newcastle could have been the big one but was over before I got started, and I was so close to the England job. I was promoting myself for England again because there was talk Capello might leave and I was better equipped for the national role than when I had my interview.

I sensed it was coming to an end at Blackburn and had to make the point that I was better than the fate heading my way. The difficulty for me working abroad was learning a new language, which I wasn't very good at; and having the 'long-ball' label round my neck wasn't helpful either. No matter how much I protested, it wouldn't go away.

But the truth is I adapted my playing style to suit the personnel available and the opposition we were facing. When you have worked with players of the stature of Djorkaeff, N'Gotty, Okocha, Hierro, Campo, Stelios, Diouf, Speed and Anelka, you don't play hit-and-hope football. I counted the collection of silverware in one of the teams I sent out at the Reebok and they had 35 medals between them. Only Manchester United had more. These fellas were craftsmen, not lumberjacks.

I liked to be flexible with my formations and pragmatic too. I preferred 4-3-3, which sometimes became 4-5-1, or alternatively, 4-4-2, which became a diamond or 4-4-1-1. I even played 4-6-0 later at West Ham when we beat Spurs 3–0. Wenger and Brendan Rodgers rarely change a formation, they'll never surprise you. Their philosophy is also always to play it out from the back and even when you press them hard they won't change. Of course, Arsenal are very good on the ball, but if they're having a bad day you can rattle them by getting in their faces. Their approach has never been about 'How do we play against this team?' it has always been 'This is how we play'. There was one game where Kevin Davies headed 36 balls behind Wenger's defence. That meant we created 36 opportunities. Had we passed it around and tried to play through them, we might have got five at most.

There isn't a team on earth which doesn't hit long balls if they are losing with a few minutes to go. They can pretend they play a beautiful passing game, but they all go long when they have to. The younger managers don't like it when these basic instincts are pointed out, because they are concerned with how they are perceived by the public. But the only right way is winning, because if you don't win you get the sack. It's been the same since football was invented.

I've always regarded losing possession in your own half as a criminal offence. There are more goals scored that way than by playing it out from the back yourselves. And as the facts show, most goals are scored from four passes or less; the chances are that if your opponents rob you in your own half, there will be less than four passes before they get a shot in.

There are aspects I've always sworn by during my managerial career. Scoring the first goal is a big one. The stats say that if you strike first, then 80 per cent of the time you don't lose. Then there are clean sheets which, as a defender, I love. Chelsea won the league in 2015 because they had more clean sheets than anyone else. In nearly half their games they kept the opposition out, but scored ten fewer than second-placed Manchester City. Why did Southampton had such a good season? Because they conceded fewer than anyone else apart from Chelsea. Have a look at La Liga 2015. Real Madrid scored eight more than Barcelona but didn't win it. Barça did, who let in 17 fewer goals. Trust me, if you have a great centre-forward who scores loads of goals but you're not winning games, he'll be off somewhere else where they have a decent back four.

My whole football career has been a thirst for knowledge. I like to know how the influential figures in any sport get the best out of their teams. I was assessing player stats long before it was fashionable in football in England. Now there are owners who believe algorithms can determine whether a player will be a success or not. I would never go that far, because there are too many imponderables. The mental side of an athlete, for instance, is difficult to assess from stats but they are an excellent starting point.

They played a big part in whether I acquired a player, although I did go against it when Bolton signed Campo. Everything about his stats was awful and my backroom boys were ready to resign at the thought of him coming. But I went with my instinct. Sometimes you have to trust your judgement and be brave enough to take a risk. On the other hand, we signed prolific Brazilian striker Mario Jardel on his technical stats, even though he failed on the physical stats, and he was a disaster. He couldn't cope with the physicality of the Premier League.

The data helps you minimise your errors. Brentford swear by it and Liverpool pay great attention to it too. A player today can't escape from being measured on a daily basis in training and in games, and the more consistent his figures are, the better. If the results spike, that's not so good because it leads to both very good performances and very bad ones. The programme the sports science lads developed at Bolton, which I took with me to my other jobs, was so advanced that we worked out the physical capacity required to play in each position. Then we looked at how many possessions they had, how many crosses they delivered, how many interceptions and how many passes they performed. We established what the elite performance of a Premier League player was and measured our own players against it. We also coded games, tracking every corner, free-kick, throw-in, foul, shot, pass, and tackle to learn how to get the best out of everyone.

Fordy introduced me to Billy Beane, who was famous for using statistical data, research and analysis to sign players for the Oakland Athletics baseball team. He was at a financial disadvantage against teams with more money who could buy the bigger players, which was just like me, so to balance it up he used his expertise to bring in players with certain specialist skills in various departments of the game who were not considered star names. He was such a success that the Boston Red Sox offered him $12 million to join them and he turned it down. They made the film *Moneyball* about his career. I thought it was easier to use the analytics Billy preached for baseball rather than for football. We could sign a player because statistically he took the best corners, but that's not enough in our game; he needs other attributes too. Billy was taken on as an advisor to Dutch side AZ Alkmaar though, so there are people who think his methods will work in football.

Dave Brailsford was another backroom genius I was privileged to meet who fascinated me for his prodigious work in cycling. Brailsford swears by marginal gains, striving to improve by 0.1% here and 0.2% there or even 0.01%. He might change the material in cyclists' shorts to help them go a tiny bit faster or refine their tops because they were holding too much sweat and slowing them up. For cyclists, carrying an extra pound of sweat over, say, 160 kilometres could make a significant difference to their times. For footballers, it meant less energy expended in a game and kept them fitter for longer. I always demanded a shirt which best distributed sweat and kept players cool.

I could listen to a successful chief executive for hours, looking for any trick I might use. What was their secret? How could a man who, for instance, ran an airline come in and turn a supermarket round when he had no knowledge of the trade? It was about their people skills and the ability to put the right staff in the right places. It was why I brought in player-liaison officers at Bolton who understood the different cultures among my players and could cater for their needs, which allowed us to get the best out of them. If they needed help doing the shopping because they didn't speak English, then Matt or Sue went with them. The reason a player isn't performing is usually to do with an off-the-field problem, so you minimise them. When Okocha signed for Bolton he was well travelled and spoke four languages, but he still needed help in getting permits so his family could join him and he could relax and enjoy his football. Djorkaeff wanted an apartment in Manchester city centre because he'd lived in Paris, yet with a wife and kids you would have thought he would want a house with a garden. I learned to deal with all manner of religions too – Muslims, Jews, Protestants, Catholics and Rastafarians. Along with the chaplain at Bolton, Phil Mason, we established how religious a player was and treated him accordingly. I had a prayer room which everyone could use and made sure we had the right food for every denomination. Sometimes they didn't want any food at all if they were fasting, which could cause difficulties. You have to be physically strong to play Premier League football and there were times players were too weak to do themselves justice because of their religious beliefs. I had one player who carried round his prayer mat more than his kit bag and another who, wherever we were in the country, had to find the local church every day.

As a manager, I may seem a contradiction to the centre-half who kicked people, drank, smoked and drank some more. But as players we weren't educated about the right way to go. The only message before a Saturday match was, 'Don't drink after Wednesday.' We often stopped at the pub on our way back from a match with the chairman being ordered to get the first round in. It sounds strange today, but it was considered normal. The old adage went, 'Win or lose, drink some booze; if you draw, drink some more.' There were, though, some shining examples of what you could achieve by abstention. Stanley Matthews was one, who played until he was

50, and there was Trevor Brooking, who told me he didn't drink at all.

If you had a hangover, you put a bin liner on and sweated it out. If the coach smelt anything on your breath he made you run harder, and if you were sick, tough luck. Players are much heavier now than we were, but that's down to having much more muscle. I was probably one of the heaviest players in my day at 13st 12lb and 6ft 3in tall. Now, I would be 15st 7lb due to core strength development in the upper body which was ignored when I played. All our stuff was light, short, sharp circuit training, medicine balls and jumping off and on benches. It was thought if you put too much muscle on it slowed you down, which is now deemed to be nonsense.

● ● ●

I could put my credentials on the table with the best of them, but I wasn't desperate to get back into the game too quickly after Blackburn. Being at a loose end, I went along to the FA Cup final with my good friend Keith Pinner, who was in the sponsorship and events business and could always get you the best seats in the house. But while on my way back, Lynne rang telling me her mum was in hospital with severe abdominal pains. Now Vera was 89 so she'd had a good innings, but until the previous few weeks she'd been bright, sprightly and active. She and Lynne were extremely close and she was one of those women you thought would be around forever. She meant a lot to me too, having been there for me since I was a teenager. So I was outraged on arrival at the hospital when I found her lying in pain and in need of a pillow to help ease her discomfort. This guy, who I think was a nurse, says, 'We don't give pillows out.' This was the state of our NHS. Never be ill at the weekend with our health service, especially if you're elderly, because the chances of dying seem to increase tenfold. There was no doctor around to diagnose her illness properly and they weren't going to call one out. Vera was put on a drip and given morphine, and I had a feeling they were leaving her because she was old and, in their eyes, not worth spending too much time on. I wanted her to have tests and X-rays, but all we got back was 'You'll have to wait till Monday.'

I'd got used to private health over the years where you got quality care from the moment you walked through the front door and, having spent a lot of time in Spain, the care is so much better there for ordinary people. By the time Monday came round, Lynne's mum was getting worse.

'Can you tell me what's wrong with her?' I asked the surgeon.

'It's her age, she's old,' said the smart-arse. 'She's not strong enough for an operation.'

I wasn't falling for that, she was as strong as an ox but he'd given up on her. I could have punched him. Maybe there wasn't anything they could do, but I was shocked by his attitude. At least Vera passed away with all her family around, which is what she would have wanted.

A couple of weeks later, Mark Curtis told me about interest from West Ham. We were so consumed by Lynne's mum I hadn't noticed they were after a manager. They were in the Championship, having just been relegated, and I felt I'd done my stint at that level. Lynne was pretty fragile too, so I wasn't sure I should even bother meeting them. 'Why can't you just leave the bloody game alone?' was her blunt response when I tentatively raised the issue. The more I thought about it though, the more I wanted to talk to them. West Ham were going to be one of the best teams in the division and, having spent a few years fighting at the bottom end of the Premier League I figured it would be nice to spend some time in the upper reaches of the table, whichever division it was. After all, if I was going to be offered a Premier League job it wasn't going to be by a team in the Champions League. West Ham was a bigger club than Blackburn and in the capital, which meant it might help Lynne get over her mum's death by getting away her from the house and enjoying the lifestyle the city had to offer.

The Hammers' owners David Gold and David Sullivan worked in tandem with the vice-chair Karren Brady. Steve Bruce, who was manager at Birmingham when they were there, warned me they could be hard to work with, particularly Sullivan who took such a keen interest in the club that he could send his managers up to 30 emails a day and expected answers to every one of them. Steve's tip was, 'Don't answer them or he'll just send even more.' However, Steve did say that once a player was identified as a target, Sullivan was good at quickly sorting out the deal.

Brucie's been a good sounding board for me over the years. I first came across him when I was playing for Millwall and he was in central midfield for Gillingham. He moved on to Norwich and must have played about 400 games before getting his chance at United when he was 26, which is not the conventional route to the top. He tells me he had a trial at Bolton but Greavsie thought he wasn't good enough. That was fortunate; he might have taken my place. I got to know Steve better through my friendship with Bryan Robson, when we all hung out at Benny's in Radcliffe which had a bar called Robson's named after Robbo. Maybe we were kindred spirits, because we both knew our way around lower league football. Brucie could have bombed at United but was one of those who got better in that pressurised environment and had the character for it. He should have played for England. Brucie made the right decisions in his career, while I wonder if I'd gone to Derby and learned alongside a great centre-half like Roy McFarland instead of joining Sunderland, whether my career would have worked out better too. We'll never know.

I went with Mark to the meeting at Sullivan's house. We had a long chat and I got a good feeling about it. I realised the wage bill had to be reduced and players moved on, but equally they knew I needed a certain amount of funding to mount a realistic promotion bid. The job was mine if I wanted it, but I warned that if Lynne was still too raw and didn't want to move with me, that I wouldn't take it. We had to be together, I didn't want her staying in Bolton, with me in London. We'd done all that living apart.

Lynne didn't want to go. It wasn't about West Ham, she just didn't want me going back into football. I asked her to think about it as a new adventure. 'Come down and have a look round and if you don't like it I promise I won't take the job.' It was the first time she'd ever put her foot down and said she didn't want me going anywhere, so I knew she was serious. It was a delicate time, but Craig and Rachael thought we should go for it.

So we travelled down to a hotel and I drove out to see the training ground at Chadwell Heath. I took one look at the place and suddenly it was more me than Lynne wondering about the wisdom of taking the job. What a hole. It took me right back to the early Bolton days. This was one of England's major football clubs with lower league facilities – two-and-a-half pitches with a load of portakabins. There was another site down the road at Rush

Green which they had earmarked to move to one day, and consequently Chadwell Heath kept being patched up to get it through each season. I'd need to get any new players signed up first before giving them a tour of the 'facilities' otherwise they'd run a mile. Their new home, the Olympic Stadium, will be the envy of the world, yet they still have a training ground where you would think twice about taking the dog for a walk on it.

On the positive side, we were shown a magnificent apartment in Canary Wharf with spectacular views over London. Lynne liked that and agreed to give the move a go, with the proviso that if she didn't settle I would quit. My appointment was announced on 1 June 2011 and I signed a two-year deal which suited both the club and me, as it was the timescale we'd set out to get back into the Premier League.

I said in a radio interview, 'It's a fantastic club with a great tradition and loyal supporters, but I wouldn't have taken this job if I didn't think we could bounce straight back into the Premier League. It's an exciting challenge for me and one I'm very much looking forward to.' The big debate was whether I would follow the 'West Ham Way' which nobody could define, but whatever the hell it was I apparently didn't play it. I had a bet with the media officer Greg Demetriou before my first press conference and said to him, 'If we go for a minute without any mention of style of play, I'll give you £1,000. If it's under a minute, you give me a tenner.' We timed it at 32 seconds before I was accused of being 'a bit long ball'. I felt the West Ham Way ought to be about wearing your heart on your sleeve, showing passion for the club and winning. The fans were being brainwashed by the media into thinking that, historically, the club had a particular style of play akin to Barcelona, which was potty. Did they play the West Ham Way when they got relegated under Avram Grant? I doubted it. Did Harry Redknapp play the West Ham Way? He didn't know. Did Alan Curbishley play the West Ham Way? He can't have done because he was hounded out by the fans.

My 'long ball' label didn't originate from Wenger, it was started by Graeme Souness who got upset whenever I beat him when he was at Blackburn or Newcastle and said, 'I wouldn't want to watch that every week.' I was thinking: 'Isn't it funny how we beat you.' Wenger picked up on it, as did Rafa Benitez, and the press swiftly adopted it. Bolton beat Liverpool 1–0 after Kevin Davies challenged Sami Hyypia and the defender had to go off. 'I didn't know you could play football that way,' said Benitez, who refused to shake my hand at the final whistle. These blokes couldn't take it. In my first three years in the Premier League, the talk was about me hiring mercenaries to win games, then it was 'long ball'. There always had to be an excuse for losing to a Sam Allardyce team.

There's a saying, 'If you shag one sheep, you'll always be known as the Sheep Shagger,' no matter what else you do in life. Similarly, get labelled for being 'long ball' and it never leaves you, I accepted that years ago. There was no logic in trying to out-pass Man United or Arsenal. They spend hundreds of millions on players who can thread the ball through the eye of a needle, so you have to find a way to counteract their threat. Bolton cost Arsenal the title in 2003 when we came back from 2–0 down at the Reebok to draw 2–2 and we were brilliant. But if we'd tried to pass like them we'd have been destroyed, and that applies to any smaller team. Blackpool played absolutely lovely football the year they were in the Premier League, but went down because they couldn't defend. It's a mistake trying to play the game the big boys' way but, hey, it gets you lots of praise for doing it 'the right way'. I'd rather win or draw, thanks.

I never played long-ball any more than most. It was just another tactic to me and was used by everyone from Fergie to José Mourinho when required, although in their cases it was a long pass obviously. When Alex Song signed on loan at West Ham from Barcelona, he told me that he wondered why a few of his Arsenal team-mates didn't want to travel to Bolton. Afterwards he knew why. 'You battered us,' he said. He appreciated the value of the tactics.

● ● ●

If West Ham were to win promotion, I had to work fast. Wally Downes, who was Avram Grant's assistant, had left but I brought him straight back as first-team coach, because he knew the place and I'd always liked him from meeting up at coaching courses. I also brought in Macca again to be my number two and Martyn Margetson as goalkeeping coach, who was recommended by Gary Speed for his work with Wales. I was worried we didn't have a scouting team in place though. David Sullivan felt they weren't necessary and preferred to go on stats. I, of course, also liked my stats but we had to watch players with our own eyes too. No agent ever rings up and says, 'Here, I've got a really crap player for you, do you want him?' They're always brilliant. So I got Martin Glover in as head of recruitment who had worked with me at Blackburn. It was important to have a scouting team who could put forward arguments for and against recommendations from agents, even when David was getting excited in a player and determined to sign so-and-so who was supposedly the best thing since sliced bread.

Once again, like at Newcastle, Scott Parker wanted to leave. I couldn't blame him. He wouldn't have got picked for England in the Championship and he was the Football Writers' Player of the Year, which was some achievement considering West Ham went down. But I needed to hang on to him until we got the right players in. Scott played four games for me and only signed for Spurs on transfer deadline day at the end of August after Harry Redknapp, Scott's agent and Spurs chairman Daniel Levy were all on to me to let him go. It was a good move for Scott and good business for us, getting a reported £5.5 million for a player who was nearly 31 and whose body was suffering from the rigours of Premier League football.

I knew exactly the right man to lead us out of the Championship, Kevin 'Nobby' Nolan. When I first saw him at Bolton, I wasn't convinced he would even make it as a pro. He was a terrible centre-back. He couldn't head it and couldn't tackle, and I could only think he was playing there because of his size. But when I tried him in a midfield three, he was a revelation. He got a bit carried away once he got into the Bolton first team though, thinking he didn't have to work so hard, and went out drinking with his pals and put a bit of weight on. So I dropped him and it taught him a lesson. He knuckled down and after that he was great. If you had a go at him, he came back stronger to prove you wrong. Kevin had a gift for turning up in space in the box to score, while defenders wondered where on earth he'd come from. Martin Peters used to do it, so too David Platt and Frank Lampard. Nolan never played for England but he was competing with Steven Gerrard and Lampard and wasn't quite as good as them.

But being nearly good enough for England still makes you a very good footballer, so I snapped Kevin up from Newcastle, when he had a falling out over his contract, and gave him a five-year deal, making him probably the highest paid player in the division. It was a magnificent gesture from David to back me. Kevin brought with him leadership, character and goals and would sort out the dressing room by taking over the captaincy from Matthew Upson who had gone to Stoke. Kevin is a players' man who commands respect from the rest of the team. I'd seen him grow after taking over the armband at Bolton as a youngster when Jay-Jay left. Some players lose focus when they become captain and their game suffers. It happened in cricket when Ian Botham became England skipper. But Kevin's not like that; he revels in the role and his performance is better. His shoulders and chest stick out more. He enjoys being the boss on the field.

Off the pitch, Nobby was the social secretary who arranged events for the players and their wives and girlfriends and was keen for the squad to do everything together. There was a negativity after relegation and the dressing room needed a lift. Kevin was not my nark. He only came to me on serious business, such as a player in the dressing room causing trouble for everyone. I didn't ask Kevin to do anything I wouldn't have done as a player. He believed in me and let the squad know that I would get them up if they listened to me. All the stats and fitness stuff, which some of them had never seen before, were nothing new to Nobby and he educated them about why my methods were right. Kevin would get stick off the fans wherever he played at Bolton, Newcastle and West Ham because he's not the most elegant of players. They'd think he was overweight but he wasn't, he consistently had less than 10 per cent body fat and if he didn't he would get fined. It was just his body shape.

West Ham should never have been relegated with a team including England internationals Rob Green, Carlton Cole, Parker, Upson and Wayne Bridge, who all knew the Premier League scene so well. Demba Ba had played too and Robbie Keane was on loan. Ba invoked a release clause which allowed him to leave for free if West Ham went down. We offered him a fortune to stay but were knocked back, while some good lads stayed on like Jack Collison, James Tomkins, Greeny, Carlton and Mark Noble, who was the ultimate West Ham man. They had a good attitude to the task we faced, along the lines of, 'Let's make sure we're only in the Championship for one season.' There was a massive turnover in personnel though. I think in my first year, 25 players went out of the door and 19 came in.

I sat down with every player individually on our pre-season tour of Switzerland and said to them, 'If you don't want to stay that's fine, but let me know and make sure you do your best while you're here, and when the right club comes we'll move you on.' I thought if I played fair with them, they would do the same for me. I didn't want any agitators who were constantly moaning. But I did warn them, 'If you stay but don't try and you waste my time, then we will have a problem and I'll dump you with the mushroom squad.' The mushrooms were those who did your nut in, so they trained at other times to the first-team group. They were so named because you kept them in the dark, brought them out now and again if you needed them, then put them back in the dark again until they left.

Freddie Piquionne, the French striker, got the full mushroom treatment with garnish from me and didn't seem to care. It became a joke that if you were exiled, you weren't being mushroomed any more, you were being 'Piquionned'. I did the same with Swiss international Johann Vogel at Blackburn, another one who couldn't be bothered, and those out of favour at Ewood were 'Vogeled'. Piquionne and Vogel were poison and the danger was they became recruiters and poisoned others too, which was why they had to train at different times away from the main group. But they went whingeing to the PFA, who would be on my case telling me I couldn't treat them in such a manner. It was nothing to do with the PFA, it was about players doing an honest job for extremely good pay. Those two didn't. Never mind the West Ham Way, this was the Big Sam Way.

HAMMERS AND TONGS 18

The Hammers were on the march again. I was buzzing for the start of 2011–12 season and our first game was at home to Cardiff in front of a healthy 25,000 crowd. We might have had our bubbles burst by a last-minute Kenny Miller winner which Rob Green should have saved, but we recovered from that and went on a seven-game unbeaten run, winning five, to push ourselves right into the promotion shake-up.

During that run we drew at Millwall on a Saturday lunchtime, an occasion which scared the shit out of me. The two sets of fans hate each other and all the old hooligans came out of retirement for the day. We set off on the coach with the biggest police escort I've ever seen. Even Barack Obama would have thought it over the top. People think managers should be detached and get on with the game, but it's impossible to ignore the bile spewing from the terraces and the general aggression. It was horrible. Burnley v Blackburn was noted for hatred between supporters but West Ham v Millwall took the prize.

I was learning about my squad and discovering who was up to it and who wasn't. There was a lot of talk about Freddie Sears and what a great prospect he was, but I couldn't see it. I didn't think he was good enough and he didn't help himself. He wasn't one who stayed around in the afternoons trying to improve. He was always straight off home after training and didn't understand what it took to be a top professional.

Collison understood. He was extremely dedicated but suffered something called a chondral defect in his knee before I arrived, exacerbated by playing on for too long without the correct treatment. However much the surgeon drilled round to improve the blood supply, Jack was never quite right. He was a super-talented lad, but he was like the former Spurs player Ledley King, trying to get through training in order to play on a Saturday, then struggling again. Ultimately it cost him his West Ham career, when he should have been one of the first names on the team sheet. I also found out that Carlton Cole suffered from a knee injury which prevented him training too, but he still made a massive contribution to the team. Nolan, by contrast, would train flat out every day and be fresh to go for a full 90 minutes.

I had hoped 6ft 5in Norwegian striker John Carew, who came from Villa, would play a big part in leading us back into the top flight, but the moment he signed he lost interest. Carew appeared dazzled by the London nightlife and was apparently a big hit with the ladies, but when it came to scoring on the pitch he was not so hot. We got some offers from Turkey, but he wouldn't budge. 'Gaffer, I've got millions, what do I want to go there for?' he'd say. Eventually, I mushroomed him.

I wanted to sign Dioufy again and he came to training, but David

Sullivan warned me off. There was a previous incident where he allegedly spat at West Ham fans while playing for Liverpool but was subsequently cleared of all charges. I abhor spitting. Although I'd fined Dioufy at Blackburn for spitting, I didn't think it was the biggest crime either. I'd rather have been spat at than have a leg broken by some loony opponent who might finish my career. Spitting in someone's face will not end their career, however disgusting it is.

So there was to be no Dioufy but I brought in a couple of imposing figures in Abdoulaye Faye and Papa Bouba Diop. Also, we signed Matt Taylor from Bolton, George McCartney on loan and Joey O'Brien on a free. I not only changed the players, I changed the food in the canteen too. Out went white sugar and white bread which is processed – basic good nutrition practice which West Ham should have known. Sugary cereals were knocked on the head too. I stressed the importance of ice baths for repairing muscles. Some of the lads went to great lengths to try and avoid them because they aren't fun. Your average man in the street would squeal like a baby if he was dropped in an ice bath. It works a treat, as does a cryotherapy unit where players stand for two minutes in temperatures of -120 degrees Centigrade (I kid you not) to heal tissue damage. Try that one! I didn't like it when the sports science team got too pally with the players, because the players abused the relationship to get out of doing their ice baths, and I gave the boffins murder if I discovered any player had wormed his way out of them. Some players will always let you down if it suits them. It doesn't matter who they are or how well you think you know them.

We were having a great November and had just beaten Derby 3–1 when I saw Steve Bruce's number pop up on my mobile at the training ground the next morning. His voice was breaking.

'Sam, have you heard? Speedo's committed suicide.'

I asked him to repeat what he said, as I couldn't have heard him right.

'Shearer's just called me and said Gary Speed is dead.'

He'd hanged himself. I couldn't take it in. Speedo was one of football's ebullient, bubbly characters. He was on BBC's *Football Focus* the previous day and looked in fine fettle, thoroughly enjoying life as manager of Wales. I'd spoken with him only a couple of weeks earlier in one of our regular chats where he liked to chew things over with me. I'd advised him to quit Sheffield United when he was offered the Wales job, and used to tease him about his fitness coach and assistant boss Raymond Verheijen who, whenever Wales won, took all the credit on social media and mysteriously went missing when they lost. Verheijen got on a lot of club managers' nerves but Speedo loved him. I kept telling him, 'You've got to get rid of that bloke, it's always about him.' Two days after Speedo's funeral, Verheijen tweeted that he wanted to be Wales manager. How insensitive could a man get?

I had to deliver the news in our dressing room, where many of the players knew Speedo well – Macca, Joey O'Brien, Nobby and Matt Taylor. There was silence, followed by lots of questions to which I didn't have the answers. If Gary had died in a car accident we'd still have been devastated, but it is easier to come to terms with than someone taking their own life. They say there are two forms of suicide – the snapper, who does it on the spur of the moment and the planner. Gary must have been a snapper, he couldn't possibly have been planning it. Speedo was an outstanding lad and a top footballer and manager. He was the ultimate pro who carried so much respect in the game and is still greatly missed.

● ● ●

We topped the table in January but started drawing too many. We didn't have enough goals in the side to turn one point into three, but Sullivan and Gold recognised the problem and I was able to bring in Nicky Maynard from Bristol City and my Bolton old-boy Ricardo Vaz Te from Barnsley on transfer deadline day. I also tried for Eder from Portuguese side Academica but somebody over there really did not want him to leave. I was warned by my mate Mickey Walsh, the former Everton and Blackpool striker who was an agent in Portugal, that there were at least two different agents involved so there could be a problem. But all was going okay when the player and the club president joined us for a meal after Eder played in a game we watched and had done well. He had a bag packed ready to travel back with us and we were relaxing with a glass of wine having concluded negotiations, when two guys came in and asked him to go outside with them. Our interpreter said they were friends, but they didn't look very friendly to me, and we never saw Eder again!

The fans were fidgety as we tried to grab on to Southampton's coat-tails with Reading coming up hard on the rails. We finished strongly by winning four and drawing two in April, but it wasn't enough to get in the top two. Reading claimed the title, having beaten us and Southampton in the run-in, so they deserved it. We'd set ourselves a target of two points a game to guarantee promotion and came up six short on 86 points.

We hadn't failed, we were re-generating a club. I'd been given two years to get West Ham back into the Premier League and now, in year one, we were in the play-offs. The two Davids were understandably disappointed but, at the same time, optimistic we could still go up, and we were pleased our opponents in the semi-final were Cardiff. They had gone all out for the Capital One Cup and only lost on penalties in the final to Liverpool, but I felt that psychologically and physically it would catch up with them. It was easier than I expected, with Collison getting two without reply at their place to set up the home leg which we won 3–0.

The final was against Blackpool who we had comfortably beaten twice during the regular season, 4–0 at home and then 4–1 away with ten men when midfielder Henri Lansbury went in goal for most of the second half after Greeny's sending off. That was the third game on the trot we finished with a man short and had won two and drawn one of them. That told me we were a resilient bunch. What concerned me was the fans thinking it was going to be easy. Blackpool were seven unbeaten through to the end of the season before knocking out Birmingham in the semis. They had also won a play-off final two years earlier so knew what to expect. Yet they were the underdogs and we were odds-on favourites. Sullivan urged us to practise penalties in case it went to a shoot-out, but some of the players thought it best to avoid them. Noble is one of the best penalty takers in West Ham's history and never practises them. He point blank refuses. 'Don't ask me to do that,' he would say. 'I'll score, leave me alone.' So you left him alone.

As Wembley was so close by, we treat it as a regular league fixture, with just the one night in a hotel together. But it was no ordinary game. There was an overwhelming feeling of excitement mixed with fear, as we approached the stadium where 80,000 fans would soon be packed in. There is not another game like it, where the outcome means so much. Its value increases every year and this one was billed as the £100 million match. It was also West Ham's first visit to Wembley in more than 30 years.

The enormity of the occasion got to us, and we were nowhere near as good as usual. Although Carlton put us ahead, controlling a cross from Matt Taylor before finding the corner, I knew at half-time we weren't right.

'Fucking hell, lads, you're bloody lucky to be 1–0 up,' I told them. 'We've got to be better than this, or we'll lose.'

I was wasting my breath. Tom Ince equalised soon after the re-start and we were in trouble. We would have lost but I made two of the best substitutions of my life, bringing on Julien Faubert for Guy Demel and George McCartney for Gary O'Neil. It shored up the team but also allowed us to get forward better, with Matt Taylor pushing on in midfield. Stephen Dobbie missed a gift to put them ahead when we left him unmarked in the box, but Nolan also hit the crossbar and it looked like we were going into extra-time, until Ricardo Vaz Te became the West Ham hero.

We signed Vaz Te from Barnsley, where he had already scored 12 goals that season, and he rewarded us with a dozen more, none as precious as this one three minutes from time. Carlton challenged the keeper, the ball ran loose and, as Vaz hit it, I had flashbacks to Dean Holdsworth's miss in the FA Cup semi-final 12 years earlier when he slammed it over the bar.

Vaz hit it high too, but fortunately he was nearer the goal than Deano and it flew in. There was a fair bit of added time, which felt like an eternity, before the final whistle went and we could celebrate. There were bubbles everywhere. We hadn't got a late goal all season but got one now when it mattered most. Macca and I walked up the Wembley steps to get our medals and we had to be cheek to cheek to hear each other. The noise was deafening. I offered a handshake to Vicky and Owen Oyston, who I hadn't seen since I was manager of Blackpool. I suppose I should have been grateful to them. Had they not sacked me, I might not have been where I was.

We drove back from Wembley to the Boleyn where we enjoyed a buffet and drinks with everybody, including my son Craig and my nephews Damian and Marc, while watching Didier Drogba win the Champions League final for Chelsea against Bayern Munich. Even Drogba could not have been happier than me. Automatic promotion is best, but you cannot beat the euphoria of going up by winning a play-off final. It's bigger than a cup final. David was in my ear immediately. 'We've got to get planning for next season, Sam.' Typical Dave.

Lynne and Rachael weren't at the game. They were in Vegas where we'd all planned to be for an Amir Khan fight which subsequently got cancelled. So I took some of the staff up to the bar next to our apartment to thank them for their efforts. We had a couple of bottles of champagne and reviewed the season through to its epic climax after 49 games. I was shattered. Winning the play-offs with West Ham was a greater achievement than Bolton, where we'd been through the experience of semi-final defeat and used the memory of that pain to get it right the next time. West Ham stepped into the unknown and the expectation was so much greater. If Bolton had lost the play-off, few would have batted an eyelid. Had we failed at West Ham, it would have been national news for days. Yet the expectation at West Ham isn't in keeping with how the club has performed in recent years. It was the same at Newcastle. The clubs are similar in that they have big fan bases who think they should be challenging Man United and Chelsea, but they don't win any trophies.

Feeling full of the joys at our play-off success, I was looking forward to my next game at Old Trafford a week later, the Soccer Aid charity match which raises millions for UNICEF UK. I'd been involved with Soccer Aid for six years since Robbie Williams and his friend Jonathan Wilkes, whose original concept it was, asked me to be a commentator at the game. This time I was going to be manager of England against the Rest of the World. I knew I'd get that England job somewhere down the line! Kenneth Shepherd, Freddy's son, was the organiser and the idea was to mix celebrities with former players and put on a competitive match. Robbie and Jonny certainly wanted to win. The players loved it and the celebs wanted to prove they should have been professional footballers. There were usually a few big names from America thrown in too who couldn't ever have been footballers, but it added to the fun. We recruited David Seaman, Martin Keown, Des Walker, Kevin Phillips and Teddy Sheringham, with breakfast TV man Ben Shephard a dark destroyer in midfield who would frustrate his opponent and was fit as a fiddle, but didn't do a lot with the ball. We also had the singer Olly Murs who, in bursts, looked like he belonged in the real England team and had obviously played a bit in his time. Both teams trained at Fulham and socialised in the evening in Chelsea Harbour where comedians Paddy McGuinness and

John Bishop had me in stitches. Bishop was a bit of a plodder on the field, but he could last all day because of all the marathons he'd run.

The Rest of the World were managed by Kenny Dalglish and weren't short of quality, with Edwin van der Sar, Jaap Stam, Roy Keane, Clarence Seedorf and Freddie Ljungberg in the ranks. Among their celebrities were Michael Sheen, Gerard Butler, Will Ferrell, Mike Myers, James McEvoy, Edward Norton and Woody Harrelson. Woody didn't have a clue how to play football, but he was keen to learn. One day he wandered off and we found him practising with some kids in the park, asking them what the rules were. There were 67,000 at Old Trafford to watch and I was surprised how much of a tingle went down my spine. It was a bit of fun but nobody wanted to lose, and the celebrities were anxious not to make fools of themselves. One who definitely didn't was Sergio Pizzorno, the guitarist with Kasabian, who scored with a magnificent chip over Seaman into the far corner to put the Rest of the World ahead. But second-half goals from Sheringham, Wilkes and Phillips saw us to victory, helped by some excellent saves from the actor and presenter Jamie Theakston who replaced Seaman at the break. I managed England again two years later but lost to a José Mourinho team. He wanted to win so much he came onto the pitch and chopped down Olly Murs to stop him getting free on the wing. He also sneaked 12 players on without the ref noticing.

Dalglish and Mourinho do a lot for charitable causes which often go under the radar. I've long supported Kenny and his wife Marina who organise funding for a cancer unit in the North West. Not only have they helped build the unit, they have to raise millions to run it because they get no help from the government. And Ronnie and Gail Wood hold a Cancer

Research ball at Christmas which raises up to £100,000. It's been going 25 years and most years I do a turn. I've done Freddie Mercury, John Travolta, Mick Jagger and Michael Jackson in *Thriller* which I think was my finest effort as I squeezed into some very tight black pants and nailed the Moonwalk. We performed the Peter Kay version of 'Is This the Way to Amarillo?' with Sammy Lee knowing exactly what his role was going to be: 'I bet I have to play Ronnie Corbett,' he said, with a sigh of resignation. He did and he was brilliant at it. He got the moment where Ronnie falls over down to a tee. A group of us also did Michael Flatley's *Riverdance* and I've even dressed up as Cheryl Cole and a character out of *Hairspray*. Strangely, my mates thought I was a little too keen to dress up as a woman.

At West Ham, the club embraced Stephanie Moore's bowel cancer charity in honour of her husband Bobby who died of the disease. They put on an unbelievable dinner created by five Michelin-starred chefs which attracts lots of football faces and is a major fundraiser for the organisation. I got to know Stephanie well in my four years at the club and learned that had Bobby been diagnosed sooner he would have lived a lot longer, but he didn't get checked out as early as he should have done. It's a message for all of us.

West Ham were masters of charity work and pushing their community programme, led by the chief executive of the West Ham United Foundation Joe Lyons. Joe came from Spurs and had terrific vision for how the club could help improve people's lives, whether it was aid for the disabled or helping people gets jobs. He worked with businesses urging them to give members of the local community careers, even in high-flying jobs like banking in Canary Wharf. There are 100,000 people employed in banking on West Ham's doorstep, so Joe saw no reason why some of those jobs should not go to locals. It's supposed to be the government's responsibility but they aren't doing it, so great blokes like Joe have taken it on themselves to make it happen. We helped him promote his work by sending players into the community and made sure everyone did their bit. Some were put upon more than others though. Poor Mark Noble barely had a minute to himself, but he felt an extra responsibility, being a local lad.

West Ham had a community feel even though it was a London club. Like Bolton, there were many people attached to it who had been fans all their lives. Men like Jimmy Frith are part of the fabric of the place and it seemed like he had been there since the club was founded. Jimmy did a bit of coaching with the academy and a bit with me, and wherever he was needed he was there. He couldn't survive without West Ham; it means everything to him. He's got to be getting on for 80 but he's fitter than blokes half his age. When West Ham move to the Olympic Stadium and usher in a new era, they must never forget people like Jimmy who make the club what it is.

● ● ●

We had to build for the 2012–13 Premier League season, and making sure we didn't go back down again was our priority. First of all, I needed a keeper. Greeny was out of contract and was off to QPR after turning down three improved contract offers. He went with our best wishes after doing a brilliant job, despite being handicapped by a finger injury. The physio was worried that if the finger got damaged again it could finish him, so we had a glove made with four slots in it so that two of his fingers sat together.

I had just the man to replace Rob in Jussi Jaaskelainen. Jussi had lost his place at Bolton to Adam Bogdan, who to me wasn't as good, and they'd just been relegated. It was assumed I was bringing Jussi in as a back-up given that he was 37 years old, but I wasn't. I needed someone who knew what the Premier League was about, could organise a defence and would slot in straight away. I had to find a top-class striker too, which is every newly promoted manager's number one headache. If you find one, and he stays fit, you are guaranteed to stay up; without one you will most likely go down. I took a keen interest in the vibes coming out of Liverpool from the man who had taken over from Kenny Dalglish, Brendan Rodgers, who didn't seem to fancy their £35 million front man Andy Carroll. Carroll had finished the previous season strongly, scoring the winner in the FA Cup semi-final against Everton, which made him an Anfield hero, and another in the final defeat by Chelsea. He also netted a sensational header for England against Sweden at Euro 2012, so he wasn't exactly out of form.

I knew Carroll from my time at Newcastle when he was a brave, admittedly raw, 18-year-old, trying to establish himself at St James' Park. In a friendly against Juventus in the summer of 2007, Andy scored and soon after was taken out with a knee to the face by the Italian international keeper Gianluigi Buffon. Buffon said it was an accident, but to me it was like the Harald Schumacher assault on Patrick Battiston at the 1982 World Cup, which is generally acknowledged as the worst foul by a keeper of all time. Somehow, Andy got up from that to play on when he was lucky not to be in hospital

Carroll was 6ft 4in and good on the floor as well as in the air. He scored more with his feet than his head and had a much better touch than he was given credit for, but sometimes people cannot see beyond how someone looks. He was the right fit for West Ham, but how on earth could I get him? Surely Liverpool weren't prepared to dump a player who cost so much? But the more I listened to Rodgers on the radio and TV trying to evade questions about Carroll, the more I realised he didn't want him. Take this quote: 'I would have to be a nutcase even to consider letting Carroll go at this moment, unless there are other solutions for that.' He didn't say he'd be a nutcase to let Andy go, just that he'd be a nutcase to do it at that moment.

Newcastle were in for Andy too and wanted him back either for a third of the price they had sold him for 18 months earlier or on loan. Liverpool viewed this as an insult and thought Newcastle were taking the mickey out of them. But would they think it an insult if we proposed a loan deal? Just before the transfer window shut, we got our break and signed Andy on a season-long loan with Liverpool apparently having lined up Clint Dempsey from Fulham as his replacement. I was shocked we were able to pull it off, even more so when Dempsey went to Spurs instead, leaving Brendan short of front men. Brendan later admitted he would never have let Carroll leave had he known the Dempsey deal would fall through.

Andy still wanted to make a go of it on Merseyside and told me he planned to go back at the end of the season. In fact, until Rodgers spelled it out that he wouldn't start any games, he wasn't interested in joining us at all. It took Nobby Nolan, Carroll's mate from their Newcastle days, to give him a hefty shove in our direction after it eventually dawned on him that he would get plenty of games for us and none if he remained at Anfield. If the West Ham coffers had stretched to it, I would have signed Jordan Henderson, Stewart Downing and José Enrique from Liverpool too, because Brendan was prepared to let them all go. The reason we ended up having such a good season was Carroll, no question, because the other striker I signed, Modibo Maiga from Sochaux, didn't cut it. Maiga couldn't cope with the physicality of the Premier League, whereas most opposition defenders couldn't deal with the physicality of Carroll.

I brought James Collins back from Aston Villa to strengthen the defence and Mo Diame from Wigan to stiffen up the midfield, while we got Matt Jarvis from Wolves for around £10 million at the end of August to give us some pace on the wing. We won our first game back in the Premier League, 1–0 against Aston Villa, thanks to a goal from Nobby, and it was more comfortable than the score suggests, as we were denied a stonewall penalty for a foul on Carlton Cole. The supporters enjoyed themselves, and the fact we kept a clean sheet, which always makes an ex-defender like me happy, added to the achievement. But we were well beaten 3–0 at Swansea next time out, due to some awful errors at the back. Carroll's debut came in our third game against Fulham and he absolutely terrorised them, setting up two goals as we won 3–0. We were five seconds from taking Andy off and getting Carlton on when Andy damaged his hamstring, but he only missed a couple of matches and returned as sub for our 2–1 victory against QPR. I knew if Andy stayed fit, we would be fine. He brought the rest of the team into play and had a telepathic understanding with Nolan who was on the end of everything he set up. He was vital to us. You only had to look at our points gained when Carroll played, as opposed to the points lost when he didn't. He was out for a nine-game stretch over December and January and we only won twice.

Andy could be even better if he pushed himself and put the work in. He tells you he does, but he doesn't always do it. He doesn't really like watching football either and isn't interested in the history of the game. He certainly wouldn't be in your football quiz team, but it's surprising how many players are like that; there are more than you might think. I had Hidetoshi Nakata at Bolton, who was a Japanese icon and one of the most famous players in Asia. He got bored with football and quit at the age of 29 to travel the world. Carroll does care about the team but treats life a bit too casually. He also gets himself into situations off the pitch too which a manager could do without and so could he. He needs to be more responsible and realise that a football career passes in the blink of an eye. You don't realise it at that age, I certainly didn't. Injuries have robbed him of valuable time in the game and he has to take more care with his rehab, otherwise he'll be finished before he knows it.

Carroll loves being the main man when he's on the pitch though. He never goes hiding. When fit he should be England's regular centre-forward, because we've missed having enough quality strikers in recent years in the mould of Gary Lineker or Alan Shearer. Wayne Rooney has had to carry the country's hopes, and we need more than him if we are ever to win a tournament. But the way Carroll plays means his body goes through a lot of trauma. Andy leaps higher than anyone, he has a great spring, and is one of the most elegant sights you'll see when flying through the air. But that supreme aerial ability means he also lands hard, putting pressure on the base of his feet, his ankle ligaments and knees. According to Freddie Flintoff, the cricketer, who had a similar build and experienced injuries from bowling, there is six or seven times your body weight going through you as you land. That is a hell of a lot of pressure hitting the ground.

It was that pressure in the final game of the season which resulted in Andy tearing his plantar fascia, the tissue which runs along the sole of the foot to the heel. He was still a Liverpool player, but we were hoping to make the deal permanent and the fans were singing 'Andy Carroll, we want you to stay' as we went on a lap of honour, having beaten Reading 4–2 with a hat-trick from Nolan to earn a highly respectable 10th place finish. Andy pulled out of the England squad for their end of season friendlies against Ireland and Brazil, but the medical diagnosis was that his injury had only a 4 percent chance of recurring. So I took the risk and we pressed on with his signing, giving him a six-year contract and paying Liverpool what was, by West Ham standards, a bank-busting fee, widely reported in the media as £15 million.

Unfortunately, Carroll didn't play for us again until the New Year, after breaking down in training at the start of September with a rupture to the medial tendon in the same foot. The physio gave me the grim news and there was a horrible empty feeling in my stomach. Andy had become one of the 4 percent. We had blown most of the budget on him and we'd spent the rest on Stewart Downing to supply his ammunition. Now we were in the mire, with no timescale on when Andy might be back. I was fuming with the medical staff who had advised me of the low chance of a fresh injury. I was even more angry because I'd passed on the chance to sign Wilfried Bony in order to pursue Andy, and Bony ended up scoring 16 for Swansea. The chairman and I agreed Bony was a bigger risk than Carroll based on our experience with Maiga, but I would never have signed Carroll if I'd known what was to come. David Sullivan wasn't happy that Andy was on the sidelines and I had every sympathy with him.

Sullivan was committed to getting Andy fit and sent him to Holland for further treatment. It can be hard persuading a chairman that it's worth £30,000 sending a player to a specialist abroad. Their argument will be, 'Why can't you send him to the bloke down the road?' But you learn over the years who are the best at dealing with each particular injury, and experience says it is a wise investment which gets a player back quicker and stronger. If your most expensive star comes back six months earlier it's good business, because every game missed means you are wasting money. Although the trip to Holland worked, we were told that even once Andy got fit he would feel the injury for some time to come.

Bloody marvellous being a football manager. Why on earth do we put ourselves through all this?

19

The best managers never shy away from the toughest decisions, even when it looks like things are going smoothly. Their legacy endures and becomes part of the fabric of their club. So when it was announced in May 2013 that Sir Alex Ferguson would be retiring after nearly 27 years in charge at Manchester United, it seemed like the end of an era in British football.

I couldn't believe it was happening, it didn't seem right that he wouldn't be there in the dugout anymore. Fergie was the greatest manager we'd ever known. He had an unflinching determination to make United number one in England and Europe and possessed an acute sense of timing about when to overhaul the squad or make changes in his backroom staff.

I built probably two teams at Bolton but Fergie created six or seven at Old Trafford, with four or five backroom changes too. He could re-motivate and re-energise United year after year, which takes some doing when you've been in charge as long as him. As exceptional a manager as Arsene Wenger is, he found that difficult to do, and couldn't defend a title whereas Fergie did it time and again; and remember United hadn't won the top division for 26 years until he lifted the first Premier League trophy in 1993. Wenger, on the other hand, joined a club which was much more familiar with being top dogs.

Fergie moved with the times too; as the game changed he changed with it. He was one of the first to embrace a rotation system, knowing when to rest players from the team or give them little breaks during the season to keep them fresh. He also kept his ear to the ground about new innovations to do with training or diet, and never felt he knew it all.

I could ring him up and he would always be available if I needed advice over a problem with the board or a player or about a possible signing. I would still make my own decision, but his input was invaluable. I had so much respect for a man who had always been willing to help out fellow managers like myself and we just seemed to click. He defended me over my leaving Notts County, and as a committee member he told the LMA to support me. He wanted better protection for managers at every level of the game and we all owed him our gratitude. At Bolton, he spoke at one of our charity dinners and told Phil Gartside and the board to get their hands in their pockets and provide the money to assist in the transfer market. Gartside shouted, 'He wouldn't know what to do with it!' which was nice of the chairman. For the record, I would have done.

Sir Alex ruled United like no other manager anywhere else and created a dynasty by taking an interest in every level from first team down to the Under-9s. His Class of '92 was exceptional and may never be repeated.

He made United the go-to place for the best kids, which wasn't always the case before he arrived. Whenever I was out with Fergie though, he would tell me, 'Sam, managing United is hard work. You lose two in a row, it's a disaster.' He earned his retirement after given the game so much. The way he finished his career, winning the title by 11 points with a team which wasn't the best he ever had, spoke volumes.

Whoever followed Fergie into the Old Trafford hot-seat was going to find it almost impossible. Any new man wants to do it his own way, but you can't change everything, nor should you. Change has to be happen gradually, as I learned from my Newcastle experience where I tried to do too much too soon. Equally though, it's a job you cannot turn down. My former manager Ian Greaves, who was an ex-United player, got the Old Trafford job in 1977 after Tommy Docherty was sacked for having an affair with the physio's wife. Ian had brought all of us youngsters through at Bolton in the 1970s, the way Fergie did with his in the early 1990s. But when it was discovered Ian had just left his missus, they withdrew the offer because they thought it hypocritical to appoint him in the light of why they'd sacked Docherty. Greavsie was gutted.

David Moyes was Fergie's recommendation to succeed him and I thought he was the right choice. David had enjoyed 11 years at Everton but was ready for the next level, and it didn't come any bigger than United. I'd known David since driving all that way to watch him in Scotland and get him signed by Preston when no-one knew who he was. Now he had the best job in the game. Moyes was a centre-half and captain at Preston and always came across as a good organiser. When he became their manager, he almost got them into the Premier League only to be beaten by me in the play-off final, but his abilities were recognised by Everton and he more than lived up to their expectations. I invited him onto the LMA committee because I thought he would be an important voice for managers. He had plenty of opinions, wasn't shy in coming forward, and was another who cared about the plight of bosses in the lower leagues because he'd been there.

I didn't know he was getting the United job until the day it was announced. Both he and Fergie kept their cards close to their chests, but obviously Sir Alex saw in David someone who built teams the way he did and who could carry on his legacy without ripping apart the infra-structure. A foreign manager tends to be more short-term, coming in for two or three years, then moving on to the next project while British bosses aren't like that, unless they get sacked. It's easy to be wise in hindsight about why it didn't work out for Moyes, but he was unlucky that David Gill, the managing director who worked so closely with Sir Alex, left at the same time. Ed Woodward, who took over from Gill, was finding his feet too and they missed the boat in the transfer market over the summer. Then, after Moyes got sacked and Louis van Gaal arrived, the Dutchman was given hundreds of millions to spend. I'd have been pretty upset about that if I'd been Moyes.

Nobody was more disappointed it didn't work out for David than Sir Alex, and I'm sure there are some things Moyes wishes he'd done differently. When I spoke to him a few days later, he was very upset about it, especially as, unlike me, he'd never been sacked before. He felt he should have got longer than ten months in charge and that he would have got it right, but there is precious little patience in football today.

That's the volatile nature of the industry, and however unjust you feel the decision is, you have to deal with it and move on. It was sensible of David to go and work in Spain and get away from the attention in England. He could never have taken another Premier League job straight after United, because all the press would have been about his time at Old Trafford. Spain gave him the chance to breathe and come back a better manager.

● ● ●

With West Ham finishing so high in the table in our first season, it built up the fans' expectations. Our 46-point haul would have placed us only 13th the year before, which was more realistic of where we were in English football's hierarchy. If we were going to improve on 10th, that meant we would be pushing for a European place and I didn't feel we had anything like the quality to do that.

Joe Cole had returned to the club the previous January on a free from Liverpool and he helped get us off to a winning start to the 2013–14 campaign, scoring in our 2–0 home win over Cardiff. We then failed to win any of our next five, losing three as we plunged down the table. Maiga wasn't working as our front man, so as we prepared to face Spurs at White Hart Lane in October I came up with a plan – no strikers at all and a 4-6-0 formation. This was fraught with danger and I knew would invite enormous criticism if it didn't come off, but I thought it might just catch Tottenham out. Their manager André Villas-Boas was relatively inexperienced and planned meticulously, drilling his players exactly how to perform in different situations. But I was confident he wouldn't have planned for this and it would throw him. I couldn't have dreamed it would go so well, as we won 3–0 with all our goals coming in the second half, including an amazing solo special started from inside his own half by Ravel Morrison, a young man who was much talked about but rarely delivered due to his 'I'll do what I want, you won't tell me what to do' attitude. I told the television interviewer, 'Maybe the penny has finally dropped with Ravel.'

It was hoped that goal would spark life into Morrison after he was dumped by Manchester United. Fergie warned me he was a handful, but Sullivan wanted him and thought the risk was worth it. He reckoned I could change him based on what I'd done for similar types in the past. But I thought, 'If Fergie couldn't handle him, how am I going to do it?' Yet, after being on loan for a season at Birmingham, Rav seemed to knuckle down when he came back to us. He was getting out of bed on time, turning up to training every day, chasing people back and not just floating around in midfield, and generally applying himself correctly. The players went from not fancying him at all, or wanting to be anywhere near him, to, 'Okay, it looks like he's changed, let's see what the kid's made of.'

Stories emerged of a high-value release clause in his contract and that we had to quadruple his wages to £60,000 a week if we received a £10 million bid from another club. It was obvious Rav's agent was trying to cook up a £10 million offer to put pressure on us, but Karren Brady persuaded me and David Sullivan that it was too soon to give him a new deal. It was a big decision which proved to be correct. We were calling Rav's bluff and gambled that until he put in a series of consistent performances, no club would take that £10 million punt. His game went off the boil and the end for me came over Christmas when, after we'd played at Manchester United, Rav stayed up North to see his family and didn't come back. He wasn't injured, he just didn't fancy getting involved in our festive relegation battle. We couldn't get hold of him on the phone and then the lads saw a picture of him on Facebook enjoying Christmas lunch with the family while they were preparing for our Boxing Day game against Arsenal. Words can't describe what they thought of him. That was it for them and for me. Rav only had 18 months left on his deal and there was speculation he would leave in the January window, but nobody wanted him. David was convinced we could still change him but I said, 'You can get him going for a few games, but he will always go back to his old ways. He's not worth the trouble.'

When Rav returned, I sent him to train with the kids and eventually Harry Redknapp took him to QPR on loan, where he was driven round the bend by Morrison as well. Rav had these pals who were from outside football and would come down from Manchester to lead him astray – and he was easily led. Fergie thought the only chance I had of making Ravel see sense was getting rid of that gang of hangers-on, which I hadn't been able to do because they all lived in Manchester. But it made no difference in London, they just followed him and Ravel paid for them to do everything. These were even rumours that Rav was driving his friends around, which was interesting considering he didn't have a driving licence. But Rav always insisted he had a qualified driver with him, just like any other learner driver.

There's only so many times you can give someone a chance and only so far you can go. He had his idiosyncrasies too. When we went abroad he wouldn't eat the food or drink the water and would pack all his bags with baked beans and other tinned food. He also had absolutely rotten teeth. He wasn't capable of looking after himself and there was no one to do it for him. If I'd fined him every time he didn't turn up, he'd have had no wages at all.

Rav has plenty of ability, and was potentially a £50 million player, but he's blown his career. It is unlikely to happen for him now. He was likened to Paul Gascoigne and had Gazza's skill, but the comparison is unfair on Paul. Gazza wanted to play and train, Rav wasn't bothered. I do feel sorry for him, because he had a tough upbringing and didn't learn any life skills. I had endless conversations with him where he would nod, say 'Yes' and 'No problem, I'll do it,' but the minute he was out of the door he was back to his destructive ways. There were more important ways to spend my time than on someone who patently didn't want to change.

His attitude annoyed me all the more because we had a lot of injuries around Christmas, losing defensive stalwarts like James Collins and Winston Reid, so we were stretched as it was. We were in the pressure zone, 19th in the table and, with most of the football writers and their bosses seemingly West Ham fans, I was getting plenty of flak in the papers.

The integration of the media and football has changed. There are not so many close relationships between the press, managers and players any more. Both sides would probably blame each other, but it's the way the world is now. Younger journos build up contacts with agents, press officers and PR people rather than coaches and players and get a lot of their stories from websites and Twitter rumours. Most players would avoid journalists completely if they could, whereas we used to actively seek them out and I still have a lot of good friends in the industry: for the last 30 years I've regularly attended regional events with journalists and sports writers. But I would argue that the press focuses too much on off-field controversy, when in the past all you got criticised for was how you played. Very few of them can take criticism, even though they are always dishing it out. It makes me chuckle when they get on the defensive. The press boys are like managers though; the game's a drug to them and they cannot leave it alone. I've got far more respect for the ones who get out and cover the games and go to the events than the ones who've never left the office in their lives and write the poisonous stuff based on tittle-tattle.

Back in my management days at Bolton, I'd asked Alastair Campbell, the Labour spin doctor, for help in handling the media. I wanted to set the agenda rather than allow my inquisitors to do it, and who better to help than a man who'd been a key figure in national newspapers and in politics. He told me, 'You've got to think of the questions that are coming, Sam, and prepare yourself. If you don't want to answer a question, say anything which distracts and confuses them. When they complain "That's not the question I asked" make sure you're already moving on to the next point.' It was good advice and I learned to do it subconsciously, always conveying the message I wanted to deliver, not the one the media were after. If I wanted to stir it up, it was on my terms. Fergie taught me that trick. He believed the best way to take pressure off the players was to create controversy around himself, maybe by talking about the ref.

I've often wondered whether all the press attention around the Premier League makes the job appear harder than it is. Friends say to me, 'I don't know how you do it, I could never cope.' But then I think to myself, 'Is it really that difficult?' Because for all the pressures, and the ups and downs that go with it, I still don't consider football as work. From the day I started playing, it's been a joy being involved in the game. When I became a manager, I wanted to win but I also wanted my team to get as much joy out of football as I did. Players get knocked far too much. They are always being slagged off for not training hard enough, being too soft, and not caring.

Football is used as the world barometer and players are constantly criticised for earning too much money, yet when boxers Manny Pacquiao and Floyd Mayweather fight for £300 million nobody moans. Racing drivers like Lewis Hamilton are on £30 million a year, that's £600,000 a week, and there isn't a single footballer in England earning that sort of money. In fact, you can count on the fingers of one hand the number who earn half that. Golfer Rory McIlroy has a Nike contract worth £150 million over ten years. Top cricketers are earning good money as are darts players but, again, nothing's said. I know I go on about America, but no-one complains over there about what sportsmen earn in baseball, basketball or the NFL. Yet a top footballer pulls in, say, £10 million a year and there's a universal outcry. 'Oh, they are getting paid far too much.' No they're not, it's the market rate for the job.

The Premier league is the biggest sporting brand apart from the World Cup. Players make it the success it is by going out on the pitch week in week out and entertaining the public. Without them there is no game. I had a fantastic career and I don't care what the rewards are today compared to then, but I wouldn't want to be a player today. I would play in my time, not this time. You cannot take the dog for a walk today without somebody publicising it. There is no privacy whatsoever. We could have a social life, go out for a few beers, be a bit lively and nobody bothered. When players are seen with a beer in their hands now, they are instantly condemned as drunks. Everybody's watching them with camera phones and sticking it on social media. Whenever one of my old team-mates says, 'I wish I was making the money they're on now, my answer is, "Yeah, but we had a great time didn't we?" Sackfuls of money don't make up for that lack of freedom. There was a TV programme called *Who'd Be a Billionaire?* which revealed that the more money you have, the more insecure you are and the less real friends you have. I think there's a lot of truth in that.

Sullivan was another one feeling insecure – about our league position. 'Look,' I said, 'if it was my fault, I'd accept it but it isn't my fault. We can't cope with the injuries we've got, the squad's not big enough, it's that simple. If you don't want to accept that and you think it's an excuse, well that's entirely up to you. But that's the way it is. If it was my fault, I'd hold my hands up, but it's not. I'll tell you this, when we're all fit, we'll get out of it.' Despite our league struggles, another victory at Spurs propelled us into the semi-finals of the Capital One Cup. But we were thumped 5–0 in the third round of the FA Cup at Forest when I fielded a youthful team. David Sullivan wasn't happy and neither were the fans, but we didn't have enough strength to compete in two cups and escape relegation. There was also a contradiction in us being urged by the owners, fans and press to give the youngsters a chance. No wonder managers are reluctant to try it. When we lost 6–0 to Man City a few days later in the Capital One Cup semi-final first-leg, our visiting supporters really let us have it and me in particular. We were accused of lacking passion, but I didn't agree. Obviously I was desperate to get to the final, but our squad was depleted and it was beyond us. This was a City side which had already hit six against Norwich, Spurs and Arsenal, so we weren't the only ones they hammered.

There was lots of speculation that I was facing the sack as we went to Cardiff in mid-January. We were second bottom and they were three points above us. Carroll was back on the bench for the first time, with Carlton Cole, having deputised for him, opening the scoring. James Tomkins was sent off with 20 minutes left to reduce us to ten men but Noble finished them off in the 90th minute, converting Carroll's pass. It was our first win since the end of November and lifted us out of the relegation zone. Although we contrived to lose 3–1 at home to Newcastle, producing more 'Pressure Cranks Up on Allardyce' headlines, we followed up with a fantastic run starting with a 0–0 draw at Chelsea. José Mourinho didn't like it one bit. 'This is not the best league in the world, this is football from the 19th century, only one team wanted to win,' he whinged. Mourinho was blaming us for his team's incompetence but was embarrassed he hadn't wiped the floor with us, which is what Chelsea should have done when you looked at the two line-ups. I'd won the mental battle with him, my plan had been tactically better than his, with a team which cost a quarter of the price of his.

I felt we were at a turning point and said on TV, 'He can't take it, can he? He can't take it because we've outwitted him – he just can't cope. He can tell me all he wants, I don't care. I love to see Chelsea players moaning at the referee, trying to intimidate him, José jumping up and down saying we play rubbish football. It's brilliant when you get a result against him. Hard luck, José.' Then the writers asked me what I thought of his comments and I replied, 'I don't give a shit what José thinks.' Mourinho's a pragmatist like me, he knew we'd done a great job on him.

I've always found the Portuguese to be more volatile than the English, and more reactive, whereas we English are more down to earth and less likely to blow our tops. But I will concede that José is a far better manager than me. He's succeeded against all the odds and wasn't even a player. His achievements across Europe are incredible and I find it laughable when Chelsea get labelled boring. If your team wins the Premier League by eight points, it's not boring.

We followed up the Chelsea result with a fabulous February during which Nobby scored five goals in four games, all of which we won, against Swansea, Villa, Norwich and Southampton. We achieved three of those victories without Carroll, who had been sent off for swinging an arm in the general direction of Swansea's Chico Flores. It was a ludicrous decision by ref Howard Webb. Flores, who had previous for play-acting, went down holding his face, yet Andy barely touched him. We wanted to take the decision all the way to court but stepped back and had to accept a three-match ban. Those wins sent us shooting up the table to 10th to end any relegation worries. From supposedly being on the brink of the sack, I was named manager of the month.

But football was the last thing on our minds in April when our brave young Australian striker Dylan Tombides died of cancer at the age of 20. It left everyone connected with West Ham absolutely devastated. Dylan joined West Ham when he was 15 and made it onto the bench for a Premier League game against Sunderland when he was only 17. Wally Downes told me when I arrived that he was the best of the bunch in the academy. Dylan's younger brother, Taylor, was in our academy too and the whole family had moved to England to support their children's dreams of playing professional football. The alarm about Dylan was first raised when he failed a drugs test playing for the Australian youth team and it turned out the abnormal result was a sign of testicular cancer. He seemed to make a good recovery and got back playing, but our club doctor Richard Weller warned me, 'I think this may have been caught too late.'

The cancer spread to Dylan's liver and he would go away for treatment then come back with no hair, all thin, and ghostly white, and build himself back up again to play. He was a phenomenal battler. 'I want to get back training, gaffer. I can do it,' he would say. When his blood count was wrong, he went back into hospital before returning again. He was determined to keep going. I decided that if he was strong enough we'd name him among the subs for a Capital One Cup game against Wigan. Dylan got on for the last six minutes of a game where we performed dreadfully to lose 4–1, but the most important thing about that night was that Dylan achieved his goal of playing for the West Ham first team. He never played for us again, but he couldn't have fought harder. He had part of his liver cut away and his dad, Jim, told me, 'All he talks about is getting back training, that's what keeps him going.' Meanwhile the doc was saying, 'I can't tell you how much this lad must be suffering. It's sapping everything out of his body.' It was only because he was young, fit and strong that he was able to cope with the treatment, but we all knew he couldn't keep on doing it.

His family sought alternative therapy in Germany but it didn't work and Dylan passed away. We were at the training ground when the doc gave us the sad news. You see some lads frittering away a promising career but Dylan did everything he could in the face of insurmountable odds to make it in professional football. The following day we played Crystal Palace and Dylan's dad and brother walked onto the pitch with his number 38 shirt held aloft, before laying it in the centre spot. There was a minute's applause to commemorate his life and later we all went to his funeral which was extremely upsetting. We retired Dylan's number in his memory. The only other West Ham player ever to have a number retired was Bobby Moore when the club handed his number 6 shirt to his widow Stephanie, on the 50th anniversary of his debut, so Dylan is resting in peace in good company.

His passing led me to reflect on other times in my life where death affected me. Lynne's dad going at 54 made me realise you had to live for the day and enjoy it as much as you could. Gary Speed's suicide got me thinking too. Then there was the young lad who was killed outside the Reebok when I was Bolton manager. He was only 14 and was prac-tising on a motorbike at the back of the car park with his mum and dad watching. As he went round the corner, he didn't notice a chain across the entrance and flew straight into it, slitting his throat, and taking his helmet clean off in the process. I didn't see it happen but someone came running over, asking if I had a mobile and to call 999. I was trained in first aid and tried to stem the blood flow while ringing for an ambulance. The operator asked me if he was breathing but there was nothing, I couldn't do anything for him. When the ambulance turned up, the paramedics performed CPR while his parents stood there screaming. It was awful and I had nightmares about it for weeks afterwards. Another time we were in Japan on tour with Bolton when I was walking through the shopping centre in Kobe and heard a blood-curdling cry followed by a sickening thud. I looked round and there was a body lying smashed on the ground. The bloke had thrown himself off the top level. That shook me up for a while as well.

● ● ●

Back on the field, we beat Spurs for the third time in the season in our second-last game and the fans were singing, '*Can We Play You Every Week,*' but there were still rumours going around that I would be fired. Those rumours intensified when Sullivan got up on stage at our player of the year dinner and apologised to the fans that the team hadn't been good enough during the season. I felt that was unnecessary. We had guests there who had paid a lot of money to attend and he got the night's proceedings off to a disappointing start by being negative.

The *Daily Mail* said I would definitely be relieved of my duties after our final game at Man City and used a picture on their website of some fans holding a banner which read, 'Fat Sam Out. Killing WHU'. They even named the date of the meeting when I would be told by David Gold and David Sullivan that it was over. If this was true, the owners certainly hadn't told me. I saw no reason why I should be axed, but it felt like the paper was willing it to happen. Several sports journalists had a direct line to Sullivan so there was something going on, and when I went to David's house and saw the TV cameras outside, I was expecting the bullet.

'*I DID ALL THAT I WAS ASKED*' 20

It was showdown time. Karren Brady and the two Davids were waiting inside Sullivan's house and there was an extremely frank discussion. I told Sullivan how unhappy I was about his speech at the player of the year dinner while he expressed his disappointment that the season hadn't gone as he would have liked. Brady and Gold nodded in agreement.

'I don't know what you expect, because I've delivered everything you wanted,' I said. 'You gave me two years to get us up and I did it in one. You said you wanted us to consolidate in the Premier League and I've done that. If you want us to play better, give me some more money and we will play better because we'll bring in more quality players.'

They asked if I had the drive for it. I'd proved that a hundred times over. They said the fans weren't happy but, as I'd explained, that wasn't just about me, it had been the same for previous managers.

'It's how West Ham is,' I said. 'They aren't happy no matter who the manager is.' None of the players would admit it but they used to sit in the dressing room at half-time going, 'Listen to them, never fucking happy, slaughtering us all the time.' I had to tell them to forget the fans, and that they would come round if we played better. So Sullivan says: 'Give us five days while we think about it.' I could have told them to stick it I suppose, but I felt I deserved to keep my job.

A few days later, Karren rang and said, 'You're fine but give us some ideas about engaging with the fans better and how we might take the club forward.' Gold and Sullivan put a statement on the club website which said, 'We have a very clear vision of how we want West Ham United to operate under our joint ownership . . . Sam was asked to give us a detailed presentation on his vision for next season and during this he assured us that he can deliver that ethos to West Ham United and we have agreed to support him with the resources he needs. We have mapped out a way forward with him that will ensure our much-deserving fans have more to cheer about next season . . . Sam deserves credit for the job he has done thus far after securing promotion in his first year and two respectable Premier League finishes in the two years thereafter . . . The 2014–15 campaign is crucial to our future and we are confident that Sam has the passion, experience and determination to make sure it is a success.'

I had no objection to making things even better if they were prepared to support me. Their desire for an attacking coach was music to my ears.

I wanted one too. I'd let Wally Downes go midway through our first season in the Premier League because he wasn't suited to being a coach. He wanted to be assistant manager but that was Macca's job, and while I liked Wally and enjoyed his company and respected his knowledge, he wasn't fulfilling the role he was paid for. He was getting bored and complacent and it was best if he left and found himself a manager or assistant's job somewhere else. He didn't take it well. 'I can't fucking believe this,' were his exact words, if I recall. It was my decision alone, and the right one for West Ham.

I went looking for my attacking coach and thought about Ian Wright and Tony Cottee who were both former West Ham players but in the end went for Teddy Sheringham, who I'd known for years and first come across when I was captain of Millwall and he was an apprentice in the youth team. He tells me that the first time we met, he was a kid helping the kit-man with first-team duties and when I invited him into my hotel room to collect my dirty kit I was standing there stark bollock naked, as I towelled myself down. It was assumed Teddy had left the game for good and gone off to be a professional card player, but he was also doing his coaching badges with one eye on a return to football. Teddy integrated with the backroom team quickly and gave us a new perspective. Despite his pedigree as an international striker who played over 50 games for England and won the Champions League with Manchester United, he was nervous when he first started. Players will test you out, whoever you are, but I told him to be strong and believe in what he was doing and not let the players take the mickey. They had no business doing so either. Teddy's natural eye for goal was not something which could be taught, but the intelligence he had for finding space in the area, even though he wasn't quick, was something all the front men could learn from.

One thing I couldn't control was the board getting rid of my sports psychologist, Lee Richardson. I was well pissed off about that. Lee was a former player and manager in the lower leagues who tapped into the mental side of the game, but Karren didn't agree with my assessment of his value to us. The workings of the mind are important in professional sport. You only have to look at snooker's Ronnie O'Sullivan, a tormented genius to see that. Dr Steve Peters, who has worked with England's football team and the GB Olympic set-up, was crucial to him even getting to the table let alone winning. They didn't get why Lee would not reveal details about the players' thoughts. The fact was he wasn't allowed to do so because he was bound by medical confidentiality. I lived by the 5 Ps – Perfect Practice Prevents Poor Performances. Taking away my psychologist made my job harder. I knew he was effective because otherwise the players wouldn't have bothered going to see him. It takes a special type to get into the mind of a footballer and we'd lost an important member of staff.

We needed an overhaul on the playing side so we said goodbye to Joe Cole, whose contract had expired, and Jack Collison, who was such a talent but not the same player after his injury. For Cole, a Hammers legend, it was the end of his second spell at the club and one which I had hoped would work out better than it did. His agent David Geiss, who I always got on well with, told me how much Joe had wanted to come back, with the bonus that Liverpool would pay most of his wages.

It was a no-brainer. When Joe turned up at Chadwell Heath he said, 'It hasn't changed a bit, boss!' It hadn't, more's the pity. Joe was a chirpy character with medals and plenty of England caps to his name, but the challenge was to keep him fit. He suffered so many niggling injuries, a slight muscle tear here, a little strain there. They played on his mind and he would take longer than others to declare himself fit, even when the physio thought he was okay. When he was playing, though, he wanted to do it all. I had to remind him he was in his 30s, not his 20s. 'Bloody slow down, Joe!' I'd be shouting. By the end though he wasn't influencing games, wasn't getting enough touches and wasn't getting enough goals. Maybe the wear and tear caught up with him. He was only 17 when he made his Premier League debut and had played 150 games for West Ham by the time he was 21, before he was signed by Chelsea. That takes its toll in later life.

Most players only perform at their best for a decade. If you are in the team at 17, you tend to start declining after the age of 27. There are exceptions but not many. A player's body suffers throughout those ten years, especially if you're an international. The body is bound to crumble when you think of the equation 60 games x 10 years with only three or four weeks off each summer. Joe might have been better using his experience and adapting his game, but that wasn't him. When you're over 30 and you get injuries it takes a couple of games to get back in your stride, and we didn't have the luxury to allow players to do that. Joe was often quoted in the papers saying, 'I'm as good and fit as I ever was,' but it didn't look like it to me.

We found a powerful midfielder in Cheik Kouyaté from Anderlecht, a cracking left-back, Aaron Cresswell, from Ipswich, an exciting Ecuadorian attacker, Enner Valencia, right-back Carl Jenkinson on loan from Arsenal, Diafra Sakho from Metz who was one David wanted, and, on deadline, Alex Song on loan from Barcelona, and finally Morgan Amalfitano from Marseille. I didn't know it at the time, but this turned out to be my best recruitment drive whilst at West Ham.

Jenkinson's signing was interesting. He was represented by Andy Niedzwiecki, whose dad Eddie was first-team coach to Mark Hughes at Stoke. So when Andy rang me to see if I was interested I naturally asked:

'How come he's not going to Stoke?'

'We've tried that and Dad wanted him but Carl wants to stay in London,' said Andy.

I mention this merely to show how sons and fathers work together in football, just like Craig had with me. There's nothing sinister in it and Andy did a good job for us. We got Kouyaté through our Belgian head of sports science Stijn Vandenbroucke and our chief scout Martin Glover. I'd seen Kouyaté play but didn't think we'd have a chance of getting him. He was like Patrick Vieira, strong, skilful and impossible to knock off the ball. Fortunately, Stijn's wife had relatives who owned Anderlecht and we pulled off the deal. Valencia was on our radar before the 2014 World Cup and scored against England in a warm-up game which alerted a few people. But we got him when the World Cup finished. I don't mind admitting I wanted Connor Wickham from Sunderland too. He was underperforming for them, but I felt we would play to his strengths and he would get us goals and assists the way

Kevin Davies did for Bolton. Sunderland wouldn't play ball though, despite us being encouraged to go for it by his agent who was sure they would let him leave for £8 million. It turned out that wasn't the case. David Sullivan had been recommended Diafra Sakho, who was playing League 2 football in France but we were running out of options. We watched tapes of his goals which helps but is never a perfect guide, but there was something there and I told David, 'If you want to take the risk, then let's do it.' Sakho was a big success, unlike David's other suggestion, Mauro Zárate, who he had when he owned Birmingham.

The capture of Song was a surprise to the football world. He hadn't been playing regularly for Barcelona, but was a quality player with a good Premier League pedigree from his time at Arsenal. His knees weren't in the best of shape though. He was hardly ever off the treatment table and found it difficult to perform consistently, as the workload took its toll. But, in the early part of the season, he was magnificent.

●　●　●

We went to New Zealand for a pre-season tour, which was a big mistake. It's a lovely country, but it took too long to get there and we picked up seven injuries in the space of a fortnight, including another one to Andy Carroll who damaged his ankle ligaments. We lost both games too and David Sullivan's going, 'That's not very good for season tickets, Sam, we've got to do better than this.' The move to the Olympic

Stadium in 2016 added to the pressure. West Ham were committed to selling Upton Park and taking on the new facility, and it was an absolute must they were still in the Premier League two years down the line.

I knew there was a big focus on me, and that if we didn't start well I was out. I gave myself ten games maximum, possibly as few as six. There was one gone when we lost our first match of the season at home to Spurs to a goal in added time, but there was a rare Noble miss from the penalty spot and we played well so I remained optimistic. A victory at Crystal Palace the following week supported my beliefs and, although we were knocked out of the Capital One Cup by Sheffield United on penalties and slipped up at home again, to Southampton, we followed up with a well-earned draw at Hull. That game well and truly signalled the arrival of Valencia who fired a remarkable goal, from 25 yards, into the top corner without any backlift whatsoever. Enner struggled to adapt to the demands of the Premier League and the exertions of the World Cup told on him, so that by Christmas he was absolutely wasted.

Our next home game was a cracker as we stuffed Liverpool 3–1, and we had a sensational October, winning all three games against QPR, Burnley and the champions Manchester City. That got me manager of the month again, for the second time in nine months, which earned me a hug and a kiss on TV from Hammers fanatic Russell Brand. 'Give this man the credit he deserves,' said Russell. Who was I to argue? Sakho got the winner against City with a header and he was in a rich vein of form. His spring was incredible and he could hang in the air like Les Ferdinand in his prime. He was five inches shorter than Carroll but was better at getting between defenders. He just knew instinctively where to be and was brave with it too. He scored in each of his first six games to set a club record.

We were playing some great stuff, using a new diamond formation with Downing at its tip, and in Spanish keeper Adrian we had found the replacement for Jussi who was approaching his 40th birthday. Mark Curtis had tipped us off the previous season that Adrian was coming to the end of his contract and fancied a move to England. He was 26 and had only played one full season in La Liga with Real Betis, but Martin Margetson and Martin Glover checked him out and both thought he looked the part. Finally, I went to watch him play in Seville, praying 'Please don't let him be crap.' His angles, positioning, and authority were all there. One of the best parts of his game was that he saved shots with every part of his body. There are keepers who are so concerned about technique they forget that the priority is to ensure the ball stays out of the net, it doesn't matter how. If the best way to stop the ball going in was to kick it away, he would.

We took Adrian out afterwards with his girlfriend, and we made him and his partner feel wanted. The best chance of getting a transfer done is to see the player and his partner together, otherwise he might go away and think about it and you can lose him. The personal touch helped clinch the deal, which is something clubs forget. They will spend millions on a player and wonder why you've spent £400 expenses on a meal out with him. That £400 can be the difference between the player signing or going elsewhere.

Keepers mature later than outfield players, and as Adrian was free he was well worth a punt. There's nothing better than delivering a signing like that for your owners. I would have liked more money to spend, but there's real satisfaction when a deal like Adrian's proves so successful. Though Jussi was getting on in years, I was sorry for him losing his place because he had done so much for me over the years. But he was thoroughly professional about it, got his head round being number two, and when he stepped in for Adrian he never let us down. He came on at Southampton after Adrian was sent off and made three stunning saves to get us a point.

Downing meanwhile had a three-month spell where he was unstoppable, scoring goals, making them and earning a recall to the England squad. England buggered him up though. They gave him a painkilling injection in his knee before the game against Scotland and he had to be subbed at half-time. He subsequently missed the following league game against Everton, and I was really angry about that.

The diamond system leaves you open to conceding goals, and the more adventurous we became, the more vulnerable we were at the back. But we were winning more than we were losing, so we persisted with it. When we beat Swansea 3–1 in early December, with Carroll scoring a couple of headers, we were third in the league.

Ironically, that was the moment I realised they would never be satisfied at West Ham whatever I did. Carroll's return led to whispers that we were changing our style again, away from the fluid football we'd produced earlier in the season. It was rubbish; Carroll just gave us another dimension. He scored again as we beat Leicester and we went into our Boxing Day fixture at Chelsea in fourth place. I rested Song and Sakho, but we lost and there were a few grumbles, and two days later when we were beaten at home by Arsenal there was more complaining from the fans and the board. You could hear supporters behind the dugout going, 'Fucking get back up North, you Northern bastard,' which I presume was directed at me, unless it was Nobby Nolan! I didn't turn around, I didn't want to give them the satisfaction. I wish I could have done Harry Redknapp's trick. At a friendly match, he gave a critical fan a spare pair of boots and told him to go on and prove he could do better himself.

We were suffering for our early season brilliance. Fatigue was bound to kick in at some point and for the new boys like Valencia it was too much. I made up my mind this would be my last season at West Ham and told Lynne so. I knew David Moyes had been contacted about taking my job and there were probably several others. We could only go so far on the budget and I couldn't work out what the fans or the board wanted. We couldn't have performed any better than we did in the first half of the season, but still I wasn't doing it the West Ham Way. We were still too 'long ball' when we had Carroll in the team apparently, and even though he showed his skill with a great goal in our draw at Swansea, chesting it down, flicking the ball on and sticking it in the top corner, it wasn't enough to alter such stubborn opinion.

By mid-January, the flak was getting ridiculous. We'd had a tough FA Cup win over Everton during the week, which we squeaked through on penalties, and were loudly booed off at half-time against Hull before finishing up 3–0 winners. I was not in a good mood afterwards and lost it in the press conference. 'All this tippy-tappy stuff and everybody going on about the right way to play football, it's all a load of old bollocks. Getting the ball in the opposition's box as quickly as you can with quality is sometimes the best way.' We were still seventh in the table and only four points off fourth-placed Man United.

We played well in the second half of the season too, but results didn't go for us and we kept drawing games by conceding late goals, like the 92nd minute equaliser at home to Man United, or the 96th minute leveller by Harry Kane at Spurs, when the ref's watch must have stopped. In the United game, injuries meant we had to play Kayouté at centre-back, but he scored by flicking the ball up and turning, before shooting past David De Gea. United brought on Marouane Fellaini, knocked balls up to him in the penalty area and a poor header by Jenkinson fell to Blind at the death who scored in the corner. United had got away with it and everyone knew it. I said afterwards that when people claim I'm a long-ball man, they should remember what Van Gaal had done to us. 'Their equaliser just came from a long punt up the middle,' I said. I obviously got under Louis' skin and a few days later he went off on a right rant, handing reporters a four-page dossier to refute my claims.

He said: 'When a colleague of mine is saying this kind of thing, then you have to see the data and you have to put the data in the right context. When you have nearly 60 percent of ball possession, do you think that you can do that with long balls? I have made an interpretation of the data from this game and then I have to say that it is not a good interpretation from Big Sam. I am sorry, but we are playing ball possession play and after 70 minutes we did not succeed, in spite of many chances in the second half, then I changed my playing style. Then, of course, with the quality of Fellaini we played more forward balls and we scored from that, so I think it was a very good decision of the manager.'

In other words, he started hitting it long to force the equaliser. Here was yet another big-name manager who couldn't take it when I got a result against them. Just as with Wenger and Mourinho, a long ball by Van Gaal's team was a clever switch in tactics, but when I did it I was destroying the game. It was laughable.

The Spurs equaliser was even harder to take. We'd been walloped 4–0 by West Brom in the FA Cup the previous week, and there was the usual cobblers about my job being on the line. I'd agreed with the owners that we wouldn't talk about the future until the end of the season. But the press kept writing I was anxious about not getting a new deal, which I wasn't. It didn't matter, I wasn't staying. We were a different team at White Hart Lane and went two-up through Kouyaté and Sakho. But, after Danny Rose pulled one back with nine minutes left, we retreated and were hanging on before Kane went down in the box under the softest of challenges from Song. Adrian saved Kane's penalty but he followed up to score.

We played great at home to Chelsea but lost 1–0 and conceded another late one against Stoke, for whom Marko Arnautovic netted in the 95th minute to make it 1–1. As if that wasn't enough, in our last home game of the season Romelu Lukaku headed home in the 93rd minute to give Everton a 2–1 win. We must have tossed away 10 or 11 points after Christmas.

In the lead-up to the Everton match, I'd taken time out to look back on my four years in charge and defended my record. 'I have had a great time here, I have enjoyed myself, I have enjoyed London and I have done what I was asked to do, which was deliver a team that, this time round, has not only been the most successful but the most entertaining, and the most thrilling. It is the youngest squad we have put together since I have been here. If you want somebody else to do more than I have done, then I think you will have to be calling for Houdini.' I then told everyone I would begin negotiations by asking for a two-year contract, knowing full well I'd be gone in ten days.

After the Everton defeat I added, 'We've been in danger of relegation for about six weeks in three years. I'm going to get my team ready for next week and then a decision will be made. I'm 60. I don't have to worry about my position. I don't have anything to prove.'

We lost our last game at Newcastle. My mate Steve Bruce, the manager of Hull, needed to beat Man United and for Newcastle to lose, to survive relegation. I would never have forgiven myself if Hull had won and we hadn't helped him out. As it happened it didn't matter, but I still felt for him. On the basis of our position earlier in the season, we should have finished ninth at worst. Instead we were 12th, but it was still our best points return in three years in the Premier League. Mark Curtis had spoken to David Sullivan on the Friday and I'd rung David on the Saturday morning. We had a frank discussion and I thanked him for the opportunity, and we both agreed that the time was right for us to go our separate ways. 'It's right for both of us, Sam,' he said. As I headed down the tunnel at Newcastle, I approached the TV cameras to tell them I was leaving but the board beat me to it, releasing a statement the second the final whistle blew at St James' to say my contract wasn't being renewed. I didn't have to worry about the West Ham Way any longer.

TAFFS, MICKS AND JOCKS

21

My departure from Upton Park at the end of the 2014–15 season was interpreted as a victory for West Ham fans. But I never met one who told me to my face that I should go.

There was an overly loud minority at games and a few saddos on keyboards. Fans can drive you mad, but they are what make the game tick, football cannot survive without them and they've always had a go at players and managers since time began. The atmosphere they create is essential to the success of the product and football needs to realise that it has to be affordable to supporters, otherwise the game dies. It's not enough for money to be rolling in from TV income, because it looks terrible on screen if teams are playing in an empty stadium because no-one can afford to go. Football should never be complacent and take the spectator for granted.

We've got to keep the best players too and attract all the major stars to the Premier League instead of letting them go to Barcelona or Real

Madrid, or interest will decline. And we must continually strive to ensure the product is as good as it can possibly be, otherwise it will lose out to competition from other sports and activities. Fans want to get their ticket without any hassle, to travel to the ground with as little trouble as possible, to get a drink as soon as possible, and not have to stand in a great long queue for a pie. For their hard-earned money they want to be looked after, and if they aren't they become frustrated before the game starts which, in turn, makes them more angry than they should be and probably leads to unreasonable expectations of their team once the game kicks off.

Fans were treated like rubbish in my playing days, as if they were lucky to be there at all. They turned up anyway because there wasn't anything else to do, but now football has to give them a good reason to come or they won't bother. We also need to find ways of getting more families in, because that breeds the next generation of supporter. Football is sleepwalking, the average age of supporters is getting older and older. England is further ahead than many European countries in giving the fan a more enjoyable experience at games, but if they have Sky, BT Sport and go to games too, that is an expensive business. We don't want everyone becoming an armchair supporter and then switching off entirely if the product is crap.

Look at the decline in viewers for Italy's Serie A. I don't watch it at all nowadays, when at one time I was glued to it. Fortunately, we still have the best league for entertainment, not Spain. The reason the Spanish changed their TV deal to give a bigger share to clubs lower down the table is because La Liga has lost its competitive edge. There is only

313

Barcelona, Real Madrid and Atletico that matter, and I'd bet David Moyes would agree too even though he works out there. In Germany, Bayern Munich are taking over completely and it makes the league boring. In England though, every game matters, every match is an event. On a given day, anyone can beat anyone.

We must be careful we don't stop all the banter in our stadiums though, or we sanitise football too much. Of course, some chants are deeply offensive and rightly stamped on, but I remember the former French defender Frank Leboeuf encouraging people to call him 'The Frog'. In my playing days we had Taffs, Micks and Jocks in the team and that's how they were referred to – they certainly didn't take offence. Now, even if you swear during the heat of a game the PC brigade are on your case. The most burgeoning area of a football club today is the HR department. They sent round letters at West Ham saying, 'Using foul and abusive language towards a fellow employee may result in you being warned or sacked.' If they had pursued that order to its natural conclusion, there would have been no-one at the training ground. Football has always used industrial language, it is part of day-to-day life in the changing room, but those wanting to end it aren't in the real world. I was even warned at West Ham to be careful what I referred to as 'banter' because to someone else it might be deemed verbal abuse. So if a player went to HR and said, 'The manager swore at me,' I would have been hauled over the coals. Call me old fashioned, call me a dinosaur, but that's crap. Fortunately, most players are a little more sensible than that, but it only takes one disgruntled individual who's been dropped to complain about the manager's language and there's trouble.

Everyone in football is scared of their own shadow now. I said on Sky Sports that my players had got 'a bollocking' and Chris Kamara and Ben Shephard were twitching like fried eggs, apologising for any offence caused and explaining to viewers that the word meant 'a ticking off'. Come on, can't we all grow up? I see verbal abuse, racial abuse and all manner of disgraceful stuff going out on Twitter and Facebook to millions of people every day, but nobody is getting to grips with that.

We are even warned to be careful with nicknames in football nowadays in case they are deemed offensive. But if the receiver doesn't take offence, I don't see the problem. I've played with Gonk Head, Tefal Head, Dopey, Trigger, Plug, Squirt, you name them. Shall I go suing everyone who calls me 'Big Fat Sam'? Do me a favour. I get even angrier away from football when we're told we shouldn't refer to it as 'Christmas' any more, it should be 'The Festive Season'. What is this country coming to?

The big problem is that the art of conversation is dying. The subtleties and nuances of language are being lost in 140 characters. I watch the players on the coach and none of them talk to each other or, if they do, they do it by text. The minute they sit down they whip out their phones and start tapping away or listening to their music and they are lost for the length of the journey. They put their phones away for training and games but that's all, the rest of the time they are engrossed by a little screen. They are always comparing how many followers they've got, and of course there's method in the madness. If you've got six million Twitter followers, companies will pay a lot for you to promote their products. Even when they have a meal, they take a picture of it and pass it round their followers. Who wants to see a picture of someone's dinner? I know I'm sounding like a grumpy old man, but I really don't get it.

● ● ●

I went on a few holidays and did some TV work after leaving West Ham. The TV is something I enjoy and maybe I will spend more time on it, but I don't like to be controversial for the sake of it. I say what I believe. TV likes you to stir it up but that's not my style, I'm true to myself and if that proves controversial then okay, but I won't fake it. Punditry is a fantastic industry for ex-players to earn a living from, because undoubtedly some find it a struggle when they are not directly involved in the game. They can turn to alcohol or gambling and their family breaks up. The pundits today put a great deal of work into their preparation too. It's not just a case of turning up to the studio five minutes beforehand. Jamie Carragher and Gary Neville are real students of football and I like listening to them, particularly on Sky Sports on a Monday night when they can make even the dullest match interesting. The way they review all the weekend's games is both informative and entertaining, to the point where they could probably get away with just Jamie and Gary and no live match because they make compelling viewing on their own.

Pundits do annoy managers and players though. I took Robbie Savage to task for having a go about me and asked him, 'How do you know? You've never been a manager.' I may have achieved the impossible by shutting Robbie up for five seconds. In fairness, he has done well to create a niche for himself. He is his own man and doesn't care two hoots whether you love him or hate him.

When it comes to commentators I've always admired the BBC's John Motson, who is good company with a great knowledge of the game, as is Sky's Martin Tyler along with Clive Tyldesley and Jon Champion. I enjoyed doing co-commentaries with Martin, which is an art in itself, knowing when to speak, when to stay silent and how to put your information and obser-vations across. I also liked working in the studio with Andy Gray and Richard Keys when they were on Sky. They were sacked for off-air comments about lineswoman Sian Massey, but in my own personal experience they were the best double-act in TV sport. Richard is a first-class presenter and there is no better football expert than Gray.

For the record, I haven't got a problem with lineswomen. I don't notice if the person running the line is male or female and I don't think fans do either. I expect we'll see a woman referee in the Premier League one day. I don't think we'll see a woman manager in English football in my lifetime though – and that's not because they wouldn't be able to do the job but more because there are so many foreign managers in our game now that they are squeezing out the male English bosses as it is, before we even get to female ones. I don't expect to see a female player competing in the men's game either. Physically, I'm not convinced they could cope even if technically some of them are very skilled, and I don't think even women think it is a good idea. The England Women's team were outstanding in their World Cup and did so much to promote the female game that the opportunity is there for them to build on that progress. It would be nice if the men could copy them and be as successful in the 2018 World Cup.

On another pertinent subject, there have been questions about whether a gay footballer will come out while still an active player in this country. I reckon it will happen, but it's not easy being the first. It would be accepted, no problem, in the dressing room, but it's a fact of life that there would be a reaction from opposing fans and it would take a strong individual to deal with that.

As for referees, I want to see them getting more help and I'm all for more technology in the game. We are too slow to embrace it. Look how long it took to bring in the cameras to decide whether the ball was over the goal-line. It's saved a stack of trouble and should have happened ten years ago. I don't agree it would slow the game down. The referee can have a great game for 89 minutes, but if he makes one wrong decision he's had a stinker. They have to get the big decisions right which is why they need technology, but it needs thinking through so we can all decide how best to employ it. Most refs I know would welcome it.

An official needs to be able to manage players with confidence and for me that management skill has been omitted from the development and learning process of the referees today. There used to be give and take on both sides, but now it's much more regimented. In my playing days, you could have a go at the likes of Neil Midgley, my favourite man in black, and say, 'You're having a shocker, ref.' And he'd say, 'You're not playing so well yourself, Sam. I'm doing better than you.' He wouldn't book you but he had put you in your place. Jack Taylor, from my neck of the woods in Wolverhampton, was a great ref too. He officiated at the 1974 World Cup final and operated differently from Neil but was just as effective. Jack wasn't such a banter man, he was more 'Don't mess with me, I know what I'm doing, I know how to do it better than you, so you get on with your job and I'll get on with mine.'

A ref's job is much harder these days. A perfectly good tackle where the player takes the ball can result in a foul being awarded and a yellow card if the player is deemed to be showing too much commitment. How on earth can you stop yourself following through on a tackle? It's unnatural. I used to get a compliment from the ref for a tackle like that, not a booking. If somebody pulls an opponent's arm it's a straight yellow, even if it's just a little tug. The TV commentators are demanding a yellow card the moment it happens, which puts pressure on in itself.

When a penalty is awarded, is it really necessary to red-card the offender as happens most of the time? The penalty is enough in most cases, unless it's the result of violent conduct. Handball on the line shouldn't be a sending-off, the defender hasn't put anyone in danger. When games are reduced to 11 v 10, they are spoiled. We want 11 v 11 as much as we can.

As for offside . . . don't get me started on that one! Good grief, it was so much simpler when offside was offside. Now it's about whether the player is interfering with play, or coming back to onside, or was it a second phase? As Bill Nicholson, Bill Shankly and Brian Clough used to say, 'If he's not interfering with play, what is he doing on the pitch?' I don't care whether the offender is by the corner flag or in the penalty area, if he is ahead of the defence when the ball is played he is offside, end of. Let's not try to complicate the game. There is too much for the officials to process and too much doubt.

Mike Riley, the head of the referees, has a major influence and must know there are not enough top-quality officials. He should be recruiting youngsters into an academy where they are trained like players are and bring them through. There are also lots of young players who get released and could be offered the opportunity to stay in the game by taking up refereeing. They have experienced professional football, they know the game and could forge a whole new career. Isn't that better than going on the dole? It's a job which can take you round the world and you could end up reffing the FA Cup final or even the World Cup final. I don't know any top-class referee who doesn't love the job. They are like players; once they hang up their boots, they miss it.

While refs are often perceived as the bad guys, that is nothing compared to agents who get such a bad press yet are so important to every club in the world. There are good and bad ones, and my man Mark Curtis is one of the good ones. It all started at Blackpool when he rang and said, 'I believe you're looking for a goalkeeper?' and he got me Steve Banks from Gillingham. Mark was quite naive football-wise at that time but a confident bloke who was one of the first mobile phone salesmen and had that seller's patter. I liked him, especially when he went the extra mile to make sure Banksy got properly settled in the area, organising a mortgage and his house for him.

There are two types of agent, one who acts as a broker moving players around and wants nothing else to do with them, while the other type looks after their lives. When I got sacked by Blackpool, Mark invited and Lynne and me down to London for a couple of days and said, 'If I can ever help you out, I will,' which he did when he found me the Notts County job. Our relationship grew from there. Managers and players need an agent, because it prevents them being the bad guy. Send him in to do contract negotiations on your behalf and the chairman thinks, 'That agent's a bit of a bastard.'

If you go in yourself and haggle, the chairman thinks you're the evil one.

Agents are invaluable for alerting you to when certain players are available and you can check the scouting reports to see if they are what you want. They are like cats in a sack though, jealous of each other's contacts and seem to spend too much time ripping each other apart when, if they worked together, they might get more deals done. They are always complaining about being ripped-off by one another. Sometimes there are three or four agents involved in a transfer from abroad and it's a nightmare for the buying club working out who to deal with. Players make life so difficult for themselves. If every player had one official contract with an agent on a regulated website it would be simple, but it doesn't work like that. When I was at Blackburn, Chris Samba was paying four agents and would have been broke if we hadn't stepped in to sort it out. But some players are hopeless, they don't want to take responsibility, not even when they have the PFA available offering free legal advice. There is a misconception that all football agents earn millions, but the vast majority don't. Some might do only one deal a year and, if it falls through, they're skint. They've only got June, July, August and January to get business done and there's a mad panic to make things happen.

There was a lot of resentment about the relationship between me and Mark, but there are loads of managers who have particular agents who work with and represent them. Mourinho is the classic example and swears by super-agent Jorge Mendes, who has been his man since he was a young boss in Portugal. At Newcastle, Freddy Shepherd worked with Paul Stretford, who even had an office at the ground, while it was well known Spurs favoured dealing with Leon Angel. I trust Mark implicitly.

So will Mark find me another club, or have I left the game for good? I honestly don't know. I'm ambitious and I still want the England job, but I have less chance now even though I'm better equipped than ever to do it. If England doesn't happen, I wouldn't mind a national job somewhere. There was talk of Nigeria at one point, which came about because Jay-Jay Okocha is their ambassador, but nothing developed. I'd give it a go anywhere if I thought the country concerned had a genuine chance of competing. Alternatively, I might try MLS in the USA if they'll have me. I can afford to be picky. I don't need another job, the kids and the grandkids are set up financially for life. But I've always been stimulated by making a team better than it was when I started, and I've done that everywhere I've worked. I have lived the dream as player, coach and manager. To the careers teacher who thought I would never make anything of myself I say, 'Stuff you. I did it.'

LYNNE 22

Okay, you've heard plenty from me, so I thought it would be an idea to give Lynne a say. This is her take on our life together.

LYNNE: If I was going out with a footballer today, I suppose I would be known as a WAG. When I met Sam, we were both 16 and he was this big soft shy lad stood at the bar. I fancied one of his mates at first and talked to Sam as a friend, but I got to know him a bit better over a few nights out, and his mates were going, 'Big Sam fancies you.' One night in the Playmate Club, he started dancing with me. He wasn't much of a dancer, and had some weird moves, but he improved as he got his confidence. Sam was winning me round when he went off to console a girl who had just been dumped by his friend Joe Walsh. It made me realise how much I liked him, I didn't want him with any other girl. From then on we were an item, although I don't remember either of us saying, 'Shall we go out together?' It just happened.

I didn't know he was a footballer with a professional club; he told me he mended record players and played football on a Saturday. It was only when I saw his picture in the paper that I realised he played for Bolton youth team. I told him off for lying and finished with him, but he said he was worried if he'd told me he was a footballer I'd think he had lots of money, when actually he didn't have anything at all. He was only on £4 a week. I used to go and watch him playing for the reserves, I wasn't bothered whether the team were winning or losing, I just wanted him to do well. I didn't thinking of him as a star footballer. I just wanted him to be a success in his job.

We were engaged at 18, married at 19, and by the age of 20 we'd had Craig. It was all very quick. We wanted kids, of course we did, but we were a bit naive about the responsibilities. Sam had only just got in the team and was a bit of a minor celebrity around town while I was at home with the baby, and I think I suffered from post-natal depression. I'd also just lost my dad which made the situation worse. When I look back, I can see I didn't cope very well. Sam went out at Christmas without me in a bumble bee costume for a fancy dress party and I remember shouting, 'Do you not get enough attention without dressing up as a bloody bumble bee?' I knew all the players attracted a crowd of women when they went out. I wasn't stupid and I felt vulnerable, being a young mother at home. Even when we did go out together, girls didn't notice I was there and would brazenly chat to him. And this was when he was playing for a team in the second division, not the first.

We didn't live an extravagant life but financially we were okay, especially if Sam got a win bonus which could double his wages. We didn't though have anything like the money players do today. I wouldn't have been able to afford the Louis Vuitton shoes and handbags. Chanel and Armani gear was for the rich, not us. I bought my stuff at Marks & Spencer and was always one for a bargain. Even now I get infuriated if I see an item which is twice the price of what it is being sold for in the shop round the corner. I'd have hated as well the attention the partners of players get today. They are in glossy magazines as much as their husbands and boyfriends with their fancy hair-extensions, make-up, nails and eyelashes. I was a jeans and jumper girl. No-one had a clue who I was, and that's how I liked it.

I've always been able to stand up for myself and I'm known for being feisty when I need to be. There was a hierarchy at Bolton among the players' partners and you had to work your way into the gang. I remember asking if anyone was sitting in a seat before one of Sam's early games and an older player's girlfriend looked down her nose at me and said sarcastically, 'Is there a name on it?' I didn't like her attitude. When I got older I made it my business to welcome the girlfriends of the younger players and integrate them into the group and we built up a great cama-raderie. It was difficult when Sam went to Sunderland because those friends drifted away and we had Rachael as well by then, so I was left at home with two young children. Rachael didn't understand what was going on when Sam was driving off to the North East, but Craig got in a right paddy. One time he put his foot through the door when Sam went out to the shops because he thought he was going away for the week. We ended up in hospital getting Craig's foot bandaged up.

When Sam joined Millwall, we moved the whole family down south.

I was terrified at first, having never been out of Bolton, but we lived in a lovely community in Sevenoaks and thoroughly enjoyed it. We also had some great times in America, going back to Florida for ten years on holiday and when Sam played for Tampa. Living on a complex with the Tampa Bay Buccaneers NFL team, I got to know all the families. Craig would go off fishing with the American footballers, who were twice his dad's size, and developed a broad US accent within a week. He'd be all 'Hey guys, you comin' out?' I always thought it was hard when footballers got transferred, but in the NFL it's dreadful. They get traded at a moment's notice. One day you are chatting and really getting to know them, the next morning they are off to the other side of the country. The wives would be in tears, knowing they had to build yet another new life.

I'm proud of what Sam has achieved in his career, but he would have done any job to provide for his family. During those awful times when he was finishing playing and the pub restaurant was going under, Sam would have swept the streets to put food on the table. When he was managing Limerick and we were scratching for every penny, we sat down with our bank statements and cancelled every direct debit we didn't need. I was a nervous wreck. I was even working in the pub to help keep us afloat.

I was upset for Sam when he didn't get the Preston job. Then John Beck made Craig's life a misery and forced him out, while Sam had to stay on because we needed the money. Sam hated working for Beck but he didn't sit around crying, he got on with it. It was me who felt like bursting into tears. Friends would come up to us saying, 'Sorry you didn't get the job, Sam,' and it took a lot to stop me breaking down on the spot. When you are 19 you don't think about what happens when a footballer's career comes to an end, but it's amazing how quickly it catches up on you. By the time we hit mid-thirties, it was panic stations.

When he was appointed Blackpool manager, it was like all those years of worry evaporated. The champagne we opened that night was the best bottle I've ever tasted, but the high was short-lived. I was on tenterhooks the whole time. Billy Bingham would come out of the boardroom and if they'd won would walk past me saying, 'He should be alright this week.' Maybe he thought it was a joke, but I never saw it that way. If they lost, he never said a word to me. We went out with the board on Saturday nights and the chairman, Owen Oyston, would ask us to give marks for every player's performance. I gave everyone a six to be on the safe side. Sam was in his own world in those early Blackpool days. I felt desperately lonely, even when he was at home. It was football morning, noon and night and missing out on the play-offs was a real blow to him after all his hard work. But we thought he was going to get a new contract and when he went out the door I remember saying, 'Don't accept one year, make sure you get two.' Instead, he got the sack.

I could feel the pressure Sam was under when he got the Notts County job. He had to make it work or he might never have managed again. He rented a bungalow in Nottingham while I stayed in Bolton, and the chairman, Derek Pavis, never let him come home. He had a go at Sam on the phone one night for having travelled back to Bolton and my mum said, 'What a rude, arrogant man.' I sat at games with the directors' wives in this little room beside the boardroom. There were some patio doors which opened up so you could watch the match, and when I was still in there after half-time one day, Derek pushed the doors back and shouted, 'If I've got to watch this shit, so can you!' Notts County were losing every game and I was sick to my stomach. Each 90 minutes felt like three hours. I was expecting Sam to get the sack at any time. But they kept him on after they got relegated and the following season won promotion.

Sam had always dreamed of managing Bolton and all sorts of emotions were going through me when he took over at the Reebok. I took Diane and Graham along with me to his first game because I couldn't face going on my own. It was slightly uncomfortable, because Phil Brown's wife Karen was in there too. She had hoped Phil would get the job and I said to her, 'Look, I know you must be really pissed off and I'm sorry. I'd feel the same as you if it was the other way round.' We'd been friends since Blackpool days and I thought this would ruin it, but she was really good, offering her congratulations. Maybe she was thinking 'bitch' inside, but if she was it was a good act and we're still friends to this day.

I was nervous for the whole of the first four years at Bolton, every game felt like a cup final. Win and it was euphoria, lose and it was gloom and doom. I was hyper, I couldn't relax. I like to talk and I couldn't shut up when I was at the games. Winning the play-off at Cardiff to get into the Premier League was the most brilliant day ever.

I didn't go to the first game in the Premier League because it was at Leicester. I paced around and stayed away from the radio until flicking on the TV just before the final whistle to see a scoreline which read Leicester 0 Bolton 5. I'm ashamed to say my first thought was, 'They must have got that the wrong way round.' I'm a worrier who thinks disaster is always round the corner, so my next thought was, 'How can he keep that up? It's going to be downhill from here.' Despite my nerves, the early years of Sam being a manager at Bolton were my happiest associated with football. Sam was at home, he was the town hero, and everything in our life was working out just perfectly. I became a sort of social secretary, organising events for the players' families with the liaison officer Sue Whittle. Nobody knew me away from the Reebok though. I didn't get a second glance doing the weekly shop at Asda. I once popped into the Co-op for a pint of milk and some cigarettes — I confess I'm a smoker — and the girl behind the counter had a chat with me.

'Sam Allardyce gets those cigarettes, you know.'

'Does he?' I said, putting on my best amazed face.

I didn't smoke when I met Sam, but he was always a social smoker. He's packed in now but I still like a cigarette, even though everyone gets on at me to stop.

Sam's decision to leave Bolton was hard for all of us. He wasn't getting on with Phil Gartside, but I was in my comfort zone and naively I thought he'd be there until he retired. But I couldn't be selfish; if he wasn't happy then it was time to move on. I was annoyed with Phil too. I didn't think he'd given Sam much help over the England manager's job, or been supportive to Sam and Craig over the *Panorama* documentary. There were silly little things too, like banning Craig from playing head-tennis at the training ground. He drove a wedge between the board and our family. I was friends with Phil's wife, Carol, but it all fell apart between us.

Panorama was an awful time. When the trailers first came out saying the programme would feature a high-profile manager, I wondered who it was about. Not in a million years did I expect a load of accusations about Sam and the trashing of Craig. We had a lot of support from friends, including Baroness Taylor of Bolton, who was previously better known as Ann Taylor MP. She said, 'Lynne, it happens to politicians, it happens to everybody,' which made me feel a whole lot better. What they did to Craig had a terrible effect on him, ruining his life. I had to convince him it wasn't his fault that Sam didn't get the England job. I just said, 'It wasn't that, it was your dad's big mouth over the years. The FA didn't like it.' I wanted Sam to sue but the cost would have been astronomical and would have taken at least a year.

When Sammy Lee replaced Sam at Bolton and I heard Phil saying, 'If Sam applied for the Bolton job now he wouldn't get it,' I was mad as hell. Sam was a Bolton player and manager for years, why couldn't Phil just say, 'He's done a great job and we're very grateful but now we have to move on.' That would have been fine, but Sam didn't get a chance to say goodbye to the fans. He didn't deserve that and it was Phil's fault for what was said in the press.

When Sam was first mentioned for the England job, my usual optimistic self thought he had no chance, but then I realised he had a very good chance. I was worried about the attention though and the fact the whole country might start hating him if England lost. Also Sven's girlfriend, Nancy Dell'Olio, was always dressed to the nines and never went anywhere without her make-up on. Would I have to do that? No thanks. I'd have been more like Cherie Blair the morning she opened the door with her dressing gown on and her hair all over the place after Tony became Prime Minister. I wanted Sam to get the job for himself, but underneath I wasn't bothered if he didn't. It sounds bad, but it was honestly how I felt. He knew before playing Steve McClaren's Middlesbrough that Steve had got the job. I said, 'Just ask him,' which he did but Steve wouldn't answer. I thought he could have been honest with him. Of course, I'm sure England would have qualified for the Euros if Sam had got it. I always back my man!

While I was concerned at the pressures the England job might bring, I didn't realise how big the Newcastle one was until we got there. Football seems to be the only thing that matters in the city. Steve Bruce's wife Janet took me to the Metro Centre for lunch one day and I swear there wasn't a single bloke who wasn't wearing black and white stripes. It was a lonely life for me in Durham and the fans turned on Sam. I saw a paper one day with a great big headline saying, 'Time Is Ticking for Allardyce' and I thought, 'Bloody hurry up and strike 12, then we can get out of here.' I was relieved when it was over. Sam rang me after he got the sack and I said, 'I'll pack the stuff and we can go this afternoon.' That's how desperate I was. The reporters were outside our gates and one rang the intercom asking, 'Are you thinking of staying in the area?' I lost it. 'Are you having a laugh? Why would I want to stay here?' I was worried that quote would end up in the papers as our parting shot. Newcastle was where I decided I didn't want to go to football any more. I couldn't take it. I had never experienced a place where virtually the whole crowd seemed to hate Sam. There's a famous picture of a guy getting out of his seat and screaming at Sam who was by the dugout and I thought, 'This is serious stuff. It's evil.'

It sounds like I'm ungrateful to football for all it's given us. I know it's provided us with a lovely lifestyle, but even when he got the Blackburn job I was cheesed off. We had planned to go to Dubai for Christmas and I was so looking forward to it. I never had him to myself at Christmas because of the heavy football programme and this was my chance. It was selfish, but I couldn't help it. When Sam was fired I was really angry though, because he'd done a good job.

I'd had my fill of football after Blackburn and didn't want Sam to go to West Ham. I didn't want an experience like Newcastle again and my mum had just died. Mum lived with us for most of our married life after Dad passed away and Sam was brilliant about it, but it worked for him too because it meant I had help with the kids while he was on his travels. I was very close to my mum, but it was still odd when Sam and I were sat round the TV with her and she'd be complaining, 'There's all this sex on television nowadays.' And that was just when Deirdre and Ken were kissing on *Coronation Street*. We were in our fifties and still felt like embarrassed teenagers!

I enjoyed our time in London. The change of scenery was probably just what I needed. We had a fantastic apartment in Canary Wharf overlooking the Thames with spectacular views of Greenwich, the O2, the London Eye and the Shard. When they told me the rent was £8,000 a month, I nearly keeled over in shock. We didn't pay much more than that for our first house, but that was the going rate, and it did have a gym and a swimming pool. I could go out in the City and see the shows, and enjoy the restaurants. I didn't need a car, I just hopped on the tube and there I was in Oxford Street, the shopping capital of the world. What more could a girl want? When the grandkids came down we went ice-skating, and took them to see the Christmas lights, Winter Wonderland and every show possible. But I didn't go to a single game in Sam's four years at West Ham. I never even went inside Upton Park, and I only met David Gold and David Sullivan twice. I went to the Olympic Stadium to see what the new ground looked like, but I doubted very much if Sam would be the manager by the time they were playing there.

We were in the States at the Bellagio Hotel in Vegas enjoying a croissant and a cuppa over breakfast when West Ham won the play-off final. Kevin Davies and his wife Emma were there with their kids too. Emma was on the phone to her dad going, 'It's 2–1, they're winning.' I was praying for the final whistle when one of Emma's kids went 'Equaliser!' but they were only joking. At the final whistle I shouted to the waiter, 'Two bottles of Laurent Perrier, please!' It was 9am, but so what? Mind you, I should have reined it in a bit, after all Kevin had just been relegated with Bolton!

I'd become obsessed with what was being said about Sam on the internet. Every day I'd log onto the Hammers fans' site 'Knees Up Mother Brown' and it drove me insane. It was like a drug which was killing me but I couldn't stop taking it. I kept telling Sam, 'They don't like you anyway, so you're better off out of it.' It took me a while to realise it wasn't lots of different fans, it was only four or five putting up hundreds of insulting messages.

Sam doesn't help himself though. He did get frustrated when everyone went on about the West Ham Way and he called the fans 'deluded'. 'Knees Up Mother Brown' went for him on that one, they called him 'The Deluded Allardyce' after that. Sam said, 'Don't worry, Lynne, I just say what I think and that's me. I live by it and die by it.' Other managers seemed to be more tactful, but Sam says some things tongue in cheek to wind the media up and comes home smiling about it. When he was in the last week at West Ham and said only Houdini could have done better than him, I was asking him, 'Why would you say that?' and he laughed. It's like throwing a maggot in the pond and all the fish having a bite. He loves doing it.

We've always been a close family, maybe because we had the children and the grandkids so young. Craig was a dad at 19 and when he told me I was going to be a grandma, I was in shock. But what could I say, considering I'd had him at 20? I couldn't wait for Harriet to be born, and was just as thrilled when Sam came along five years later, named after grandad. It was one of the most stressful times of my life when Rachael had Keaton though. She told me the baby wasn't moving and I rushed her into Bolton Hospital for tests. They told her to come back for a scan the next day and sent her home, but when she came back she needed an emergency caesarean. I remember praying, 'I don't care if Sam never wins another game, but please let this baby live.' Keaton was barely breathing and went straight to intensive care, where he needed monitoring 24/7. The paediatrician even asked Rachael if she wanted to bring the priest in to get him christened. But Rachael said, 'No, Mum, he's going to be alright. I will take him home.' She was so strong. They gave him frozen plasma and he started picking up but the nurse said, 'You won't know if he's really alright till you see him in the playground when he's five.' I checked on him every day but he turned out fine, he's gorgeous and we love him to bits. I was worried when she was having Ollie but fortunately that was less traumatic, although his birth required another caesarean and he was born with what they call a true knot in the umbilical cord which fortunately didn't cause any problems. I told Rachael, 'Please don't have any more, I can't take it.' I get so much joy out of the grand-children but I get worry about young Sam, who's at Man United juniors, because I know what Craig went through fighting for a career in football.

Big Sam can be an old romantic when he puts his mind to it. He organised a Caribbean cruise to renew our vows on our 25th wedding anniversary but he couldn't keep it a secret, knowing I wouldn't have had the right dress to wear, so he had to tell me. The ceremony was held in front of a few friends we'd made on the cruise and I enjoyed it more than the wedding day because there were no nerves. He also listened when I was watching Celine Dion on TV and said, 'I'd love to go and see her.' The next time he had a break during the season, he took me to Vegas and bought us tickets for her show. I know Sam and I would always have been together, whether he was a footballer or a plumber. In fact I used to say to him, 'Why can't you just get yourself a job where you start at nine and leave at five like most people?' He'd have been bored with that. In football, you never know what's coming next. Actors seem to have this thing about dying on stage being the best way to go, but I don't want Sam dying on the touchline. He's more relaxed now, the heart scare at Blackburn made sure of that. But football is in his blood, it's an addiction, and I'm not convinced he's finished with it yet.

THE BEST 23

I've worked with many outstanding players over the years and, after much deliberation, I've come up with my all-time best XI in a 4-3-3 formation. Apologies to those I missed out – it's nothing personal.

GOALKEEPER

While at Newcastle, I had Shay Given who was absolutely top class, but I never saw him at his best because he was still getting over a nasty injury sustained the previous season. He suffered a split bowel in a challenge with Marlon Harewood which nearly killed him. At Blackburn, Paul Robinson showed his international class at times but was scarred by a mistake for England which knocked his confidence. So the decision falls between Adrian and Jaaskelainen. Jussi edges it for his longevity. At Bolton we were in the top eight for four years in succession and much of that was down to the flying Finn. He was ever present in three of those four seasons and only missed two league games during that entire period.

RIGHT-BACK

For a lot of my time in management, I had to play individuals at right-back for whom it wasn't their natural position. Right-back is one of those spots where you sometimes make do, but ideally you want a specialist. Michel Salgado, the Spanish international who spent ten years at Real Madrid before I signed him for Blackburn, was outstanding but by a whisker I'm going for Habib Beye who we brought to Newcastle from Marseille. He was an absolute bargain, a stylish defender who could set up attacks too. Although I didn't have the pleasure of working with him for long, the Newcastle fans voted Habib player of the season at the end of his first campaign at St James' Park. They even had a song for him after the hit US comedy series *Happy Days*. It went '*Monday, Tuesday, Habib Beye* . . .' When the fans give you a song, you know you've cracked it.

CENTRE-BACK

At Blackburn we had a terrific combination in Chris Samba and Ryan Nelsen, and we had the emerging Phil Jones although I tended to use him in midfield. At Bolton, I could always rely on Gudni Bergsson, who was still going strong at 37, and at West Ham my favoured combo was James Tomkins and Winston Reid. Tomkins was good but on occasions was more concerned with how he looked bringing the ball out of defence, then wondered why players got round him on his blind side. They don't produce many top-class footballers in New Zealand but in Reid and Nelsen the country had two to rival any pairing in the world so, consequently, I've put them together in my all-time team. Nelsen was a good captain, great professional and steady as a rock. You knew exactly what you were going to get from him week in, week out. Reid was a bit raw at first but learned quickly. Both Nelsen and Reid knew their priority was to defend, whereas Tomkins took a while to realise it.

LEFT-BACK

Ricardo Gardner wins this shirt hands down. I converted him from a left-winger at Bolton and he was a fantastic pro. He still visits when he comes over from Jamaica and his dreadlocks are longer than ever. I love the lad. His goal in the play-offs against Preston is my all-time favourite of any goal scored by any player in any of my teams. He picked it up in his own half, went on a mazy dribble and smashed it into the corner. When Sammy Lee took over, and then Gary Megson, they both put Ricardo back on the left of midfield. I'll never work that one out. He'd been converted into one of the best left-backs in the Premier League, but what did I know?

MIDFIELD

What a trio this is – Jay-Jay Okocha on the right, Fernando Hierro in the middle and Gary Speed on the left. Those three would grace any team in the world. Okocha's tricks were mind-boggling. There was nobody in the Premier League who could do what he did. Give yourselves a treat, look him up on YouTube. His first three years at Bolton were special. Hierro didn't even play a full season but still became a cult hero. During his short time in England, he was the best passer in the Premier League, no question, and they weren't show passes, they cut defences apart. Anyone can pass a ball 15 yards sideways; it's a lot harder to find your man passing forwards all the time as he did. His reading of the game was second to none. Speedo, meanwhile, was the pro of pros. He was a Premier League winner with Leeds at the age of 22 and was still playing in the top division as a midfielder at 38. He gave it 100 per cent from the day he started to the day he finished. I said earlier in the book that most players only have ten good years in them, Speedo had nearly twice that. He was the perfect all-round midfielder: he could defend, head it, pass and get in the box to score.

ATTACK

I thought about El Hadji Diouf but I've plumped for Stewart Downing on the left. Maybe Stewart hasn't achieved all he should in the game but his talent is immense, and when he's on song he's one of the best. He lacks self-confidence, which holds him back and stops him being a greater player than he is. If his first two or three crosses don't come off, he goes into his shell. You have to get an arm round him and tell him how good he is. A rocket from the manager doesn't work with him, but with more self-belief he'd have been an England star. He went back to Middlesbrough in the Championship after I left, and to me that's an indication of that lack of belief. He belongs in the Premier League. Down the right would be Youri Djorkaeff. Wenger called him 'The Snake' because you never knew when he would strike with venom either by a defence-splitting pass or with a goal. Down through the middle, I'm going for Nicolas Anelka. He was bigger than Bolton, shown by the fact he was bought by Chelsea for £15 million which was nearly double what we paid for him, and he went on to win the title and two FA Cups. He was a goal-scorer, goal-maker and a quality footballer.

So there it is, my all-time top team of players I've managed, costing a little more than £20 million. It was hard leaving Dioufy, Kevin Nolan and Kevin Davies out, but I think it's a well-balanced side which, in its heyday, would have given anyone a game. It would never be out of the top six, that's for sure.

My all-time team (4-3-3): Jussi Jaaskelainen; Habib Beye, Ryan Nelsen, Winston Reid, Ricardo Gardner; Jay-Jay Okocha, Fernando Hierro, Gary Speed; Youri Djorkaeff, Nicolas Anelka, Stewart Downing.

● ● ●

Looking at the best XI I've managed against, it's hard to deny the inclusion of so many Arsenal players. The Invincibles of 2004 were phenomenal, probably the best team unit ever seen in the Premier League. They not only had great technical ability but they were big and strong too, from David Seaman in goal through Martin Keown and Sol Campbell at the back, Patrick Vieira in the centre, and Thierry Henry up front. Then you had Freddie Ljungberg, Robert Pires and Dennis Bergkamp playing around them. You could only admire the football they played. They were prepared to mix it too. If you tried to kick them, they would kick you back which is why they had the worst disciplinary record in the league, a fact that gets forgotten. I've faced some exceptional Man United teams too with players like Ruud van Nistelrooy, Paul Scholes, David Beckham, Ryan Giggs, Cristiano Ronaldo, Roy Keane, Wayne Rooney, Gary Neville and Rio Ferdinand in their ranks.

I'm going 4-4-2 with this team but it could easily switch to 4-3-3.

GOALKEEPER

I would have gone for Peter Schmeichel but he was coming to the end of his career when I started managing in the Premier League, so I'm going for David Seaman who had huge hands and an ability to block the entire goal just by standing in front of it. He was pilloried for a couple of high-profile mistakes, but that's only because they were so rare – most of the time he was unbeatable.

RIGHT-BACK

I lived in the same area as where the Neville brothers grew up and it was always reckoned that Phil Neville was more talented than Gary. Phil had a great career but Gary had such an extraordinary will to win and determination. He was a good lad and an honest pro who got every ounce out of his ability and nobody could shift him from the Manchester United side once he got in it.

CENTRE-BACK

My first choice is Tottenham's Ledley King. It's a real shame he was struck down by injury at such a young age, which prevented him being able to train properly and curtailed his career. A fully-fit Ledley would have been the first name on my team sheet. He reminded me of Kevin Beattie, an equally gifted defender from my playing days, who was also plagued by injury. King read the game better than anyone and never looked rushed, everything seemed to be so easy for him. I'd play King next to Rio Ferdinand, which is a big call because John Terry has a very strong case. You might say a Terry-King combination would be more natural, but I think Ferdinand and King could cope with any situation, on the ground or in the air.

LEFT-BACK

It has to be Ashley Cole. For ten years there was no equal in the Premier League, and he was the best left-back in the world. Cole got up and down with so much energy and did his job to perfection. You could spend hours working out how to expose Cole down the flank, but there was no solution. You were better off going down the left-wing instead.

MIDFIELD

Paul Scholes and Patrick Vieira is a dream midfield pairing. They had some battles on opposite sides of the pitch but together would have been a formidable force. Scholes and Keane were a great duo for United, but I think Vieira had the edge over Keane. Although both had moments where they lost their cool, Vieira was not so much of a hot-head and let his football do the talking a bit more. Scholes was the outstanding midfielder in the game in my time as a manager. He wasn't the greatest tackler but he made up for that with his passing, which was second to none, and his goals. On the left-wing it has to be Ryan Giggs, the nearest thing I ever saw to George Best. I played against Best once and couldn't get near him, and Giggs was equally elusive. He played at the top of the game on the wing and later in the centre for almost 25 years. That's just crazy. On the right-wing, I'd go for Cristiano Ronaldo, who gets in ahead of David Beckham. He got 42 goals one season from playing out wide and could beat a man in his sleep which wasn't Becks' game. He set them up too and entertained every time he had the ball. Mind you, no-one delivered a better deadball than Beckham, not even Cristiano.

ATTACK

My front two scored goals for fun – Alan Shearer and Thierry Henry. Shearer is the Premier League's all-time top scorer with 260 goals while Henry is fifth with 175. They were two unbelievable finishers but had different strengths. Shearer was exceptional in the air and a great out-ball for any defender because of how well he held it up and had a blockbuster of a shot on him. Henry couldn't head it, but boy could he use his feet and twist an opponent inside out, and he created as many as he scored. He liked lurking outside the box, whereas Shearer did most of his damage inside the penalty area. In his early days, Shearer used to work the channels but changed after picking up a few injuries and became a pure 'down the middle' target man. If Alan had played for Manchester United, he would have got 300 goals. I know there was this pull to play for his boyhood club, but professionally he made a mistake and belonged at Manchester United. What has he got to show for his career in terms of silverware? One Premier League winners' medal, and he got that with Blackburn, not Newcastle. Shearer was unlucky not to win a trophy with England though. They should have won Euro '96 and could have won the World Cup in '98 but that's penalties for you.

My best opposition XI (4-4-2): David Seaman; Gary Neville; Ledley King, Rio Ferdinand, Ashley Cole; Cristiano Ronaldo, Paul Scholes, Patrick Vieira, Ryan Giggs; Thierry Henry, Alan Shearer.

I think I can safely say there is not a team on earth which could beat that lot.

ENDGAME

31 August 2015

It's been a relaxing summer, which is what I'd always planned, without the phone ringing every five minutes with queries from the chairman, the backroom staff or agents wanting to flog players. Absolute bliss. Now the season has started up again, I'm in demand for TV work with BBC, Sky, BT, Premier League TV and BeIN Sport. I could be on screen every day if I wanted to, but that's maybe too much for anyone!

I was doing TV analysis in Doha on the first weekend of the new season and enjoyed watching the performance of Reece Oxford playing in midfield for West Ham in their 2–0 win at Arsenal. Reece is only 16 and became the second-youngest player to start a Premier League game. It is unwise to predict the future for someone so young but it was clear

Reece had all the attributes to become a top player in my time at West Ham. He started training with the first team during the school holidays a year ago and wasn't the least bit daunted by it. He was like the new Rio Ferdinand, similar in height and frame, elegant in his stride and looking to bring the ball out of defence. I had Phil Jones at Blackburn and, if anything, Reece was the better player at 15.

The worry for West Ham at the time was whether they could keep him. Terry Westley, the academy director, and Nick Hancock who looked after the Under-18s both told me, 'We mustn't let Reece leave.' I passed on the message to David Sullivan that, whatever it took, we couldn't afford to lose him and David made sure he stayed. My hope is he remains at West Ham for a good few years and doesn't get bought by one of the big clubs and then loaned out. That is happening too often and is having a detrimental effect on our youngsters, because many of them never get to play in the first team of their new club. Then they become disillusioned, get released, and don't have the motivation to go and play in the lower leagues. They have probably been earning £3,000 to £5,000 per week and then get offered £300 per week, so they pack it in and do something else. I'm not saying that will happen with Reece because he has a good head on his shoulders, but it's a concern for any talented youngster.

Watching all the games live in the TV studio, as I've been able to do, has given me a different perspective, and also means I'm right up to speed should any new job offers come along. I'm not saying I will go back into management, but I wouldn't dismiss everything out of hand. I will consider what, if anything, comes along and assess my chances of making a success of it, but I'm not chasing a job. You can build a reputation in ten years and destroy it in three months if you make the wrong choice. My former assistant Phil Brown did a superb job at Hull, saving them from relegation from the Championship, taking them into the Premier League and keeping them up in his first season. But he was given the chop the following year, had a tough time in charge of Preston and has had to prove himself again at Southend where he won the Second Division play-offs last season. It's a long road back.

I lost two great friends over the summer, Keith Pinner and Neville Neville. Keith was the founder of Arena International, a hospitality and sponsorship company which had a lot of links in football. He was a lovely man with a great sense of humour and an incredible ability to get negotiations done by seeing both sides of the debate. Nev was well known as the father of Gary and Phil, the footballing brothers, and Tracey, the coach of the England women's netball team. What proud parents Neville and his wife Gill were to have such talented offspring. I'd known Neville for many years, going right back to when Craig played against his boys in youth football and when he was commercial manager at Bury. Football is all the poorer without Keith and Nev involved.

I have realised during this break that I'm not someone who can sit around all day doing nothing. You have to have a reason to get up in the morning. So, apart from TV work, I've become a brand ambassador for MyClubBetting which helps grassroots sports teams generate income for themselves by taking 20 per cent of profits from the betting site. They can also get free kit and equipment. It's a great idea and one that I expect to grow in popularity.

Christmas seems a long way off but Lynne's got a special family gathering planned with the children and grandkids because we've never been able to do it before due to football commitments. I'm looking forward to it, unless . . .

INDEX

AC Milan 121, 145, 178, 196

PLATES PICTURE CREDITS

Action Images: 3 top right (Sporting Pictures/Joe Mann), 10 centre left (Paul Currie Livepic), 11 top (Jason Cairnduff Livepic), 11 bottom right (Alex Morton/ Livepic), 13 centre (Jed Leicester Livepic), 15 bottom (Tony O'Brien Livepic), 16 top (Henry Browne Livepic)

Corbis: 13 top (Eddie Keogh/REUTERS)

Daily Mail/Solo Syndication: 12 bottom left (Andy Hooper)

Getty Images: 3 bottom (Evening Standard), 8 bottom (Laurence Griffiths), 9 centre left (Clive Rose), 10 top left (Matthew Peters/Manchester United),

13 bottom (Richard Heathcote), 14 bottom left (Jamie McDonald), 14 bottom right (Ian Kington/AFP)

Press Association: 9 centre right (Martin Rickett/PA Archive), 11 bottom left (Scott Heppell/AP), 14 top (Nick Potts/PA Archive)

Rex Features: 7 top (Brian Bould/Daily Mail)

TGS Photo: 15 top (Rob Newell)